FAITH AND
MAGICK IN THE
ARMED FORCES

About the Author

Stefani Barner (called Spiral) has been a practicing Witch for over fifteen years and a military wife for ten. She is married to a two-tour Iraq War veteran and a member of a Gold Star family, and she is a professional mediator specializing in community and family conflict. An early and active member of Military Families Speak Out, Stefani has spoken on issues relating to military affairs, family support, veterans' care, and Iraq War policy before groups numbering from a few dozen to over a thousand, has lobbied Congress, and has been a regular commentator in the media, including both local and national newspapers and television outlets. She is a featured columnist for The Pagan Activist website (www.thepagan activist.com), where she writes an ethics column called "Rede+Right," and a freelance editorial contributor to the *Air Force Times* newspaper, and she has been a featured guest on National Public Radio to discuss military advocacy. Stefani has taught classes on conflict within the Pagan community and on Paganism in the military and has led women's rituals at several ConVocations. Currently she is maintaining an active presence in both her local Reclaiming and Unitarian Universalist communities and preparing to enter the seminary. For more information, please visit her website, www.faithandmagick.com.

FAITH AND MAGICK
IN THE
ARMED FORCES

A HANDBOOK FOR
PAGANS IN THE MILITARY

STEFANI E. BARNER

Llewellyn Publications
Woodbury, Minnesota

First Edition
First Printing, 2008

Cover design by Gavin Dayton Duffy
Cover images: dog tags © stephen Mulcahey / Alamy; background © Brand X
   Pictures
Interior book design by Joanna Willis
Interior illustrations by Llewellyn art department

Llewellyn is a registered trademark of Llewellyn Worldwide, Ltd.

The author and publisher would like to remind readers that military regulations are changed frequently and that no print resource will be able to maintain 100% accuracy over time. Recognizing that access to well-stocked libraries or bookstores may be limited by a serviceperson's duty station, many electronic sources have been provided to allow the reader to seek out updates and further information.

Library of Congress Cataloging-in-Publication Data
Barner, Stefani E.
  Faith and magick in the Armed Forces : a handbook for pagans in the military / Stefani E. Barner.—1st ed.
     p. cm.
  Includes bibliographical references.
  ISBN 978-0-7387-1194-2
  1. United States—Armed Forces—Neopagans—Handbooks, manuals, etc.
  2. Neopagans—Religious life—United States—Handbooks, manuals, etc. 3.
  Spiritual life—Neopaganism—Handbooks, manuals, etc. 4. United States—
  Armed Forces—Religious life. I. Title.
  UB418.N46B37 2008
  299'.94088355—dc22

                                                                    2007052778

Llewellyn Publications
A Division of Llewellyn Worldwide, Ltd.
2143 Wooddale Drive, Dept. 978-0-7387-1194-2
Woodbury, MN 55125-2989, U.S.A.
www.llewellyn.com

Printed in the United States of America

Dedicated to those who wear the uniform
And fight each day in defense of our rights;

And also to those on the home front,
Who fight for the rights of those in uniform.

May peace, through justice, prevail.

HOMECOMING
(A Poem for the Fallen)

I walk along the starlight path where the triple crossroads meet
And midnight jasmine blooms.
The scent of it envelops me like moonlight
And I finally know what peace is.
My wonderment at this journey is tempered
With the knowledge that all is as it is meant to be,
And the footprints of those who have gone before
Remind me that I am not alone.

I walk upon the starlight path where the triple crossroads meet
And the still, clear river flows.
It is cool, and it rinses away my fear and pain,
The detritus of my mortality.
I am refreshed and reawakened to the mystery
Of my travels from life to death to life beyond.
That where I've been is not all that is,
And I've only begun the trip home.

—*Spiral*

Contents

Introduction   1

I. TO KNOW
1. Know Your Options   11
   PAGAN PERSPECTIVES *Adult Child of a Veteran   28*
2. Know Your Rights   35
3. Know Your Basics   61

II. TO WILL
4. Willingness to Stand Up   83
5. Willingness to Serve   101
6. Willingness to Sacrifice   109
   PAGAN PERSPECTIVES *The Military Wife   122*
7. Willingness to Kill   131
   PAGAN PERSPECTIVES *The Coalition Partner   144*
8. Conjuring Peace in a Culture of War   151

III. TO DARE
9. Daring to Deploy   161
   PAGAN PERSPECTIVES *The Combat Veteran   189*

10. Family Life During Separation   193

    PAGAN PERSPECTIVES *The Dependent Child*   *203*

11. Daring to Confront Danger   207

IV. TO KEEP SILENT

12. Coming Home   221

13. The Unending Battle   233

    PAGAN PERSPECTIVES *The Military Widow*   *254*

Blessings and Acknowledgments   259

APPENDICES

Appendix A: Warrior Deities   265

Appendix B: Worldwide Resources for Military Personnel   271

Appendix C: Political Groups and Governmental Agencies   275

Appendix D: Family Support and Veterans Programs   279

Glossary of Relevant Military Terms   281

Bibliography and Works Cited   285

Introduction

O God, root and source of body and soul, we ask for boldness in confronting evil. When you are within us, we have the power to countenance all that is untrue. O Father and Mother of all humankind, may we redeem our failings by the good work that we do.

—Khasi Unitarian Prayer

"**P**agan Special Forces: From Above *AND* Below," reads the bumper sticker that hangs above my husband's desk. Beside it is another reading "Coven Security: An It Harm None . . . Permanently!" Purchased at Metro-Detroit's ConVocation several years ago, they serve as simple (and humorous) reminders of what sets him apart from his brothers and sisters in arms: namely, a worldview that's a bit . . . different . . . from that of your average serviceperson. The United States Military (on which this book will focus, with the understanding that the suggestions and exercises contained herein are applicable to military personnel of any nation) is not exactly known for being a hotbed of progressive views. According to Alan W. Dowd, writing for *The American Legion* magazine,[1] 60% of military chaplains and nearly 40% of military personnel today define themselves as Evangelical Christian. Compare this with the general population, which boasts a roughly 15% share of Evangelicals,

---

1 Alan W. Dowd, "Faith Through Service," *The American Legion*, September 2006.

and it's safe to assume that there are many challenges facing Pagans who choose to serve in the armed forces.

As of this writing, military Pagans, of any branch, do not have a chaplain of their own faith; literally, every known candidate who identifies as Wiccan or Pagan has been rejected. Pagans who are killed in combat and who choose to be buried in a veterans' cemetery were, until 2007, not allowed to have the pentacle (or any other Pagan symbol) on their tombstones. Thankfully, after a ten-year battle fought by Pagans and their allies against the Department of Defense, this protocol has finally been amended. If you are already in the service, you are probably well aware of how difficult day-to-day life can be for minority faith practitioners. If you are considering enlistment and identify yourself as a follower of nature-based spirituality, please do not allow this information to discourage or to dissuade you. As Marcus Aurelius, the great Roman general and emperor, instructed, we must enter into every decision with a clear head and a full awareness of the circumstances. The fact is, life as a Pagan in the military is lonely and frustrating, but it can also be immensely rewarding.

Many Pagans (including myself) are conflicted about military service. I can't begin to count the number of times my husband and I have had the Wiccan Rede thrown in our faces—the implication being that to serve in uniform, or in combat, is to somehow violate the charge to "harm none." But the fact remains that as much as we crave peace—truly, lasting peace— there will always be a need for a strong, defensive presence, if only to ensure that peace endures. The Swiss have been famous for their national neutrality for centuries, and yet they maintain an incredibly well-trained military. The Norwegians have an extensive arsenal, but it is designed in such a way as to be purely defensive. They have nothing that could be used to perpetuate a preemptive attack. A desire for peace and a decision to enlist are not mutually exclusive. In fact, I would argue that the latter without the former is fatally flawed. We as Pagans are in a unique position to see past the dualistic thinking that so often bogs down our contemporaries. We walk between worlds frequently and have minds adept at embracing paradox. Is it any wonder that Pagans, those who seek most to "harm none," are best suited to military service?

In writing this book, and the www.thepaganactivist.com column on which it's based, I find myself in a paradoxical position: that of both pacifist and military spouse. Many would say that these roles are contradictory or mutually exclusive, that I cannot possibly be both fully and simultaneously. I admit that it is a dichotomy I struggle with. I have come to the realization that people like me serve as a sort of sociopolitical shaman, walking between two worlds in an attempt to improve relations and assist in communication. I have many friends in the peace movement who expressed grave concerns (less politely called "condemnations") about the fact that my husband serves in the military. Likewise, I had many military friends who thought that I was hypocritical at best and traitorous at worst for taking an active role in the anti-war movement. After much time spent in meditation and activism, I came to the following realization: not only are my dual roles nonconflicting, but they actually function in a sort of symbiotic relationship.

We live in a nation with an all-volunteer military. This means that 98% of the citizens of the United States of America never have to worry about being conscripted into military service and forced to risk their lives for causes they may or may not personally support. The burden of military service is borne by the 2% of our population who choose to put themselves into just that situation because they believe in what our nation stands for . . . or sometimes because it's the only employment they can find. This right to *not* choose military service comes with a certain degree of responsibility. If our civilian population is going to rely on the military to risk their lives, to fight and die for the causes designated by our political leaders, then the civilians have an obligation to make damn certain that the cause is worth dying for. That's the symbiosis: the military fights for the civilians' right to safety, protection, and freedom, and an involved, concerned citizenry fights for the military's right to be free from service in a protracted, unnecessary war. The soldier and the protester are engaged, knowingly or not, in a careful dance of mutual protection, their common concern being the elected officials who make foreign policy decisions that ultimately affect them both. It is because of this fact that you will find many references to peace and peacemaking in a book that has been written specifically for those most likely to be sent into war. Because I firmly believe that the goal of every soldier and sailor, airman and marine, is to fight the battle in such a way as to ensure that there will not be a need to take up arms again. Everyone enters into the combat theatre with the hopes that their actions will eliminate the need for such a course in the future.

During the Revolutionary War, Thomas Paine wrote, "If there must be trouble, let it be in my day, that my child may have peace." This sentiment has been echoed in the hearts and minds of every man and woman who has served in the armed forces before or since. No one joins the military because they look forward to "going to exotic lands, meeting foreign people, and killing them" as the old battlefield humor goes. They join the military because they feel truly called to protect the peace that has for so long been the blessing of our country. They are willing to sacrifice everything for it.

At the end of World War I, the allied nations dedicated a holiday to be called Armistice Day to recognize those who had fought in the War to End All Wars. Hope was high that we had defeated those who would threaten our shores and thus had ensured a lasting peace throughout the world. "Peace on Earth" was more than a holiday sentiment—it was the fervent hope of every man, woman, and child on Earth who had seen what horrors could be wrought by war. Unfortunately, this peace was not to last.

And so, the United States sent its sons and daughters, lovers and spouses, off to battle once more, to fight against one of the most horrific tyrants of this last century. Those who served on the beaches of Normandy, in the air over Germany, or on ships scattered throughout the Pacific were fighting for the right to a peaceful world. They were fighting for a society free from bigotry and from institutionalized hatred of minorities. They were fighting to protect our nation and the world from institutionalized policies like those of the Third Reich. Peace meant being willing to fight to protect the understanding that those around us are fully human, regardless of the color of their skin, the way they practice their religion, or whom they love, and that all citizens deserve protection, to live lives free from oppression, exploitation, and death. Those who served in World War II were fighting for the very soul of the world.

The prayer of every soldier in battle has always been, as Thomas Paine said, "Let them have peace." This does not mean that they do not fight, but rather that they acknowledge that wars are the price we must sometimes pay in order to defend a peaceful nation. Ironically, sometimes the only path toward pacifism is the road to war. Everyone who has ever served in battle knows that this is so. They do not choose to go to war on a whim; they have offered their daily lives, their mortal bodies, and sometimes their very existence on the altar—not of war, but of the hope for peace.

This is why I wrote this book: To honor the sacrifice of every man and woman who has ever said, "Let trouble come in my day, that they might have peace." To honor those who were called by the draft, and who answered that call with fearful dignity. To honor those who volunteered for service, so that others with families would not be drafted. To honor those who said goodbye to newlywed wives or newborn children, turned, and boarded an aircraft bound for enemies' guns. To honor those who returned much different than when they left—having lost a limb, or a spouse, or a part of their own quiet mind. The sacrifices made by these men and women cannot be underestimated. Not one person who has donned a flak jacket or helmet has taken it off unscathed. This is why this book came about—to recognize that more and more Pagans are participating in this service and to express my gratitude to those who have returned unharmed, perhaps, but not unchanged.

Composer and playwright Jonathan Larson wrote that "the opposite of war isn't peace, it's creation." That is what these men and women in uniform have done . . . created a stronger world out of endless years of chaos and destruction. Using their very bodies as the tools of labor, our veterans have built a nation where we do not fear to go to sleep at night. We do not censor our speech, fearful of who might be listening. We do not say goodbye to our families each morning and wonder who among us will still be alive at the end of the day. This peace is the creation of our veterans, and is the constant struggle of those who serve today.

After the Korean War, Armistice Day was renamed Veterans Day in the United States. To many people, it is simply a day off from work, if even that, but to those who have served in battle, it is sometimes the only thank you they have ever received. In this era of reactionary patriotism and magnetic "Support the Troops" car ribbons, a true and honest "thank you" is a precious thing. And so, to you, my reader, I say thank you for sacrificing so much of yourself to the cause of peace. Thank you for creating a nation where we do not have to fear the rule of dictators or secret police. Thank you for giving your body, your mind, and even your life to ensure the tranquility of our nation and the safety of every citizen.

We are not the world power we are today because we have won the most wars or have the biggest weapons. The United States has been a guiding voice of the world community because our military is ultimately dedicated to the cause of peace. We do not believe in a world where laws do not apply, where borders are only suggestions of autonomy, where people live in the shadow of suffering. We are the nation we are today because we recognize that the only war worth fighting is the one that brings us one step closer to creating a lasting peace. Through World Wars I and II, Korea, Vietnam, and on into contemporary battles and wars, the military has always honored and will continue to always honor the work created by our veterans by serving only in the most honorable ways and for the most honorable of causes.

Unfortunately, many feel that this is not the case today. Military personnel and their families are facing a great deal of internal conflict regarding overseas deployments today. Our confidence in political leadership is shaken, and questions about what is a truly just and necessary mission arise more and more frequently. I have experienced this struggle firsthand, as the wife of an Iraq War veteran and career serviceperson. The sacrifices military personnel and their families are asked to make deserve a solid foundation of intelligence, confidence, and trust that many in today's military find lacking. And yet they serve—not because they are committed to any political party or ideological policy, but because they have sworn an oath to dedicate their lives to the higher calling of their nation. They are stepping forth every day into enemy fire or nature's harshest conditions, often without adequate equipment, with one goal in mind: the preservation of the peace they've left behind. Those wearing the uniforms of our armed forces today do not have the luxury of debating politics. They serve where they are asked to serve and rely on an engaged and participatory citizenry to ask the difficult questions that might keep them safe, or bring them home.

It is with gratitude that I craft this volume for them, and for you—so that our servicepeople, who are still denied the right to a chaplain who represents their own religious path, may yet have the resources necessary to carry that faith with them, wherever they are sent. Brightest blessings on our troops and their families. May your path be safe and your service honorable. May peace prevail, and may it last through the days of your children's children. Until you are home again. . . .

I. To Know

Let us have faith that right makes might, and in that faith, let us, to the end, dare to do our duty as we understand it.

—Abraham Lincoln

1. Know Your Options

Never allow yourself to be swept off your feet: when an impulse stirs,
see first that it will meet the claims of justice; when an impression
forms, assure yourself first of its certainty.

—Marcus Aurelius

The decision to enlist in the military is one of the most serious choices you can make. It should not be undertaken lightly, and all potential enlistees have an obligation to be 100% aware of exactly what they are doing, every step of the way. This means not only having a full awareness and understanding of the military—both the positive and negative aspects—but also a full awareness of the recruiting process. One of the gravest mistakes you can make is assuming that joining the military will make you an expert on military life and practices. You must educate yourself and walk into that recruiting office an expert already, versed in your rights, understanding of your goals, and aware of the potential dangers ahead. Hopefully, this chapter will help prepare you to make a decision about whether or not to enlist in the armed forces; however, it is not the end-all, be-all in recruiting information, and I strongly suggest that you draw your information from a broad base of resources, both in favor of and against enlistment.

If you are medically eligible for enlistment, then we move on to the other areas of consideration that the military takes into account in order to determine your eligibility. For example, age is a factor. Each branch of the military has specific age cutoff requirements (between twenty-seven and forty-two); however, many branches offer age waivers to persons interested in specific career fields. Citizenship is another factor considered. There is no foreign legion in the U.S. Military. In order to be eligible for enlistment, the potential recruit must be either a citizen or a legal (green-card-carrying) resident. Some branches will not take a recruit with dependents (children or spouses) under eighteen. Be sure to check the requirements of the branch that you are interested in joining prior to seeing a recruiter, since in addition to the criteria I've covered, many branches will be interested in your financial situation, educational achievement, and criminal history. After you have determined that you are eligible for service, take some time for introspection and review the goals and desired outcomes you hope to achieve through military service. What is it about the military that you find appealing?

For many, it's the desire to serve their nation, as one of the modern "Warrior Class." They see military service as a continuation of the knight/samurai traditions of old, and view the American military as a chance to, in their own way, have a seat at the "Round Table." I believe that this mindset creates the best servicepeople . . . and the worst recruits. This is because these individuals are the ones most committed to honorable service, and usually feel a deep, spiritual connection to the codes of Bushido and chivalry that inspire them. However, this eagerness and idealized vision of military life can also create a great deal of naiveté, almost gullibility, when going through the enlistment process. The desire to believe that the military is everything one has hoped it would be, both in terms of practical details and honorable intentions, can be quite a blind spot for our would-be knights in shining armor.

The second category of potential recruit is what I call the modern-day Conscript. In feudal times, as armies were passing through villages and towns on their way to battle, they would force able-bodied men to accompany them: conscripting them into service against their will. This practice of conscription is the equivalent to our modern-era draft. Obviously, there is no draft today. But this does not mean that every person enlisting in the military today is eager for military service. A great many men and women enlist in the military because of economic pressures. Coming out of underprivileged areas of the country, often with little resources for education or job opportunities, these young people enlist because the military seems like the best, or only, way out of poverty. Those in the Conscript category are often enticed into the military by a combination of pop-culture influence and economic incentives. Most don't plan on making a career out of armed service, and fewer still anticipate having to see combat. Those in this category are likely most susceptible to recruiters who are extremely talented at making the military seem like any other career move—safe, smart, and beneficial.

The final category I divide enlistees into is the Berserkers. These are the individuals who don't need a recruiter to talk them into enlisting—they've been eagerly anticipating joining the military for most of their lives. There is a difference, though, between the Berserker and the Knight, who might also have dreamed of a military career. Whereas the Knight is most interested in the glory of war, the Berserker is most interested in the guts. Berserker-type troops are usually drawn toward the Special Forces, or other career fields that allow them to work within highly dangerous, highly violent areas. If they go into Infantry, the Berserkers are going to be eager for combat and excited by the opportunity to kill and be killed. Berserkers are less concerned with trivialities like rules of engagement than Knights or Conscripts. Like the Knights, they are likely to make a career of military service. Unlike the Knights, they tend to gauge their successes by the final body count.

Each of these categories has distinct positive and negative traits. The Knights are honorable in their motivations and courses of action, yet prone to being gullible. The Conscripts are engaged and willing to sacrifice, yet often reluctant to act. And the Berserkers never hesitate to act, but must be wary of their tendency toward viciousness. To offer a (perhaps flawed) example of each, the soldiers at Iwo Jima were Knights; at Abu Ghraib, Conscripts; and at Mai Lai, Berserkers. There is no rule that says that someone with a Berserker or Conscript nature cannot excel within the military. In fact, I believe that nearly every personality type drawn to military service has the potential for excellence—so long as they are fully aware of their strengths and limitations and comfortable working both mentally and spiritually with every aspect of their nature.

I hope, however, that this exploration of archetypes will help you be more aware of your own innate strengths and weaknesses as we prepare to explore the recruitment process. Any drill sergeant will tell you that being aware of your limitations is the first step toward confronting and conquering them. I believe it is vital that you come into a full understanding of your own nature prior to committing yourself to any military contract.

What Your Recruiter CAN Promise You

The simplest rule is this: "If it goes into your contract, it can be promised." So, things like bonuses, college aid, and term of enlistment can be promised while factors like final duty station cannot. This is an important thing to realize before entering into the decision to sign a military enlistment contract. Many recruiters, with the best of intentions, will make the military seem incredibly flexible. I've had young people tell me that they were promised that the military would train them as DJs or photographers if they enlisted. It is understandable that people—especially young people—would become incredibly excited to learn that not only can they serve their country in uniform, but they can do so without ever serving in a "dangerous" place *and* they can pursue their dreams of (insert groovy civilian job here) while earning money for college. It may come as a shock to realize that this is not always the case.

Honestly, the best candidate for military service is the one who wants to serve in the military. This may seem rather obvious, but there are a great number of recruits joining the military today not because they want to serve in Iraq, Afghanistan, or some other combat theatre, not because they are interested in training for a military career as a rifleman, convoy driver, or gunner, but because they need college money or need a job and see the military as a steppingstone toward their ultimate long-term *civilian* aspirations. These people are not dissuaded by the military recruiter. No one in the recruiting office is going to inform them of the other options they have available to them in order to succeed in their civilian goals. Military recruiters are, at their essential core, salesmen. And much like the guy selling cars, houses, or appliances, their job is to make sure that what they're selling looks like what you want to buy.

I don't want anyone to think that I'm insulting recruiters—they perform a necessary function for the military today and are a great help to those potential enlistees who are truly interested in a career in the armed forces. Recruiters are quite helpful at explaining enlistment standards and regulations, and if you have grown up knowing that you will never be happy unless you put on that blue or green or white uniform, the recruiter is your best friend. They will do everything in their power to help you succeed in your military aspirations. But if you fall into the former category—the person who desperately wants to be in radio, the arts, medicine, law, or journalism, and sees the military as a simple and relatively easy path toward that goal—then caveat emptor. The recruiters have goals and quotas of their own to meet, and they will do everything in their power to shape the image of the military into whatever you most want it to be, regardless of what the likelihood or the benefit truly is. Know yourself and your goals before you set foot into the recruiter's office. If you want nothing else in life than to serve in the armed forces, you are in the right place! If, however, you are viewing the military as a tool rather than as a goal, spend some time evaluating your motivations and your alternatives before you sign on that dotted line.

What Your Recruiter
CANNOT Promise You

"Laws and regulations that govern military personnel may change without notice to me. Such changes may affect my status, pay, allowances, benefits, and responsibilities as a member of the Armed Forces REGARDLESS of the provisions of this enlistment/reenlistment document."[1] This is just a bit of the fine print on the back of a standard enlistment contract. It is vitally important that everyone considering enlistment understand that the act of enlistment is a commitment to the unknown. Regardless of what the recruiter says, the playing field can and probably will change at some point in your career. It is up to you to decide if this is a situation you can live with. Military enlistment is a deeply personal decision and one that must be entered into with eyes open, and with an alert and discerning mind.

When, after research and contemplation, you have decided to sit down with a military recruiter and discuss your potential military future, it is important to be aware of what a recruiter can and cannot promise you. I would like to thank Rod Powers, the U.S. Military Guide at About.com, for his assistance with this section. Mr. Powers was an invaluable resource and aid to me throughout the research process, and I cannot thank him enough. I highly recommend that anyone considering pursuing a career in the military spend as much time as possible reviewing his site; it's an absolute wealth of information.

One of the first things to understand is that recruiters are required to meet certain quotas in order to maintain their military record. This means that their primary goal is to get signatures on contracts—not to act as a career planner or to look out for your personal interests. Most recruiters are honorable, honest people who are simply doing the task they've been assigned to fulfill; however, that task involves getting more people into a uniform—everything else comes second. Recruiters operate under a great deal of pressure from their commanders, and this stress can unfortunately lead to instances of less than upfront or honest behavior. I strongly rec-

---

1 Obtained from "Advice to Those Considering Enlistment" as published by the Center on Conscience & War. Available at http://www.centeronconscience.org/literature/pdf/enlistment_advice.pdf (accessed January 10, 2008).

ommend that anyone planning on meeting with a recruiter (and everyone joining the military will have to do so at some point) remember the following tips:

1. Get everything in writing. If it doesn't go into your enlistment contract, then it doesn't count. Verbal assurances from your recruiter count for nothing when it comes to determining your career field, duty station, and a great many other factors that the average recruit is concerned about.

2. Take someone with you. I cannot stress this enough! I am a firm believer in using the buddy system when meeting with recruiters, and I personally feel that the person who accompanies you should be someone who is not personally considering military service. You need a critical ear, a voice of reason on your side, because the recruiter is there for the hard sell.

3. No matter how well the meeting goes, or how appealing the facts presented are, take some time to think about it before you sign an enlistment contract. Never, ever sign anything on your first trip to the recruiter. Take a few days or even a week or two to talk to family and friends, and, if possible, meet some current service personnel and ask their advice.

Once the decision has been made to enlist, you'll want to know what a recruiter can and cannot promise. The following sections offer a brief overview of what you need to know before you sign on the dotted line.

In 2005, all military recruiters were required to undergo ethics training, in response to an embarrassing rash of "less than honest" recruiters making national news. Again, I want to stress that the vast majority of recruiters are honorable, honest people. However, there are times when the stress of the recruiting numbers game wears them down and it's all too easy to slip into habits of not really lying but not really telling everything. So, in the interest of making sure that everyone who joins the armed forces does so as a fully informed, educated, and prepared adult, I will discuss a few of the most common inaccuracies used by recruiters.

"You won't see combat." The fact is that you are joining the *military* and, frankly, odds are good that at some point in your career you will see some kind of hostile duty. Regardless of whether you are joining the military for the college benefits or because you truly want to build a career there, you must understand exactly what you are signing up to do. Many young people considering enlistment think that if they don't sign up for a career in Infantry, Special Forces, or Armory, then they'll never be sent to the front lines. The unfortunate reality of modern warfare is that there are no front lines—when you are in country, the front lines are everywhere. A sobering reminder of this is the fact that Shoshanna Johnson, one of the first prisoners of war (POWs) captured in the Iraq War, was a member of the 507th Maintenance Company. She was a woman (technically "barred" from frontline combat) and a cook, and yet not only did she "see combat," but she was captured and held prisoner for twenty-two days. Yes, career paths matter. You might never be asked to carry a weapon. But the fact remains, **if you wear the uniform, you might see combat. There are no exceptions.**

"You're more likely to be murdered in any American city than to be killed in combat." This is one inaccurate recruiting promise that Mr. Powers addresses beautifully. It wasn't originally on my list of "unauthorized promises," but I believe that it should be addressed. I'll quote Powers directly: "On average, 50 military members are killed in action and 481 are wounded in action each month in Iraq. The Army and the Marine Corps bear the brunt of these casualties. While the numbers fluctuate somewhat from month to month depending on rotation schedules, there are about 133,000 troops deployed to Iraq at any given time. If you live in a city with a population of 133,000 and you have 50 murders per month and 481 violent crimes per month which result in injuries, I'd move, if I were you."[2] His analysis is absolutely correct. There are certain groups that are called "heroes": police officers, firefighters, and military personnel among them. They are called heroes because they face incredible

2 Rod Powers, "Top 10 Lies (Some) Recruiters Tell," http://usmilitary.about.com/od/join ingthemilitary/a/recruiterlies.htm (accessed May 21, 2007).

danger every day in order to do their job. They risk their lives to save or protect others. Ultimately, regardless of what career field you enter into, **the military is an inherently dangerous job.**

"The military will accommodate whatever career path you wish to pursue." In most cases, this is true, with a few exceptions. If you undertake training for your selected career field and fail the required courses, then you may be reassigned to any needed MOS (Military Occupational Specialty) position at your commander's discretion. However, even if you complete your training, pass the courses, and obtain the ratings necessary to work in your chosen field, you may get to your duty station and find out that the unit has too many already, or that your career path has been eliminated. In these cases, you'll be retrained for another function—again, one of your commanding officer's choosing. Finally, in combat situations, all bets are off. If a task is needed, the position will be filled, and the fact that you were trained to be a radio operator (for example) will mean very little when they hand you the keys to the Humvee and tell you to hit the road with the next convoy. Most of the time, your career choices will be honored, but it's important to be aware of the exceptions as well. **Make sure your career preference is written into the enlistment contract exactly as you express it, but understand that extenuating circumstances will sometimes prevail.**

These two go hand in hand: *"If you don't like the military, you can always quit"* and *"If you try to back out of your contract, you'll go to jail."* The secret is that you have every right to change your mind up until the day you leave for basic training. They will not arrest you, deport you, revoke your citizenship, or ruin your life in any other way. They will put a *lot* of pressure on you to stay. They will remind you of the educational benefits, career training, bonuses, and lots of other potential perks (be sure you've done your independent research!), but they cannot have you arrested for changing your mind. As long as your decision is made before you get on the bus. Once you arrive at basic, the story changes. You cannot simply "drop out" of basic. Yes, there is such a thing as "failure to adapt," which can result in your discharge from the military before completing basic, but keep this in mind: it is a drill instructor's job to break down all your civilian habits, patterns, and ways of thinking in order to create a soldier, airman, sailor, or marine. In short . . . drill instructors are there to *make* you adapt, and they will use every technique in their book to do this before they ever consider you for a failure to adapt discharge. This makes perfect sense when one considers the amount of time and financial resources that are put into every recruit, even prior to their arrival at basic. It is in the best interest of the military to ensure that this investment is not lost. Therefore, those who do not adapt easily (or at all) to their new environments can face being "recycled" through training over again in the hope that they can indeed adapt if given enough time. Those hoping to exit the military after they've arrived at basic face an uphill battle, and, while it's not impossible, they must be absolutely unshakable in their desire to leave. The drill instructors are used to dealing with fear, rebellion, and anxiety, and they do not give up on their recruits easily. Any potential to create a solider will be exploited—that is, after all, the goal. **You have rights and options available to you after you sign your contract, but you must exercise them before you begin your training.**

"You can sign up for just a year or two, and when you're done, you're done." The reality is, any enlistment contract (even the new short-term "trial" enlistment) actually commits you to a potential eight years of service, in the active-duty military, the Reserves, or the Individual Ready Reserves (IRR). The IRR allows the military to recall you to active duty for several years after your enlistment contract expires. The Department of Defense has also been issuing "stop-loss" orders, which allow personnel in the field to be retained by the military involuntarily for an indefinite period of time, until their services are no longer required. Stop-loss orders have been used by all branches of the military at one time or another, but only the Army and the Marines have exercised this option in recent years. **Regardless of what your enlistment contract states, you are signing up for a total of eight years of potential military service.**

If, as you pursue military enlistment, you encounter claims from recruiters that sound too good to be true, they very well might be. I highly recommend Mr. Powers's website, usmilitary.about.com, as well as www.military.com and www.militaryonesource.com to fact- and reality-check their claims before you sign anything.

Important Questions to Ask

1. What is the minimum enlistment commitment?

2. What physical fitness and vocational/educational benchmarks must I meet to be eligible?

3. What is the expected pay for my chosen career field? Are there bonuses or special enlistment programs I may be eligible for? Are there differences between the branches in terms of what I can expect to make?

4. What employment and career training is available to me?

5. Am I likely to be stationed overseas? In combat?

6. What is the basic training experience like?

7. Are there any military expositions or events coming up that I could attend?

8. What college or educational benefits would be available to me?

9. What happens next?

10. Can you put your answers in writing for me?

Alternatives to the Recruiting Station

Many Pagans are familiar with the adage "all rivers lead to the sea." The same is true, to a large extent, about joining the military. While the most common point of entry is through the assistance of a recruiter, this is by no means the only path into military service. Here, we will briefly discuss a few of the other ways one can become a part of the armed forces.

United States Military Academies

There are several ways into the United States Military. The most prestigious route is through entry into a military academy. Each branch of the armed forces operates a university dedicated to the training of future military leaders: the elite of the Officers' Corps. These schools are as old as the country itself—the U.S. Naval Academy was commissioned by George Washington, and West Point trained some of the most prominent historical figures of modern warfare. In addition to a rigorous academic curriculum, these universities provide training in military history and strategy, leadership, and other specialized education for the future crème de la crème of the military establishment. These schools (West Point, the U.S. Naval Academy, the Air Force Academy, and the Coast Guard Academy) count as their alumni many of the most famous figures in American military history.

Needless to say, the admissions standards for these schools are extremely high. The Air Force Academy, for example, only accepts 1,300 of the 12,000 applicants who apply each year.[3] But if you are able to get in, the payoff is enormous: free tuition, room and board, books, and meals for the duration of your education[4] . . . plus the ability to learn at the feet of some of the most prominent scholars of military studies. All this, and the knowledge that you will be guaranteed a commission as an officer in the United States Military after graduation. Each school has its own standards and admissions criteria, making the subject of "getting in" impos-

---

3 Rod Powers, "The Perfect University," http://usmilitary.about.com/od/joiningthe military/a/academies_4.htm (accessed May 21, 2007).

4 The Coast Guard Academy does charge a $3,000 fee.

sible to cover in any depth here, but there are certain standards in common. All of the academies require that an applicant be the following:

- At least seventeen but not yet twenty-three by July 1 of the year admitted
- A U.S. citizen at the time of enrollment (exception: foreign students nominated by agreement between the United States and another country)
- Of high moral caliber
- Unmarried
- Not pregnant or legally obligated to support a child or children
- Nominated by a U.S. congressperson, senator, or the vice president of the United States

There are two exceptions to the last requirement. You do not need a letter of nomination if you are already an enlisted member of the military or if you are applying for entrance to the Coast Guard Academy. It is interesting to note that home-schooled students are eligible for consideration, as long as they can document a comprehensive academic core and sufficient extracurricular activities. Each school has a questionnaire that applicants must complete as a part of the admissions process. More specific information on the application process and standards for each academy can be found through its website:

The United States Naval Academy: www.usna.edu

The United States Military Academy (West Point): www.usma.edu

The United States Air Force Academy: www.usafa.af.mil

The United States Coast Guard Academy: www.cga.edu

It is important to understand that military academy educations are tuition free, but not without their price. Each school has a contract that incoming students must sign that contains specific military service commitments in addition to the usual honor code and conduct conditions.

However, typically those who pursue this course are dedicated to the pursuit of a long-term military career, so this should come as no surprise.

Keep in mind that military academies are not the only road into the Officers' Corps. Many earn their commission through participation in the Reserve Officers' Training Corps (or ROTC), which will be discussed in the next section. Others enter the military as traditional enlisted personnel and then rise through the ranks by way of educational and career achievements. This last method is most common in the National Guard and Reserves. Officers have career opportunities within the military that are not available to enlisted personnel. For example, if you wish to be a pilot, you'll need to be an officer. Recruiters can explain the various career options available to you and how best to achieve your goals. However, if you aspire to a military academy, it's best to begin your preparation (physically and academically) as soon as possible—preferably no later than your sophomore year of high school.

ROTC

The Reserve Officers' Training Corps or ROTC (often pronounced "rot-see") is another point of entry into the military. Established programs on college campuses, and even the Junior ROTC in some high schools, allow students to use their academic study time for preparation and training for military service. The Army, Navy, and Air Force all offer ROTC programs to students, providing an experience that is somewhere between military basic training and a scouting program. Anyone who has spent time on a college campus has most likely encountered the small, co-ed groups of uniformed students practicing drills, performing honor guard duties, and even occasionally engaging in cooperative activities with the regular military. These students earn money toward their education and a placement within the Officers' Corps after successful completion of the ROTC program and formal enlistment into the military.

In recent years, there has been something of a backlash against ROTC programs on school campuses, particularly at the high-school level. Some parents (and students) find the program to be somewhat of an indoctrination into the military habits and mindset at an age when many young people are vulnerable to peer pressure and desire the approval of authority figures. These are legitimate concerns, and I would agree that responsible parents need to take the time to talk to their children about their desire to participate in ROTC programming. However, if the student is serious about planning a career in the military, and wants the opportunity to experience some of what the military lifestyle offers while also paving the way toward a successful placement within the armed forces, then the Reserve Officers' Training Corps is a highly effective resource to help meet those goals.

Pre-Enlistment Divination

Most followers of Pagan faiths practice some form of divination. Primarily, this is used as a form of telescope—a way to see farther down the path you presently walk. I do not believe that our futures are set in stone; therefore, I do not believe that divination can reveal a predestined fate. I believe it only provides a clearer map of the courses we are already on. If one does not like the messages conveyed in a reading, it is a simple matter of making choices that change one's path. This view of divination is especially applicable if you are considering enlistment in the armed forces, since what you are essentially seeking is a glimpse of your future on the Warrior's Path. If the outcome is unfavorable, wait a while. It could mean that you are not at a place in your life where such a dramatic commitment is wise. It could mean you need to change the question. For example, if your query was "What does the future hold for me if I join the Army?" try asking about another branch. However, if you have repeated the divination process several times, and each time you are met with negative portents, I would advise you to think long and hard before enlisting. It could be that as badly as you may want this life, there are very compelling reasons why it is not meant to be.

This divination method is designed especially for military personnel. Many cultures consider any form of divination to be heretical, and in some cases criminal, so I wanted to create a system that could be carried with you regardless of where you are stationed. You will need one each of the following: tiger's eye, clear quartz, amethyst, hematite, rose quartz, pyrite, lapis lazuli, onyx, and a pebble. Next, you will need to draw (on a piece of paper or cloth) a circle and divide it into five sections labeled with the elements: earth, air, fire, water, and spirit. For a more permanent divination set, I suggest investing in a decent-size piece of leather that can be cut into a thirteen-inch circle. Inscribe the chart as described on the inside of the leather. When you are done, you can bind up the stones into a handy storage pouch. This should fit nicely into your duffle and be fairly unobtrusive when passing through customs. Keep in mind, though, the pyrite and hematite will show up when passing through an x-ray machine.

Now, holding all of the stones in one hand (or both hands, if your stones are particularly large), rap the paper/cloth/leather three times with the hand holding the stones and, with your eyes closed, cast them onto the chart. You will be interpreting only the stones that have fallen within the circle. Remove any that have fallen outside of the circle and put them away. Consult the chart on the next page to divine the meaning of your particular casting.

PRE-ENLISTMENT DIVINATION CHART

	Earth	Air	Fire	Water	Spirit
Tiger's Eye	Balance, steady hand, courage	Ability to discern the truth, wisdom	Impetuousness, rash decisions, regret	Stability, steadfastness, stubbornness	Protection from evil, hex-breaking
Clear Quartz	Sense of purpose, fulfillment	Deception, subjection to outside influence, pressure	Energy, power, direct action	Overwhelming emotion, chaos	Connection with ancestors, nearness to the spirit world
Amethyst	Pride, self-service, ego, greed	Calm, succor, ease of mind	Purification, transformation	Clarity, true sight, perception	Piercing illusion, check your facts, divine warning
Hematite	Earthbound, concern for physical health	Negative thought patterns, lies, curses	Strong will, courage, commitment to a set course	Judgment, submission to authority, loss of self-determination	Blood-lust, the battle-hardened soul
Rose Quartz	Calm, confidence, feelings of connection	Compassionate heart, empathy toward others	Conflicted feelings, unwillingness to part with loved ones	Strong connections to family and friends, homesickness, heartache	Compassion outweighing action, empathy overcoming conviction
Pyrite	Financial gain, stability	Fraud, deception, theft	Gambling, loss, irrational choices, risk	Building valuable relationships	Fulfillment, honor, self-sacrifice
Lapis Lazuli	Protection, good luck	Trauma, stress, fear, anxiety	Clarity of purpose, creativity, renewal through annihilation	Pain, depression	Spirit guidance, lingering memories, inability to let go
Onyx	Challenges that transform	Chaotic mind, torment by imagination	Negative energy that surrounds you	Influenced by past life circumstances	Know your mind; beware self-deception
Pebble	Solid grounding in the place where you are meant to be; connection to home	Level-headed awareness; you are unmoved by the winds of fortune	Endurance of extreme hardship, deprivation, and danger; possible loss of life	Slow erosion of sense of purpose and self; doubt, weariness, depression	True warrior spirit; strength, calm, wisdom, and restraint

PAGAN PERSPECTIVES
* * *

Adult Child of a Veteran

Name: Morgana

Branch of Service: United States Marine Corps (Vietnam Era)

Tradition/Path: Kitchen Witchcraft/Folk Magick

You are the daughter of a Vietnam veteran. How has this experience shaped your life? Has it had an impact on your spiritual practice?

I had a very strict upbringing, as far as discipline and expectations. I do know how to make a bed military style! Psychologically, I gained a very bad temper from my father. Everyone who knows him says that the war changed him—he came back with a reduced ability to feel compassion for people and about things like death, and that did have an impact on my upbringing. However, his experience also made him much more tolerant of other people and cultures, and because of that I reap the benefits of having him accept me and my faith, even though it's very different than his.

As far as my spiritual practice, in observing my father's bouts of post-traumatic stress and flashbacks, I noticed that they correlated to his desire to find the comfort and protection of God for himself and his family—especially my brother and I. He doesn't believe in a personal afterlife. And I think that in some respects he feels as if he doesn't deserve one—he carries a lot of guilt about things that he saw and did during his time of service, and I think that it's left him feeling unworthy. But for us, he wanted us to experience salvation and the love of God. That desire gave him an ability to be receptive to my own spiritual path and my journey, even though it took me far from what he had initially expected. Watching him has taught me that if you have made amends for your wrongs, you will be received by God. It makes me feel comfortable to know that there is salvation for him within my spiritual path (whether or not he believes in or accepts it), and it gives me peace to know that at the end of his life, he will find peace and acceptance with the Warrior aspects of the Deities of Paganism.

Having experienced military life through your father, did you consider joining the military yourself? How did your Pagan worldview influence this decision?

I did briefly consider joining the military in order to have access to education and health care. That was a decision that my spirituality led me away from. While I believe that the Warrior's Path is one of honor and value, I came to the conclusion, after much spiritual work and soul-searching, that it was not a path for me to take. As a Pagan and as a woman, I felt that I would be segregated and treated differently because of those facets of myself, and that was a part of my decision to pursue other paths.

The military is known as a conservative environment. Did the fact that you were Pagan have an impact on your relationship with your father or his peers? If so, how?

My father does not associate with anyone that was in the military with him. He also chooses not to participate in military or veterans' groups. He distances himself greatly from that part of himself. He is very conservative, however, and that does have an impact on how we talk to each other. When the topics come up, he is jovial and jokey in how he disagrees with me about my Paganism, feminism, and political views. I'm a socialist and he is very, very conservative, so yes, we do butt heads at times. There are many issues where we overlap though. My father completely supported the Veteran Pentacle Quest. At that point, it's not a religious or political issue; it's a matter of respecting the human being and their service. The only time my spirituality comes into play with him is when I discuss my feminist philosophy around him. Feminism is a vital part of my spiritual practice, and that, more than anywhere else, is where we disagree.

Do you feel that there is such a thing as a "Warrior's" spiritual path? Do you find that military Pagans have a different relationship with or perspective on Deity than civilians?

Yes, I absolutely believe that! Generations of people from various cultures throughout Britain and prehistory have had gods and goddesses representative of the Warrior and the Warrior Class. That is something that without a doubt has to have a special protector. If you are Christian or Jewish, it might be a guardian angel. For a Pagan, it could be the Morrigan. Every race and class of people have a special religious affinity for the Warrior aspect.

The military Pagans that I have known have been widely varied in their perspectives and their outlooks. I don't know that I could summarize or generalize them all so easily. But anyone who experiences separation from their families and life under extremely dangerous and tenuous circumstances would have to develop a special relationship with God in order to survive in such an environment. Likewise, the families left behind who pray for safety and try to support their Warrior loved ones from a distance must develop a deeper relationship with Deity and the Warrior aspects of God. It's a pattern that's been reflected throughout our human history. I think that there is a crucial difference for military Pagans though: unlike most major religions, I cannot recall a time when Pagan warriors have marched into battle in the name of their God. They might pray for protection or intercession of their Deities, but generally speaking, Pagan nations have not been concerned with conquering and converting, and that sets us apart from other faiths.

Has your upbringing influenced how you view and relate to the Warrior aspects of Deity? If so, how?

I would say so. I think that especially as I've gotten older and more attuned to my spirituality, along with the ability to see my father through the eyes of an adult instead of as a child, I have come to see that when you tap into that greater aspect of the Warrior, you are able to act more honorably and behave more honorably, and then to come home and dwell with the knowledge that you are blessed and that there is some level of reprieve for the actions one undertakes in battle.

Pagans tend to be people who passionately support their causes and beliefs. How has being a military "brat" affected the way you act upon your beliefs? Do you actively support specific military causes or issues?

I have been raised to fight for what I believe in at all costs. My father joined the military not because he was drafted, but because he didn't believe that men with young children should be drafted. So, he stepped up so that he could save someone from being drafted. He did not believe in the Vietnam conflict; he believed that laying down his life was a lesser sacrifice than that of the man with a wife and children. He has taught me to fight for what I believe even to the point of laying down my life. It's not just about political action; it's about acting morally and respectfully, even to those who disagree with you. He was greeted with disdain when he returned home, and his sacrifice was not acknowledged. He was treated as if he was something he wasn't. And so, he taught me that in every fight, you must take the high road, do the right thing, and be able to look in the mirror and say, "I did what I think was right," and I think that lesson absolutely impacts how I practice my religious and political beliefs.

Social justice is a large part of my spiritual practice. I believe that activism is a form of magick and work my religion accordingly. When it comes to military issues and causes, I do incorporate certain facets into my work. For example, the case of Suzanne Swift and the issue of command rape speak directly to my military background and my feminist witchcraft, and so this is one area where I have actively worked to raise awareness and support. I think that people have to understand what it really means to support the troops, and so I work to raise awareness of causes that really and truly benefit the troops, such as access to quality health care for veterans (including mental health care) at all stages of life and regardless of when the symptoms manifest. I also believe that sometimes supporting the troops means ensuring that they are not sent to fight for needless causes or in useless wars. I believe that by demanding that politicians and strategists view peace as the *first* step in resolving global conflict, I am supporting the troops. I'm a big believer in using the military as a tool of last resort.

Some elders in our community have a strong connection to the 1960s "hippie" or anti-war movement. Have you ever experienced conflict or discrimination within the Pagan community because of your family's Vietnam-Era service?

I have not experienced that firsthand, since I do not often share my family's experiences with others. I have, however, heard others within the Pagan community refer to soldiers as "baby killers" and find that to be one of the most horrid, vile, and disrespectful things that one can say about the military. People join (or are drafted into) the military and serve under extremely difficult conditions, both physically and emotionally. I think that most of the people that I've encountered within our community have come to see the difference between the Warrior and the war and are better able to separate the two now. Thankfully, the old-school attitudes are dying out and are being replaced by a broader understanding of what it means to serve in uniform.

Knowing what you know now, what advice would you give to someone considering joining (or marrying into) the military?

Be loving. Be kind. But also remember that who your spouse may become is not who you've married—and that's through no fault of their own. Sometimes, to support them means also to take care of your own needs. You can never know what they've been through, and there are some things that they will never share with you. But regardless of how they may change, the core of their selves remains the same.

In terms of joining the military, it is a decision that must be weighed very carefully, because it is one that will demand many sacrifices of you—financially, emotionally, psychologically, and more. Be sure that you have a strong support network around you, but more importantly, be sure that you have a strong relationship with God, so that no matter who surrounds you, or what they may understand, you always have someone to turn to. And understand that wars are the actions of men, not God, and know that no matter what you see, or do, or experience, God did not cause it and he will not turn you away because of it.

*   *   *

2. Know Your Rights

We hold these truths to be self-evident, that all men are created equal . . .

—The Declaration of Independence

Religious Freedom in the Military

In recent years, I've been pleasantly surprised by the amount of religious diversity within the military ranks. Not just among Pagan faiths, but overall—it seems to me that the military is becoming more representative of our population as a whole. There are now Christians, Jews, Muslims, Pagans, Christian Scientists, Scientologists, Buddhists, Sikhs, atheists, and humanists (just to name a few) in the service today. And this is a good thing—because for many, many years the military has been insular, predominantly conservative/Evangelical Christian, and more than a little unwelcoming to outsiders. Part of why I felt a need to write this book was to guide others through the difficulties of being a subgroup within a subgroup, especially when the latter is not known for embracing nonconformists!

What You Need to Know About the Army Chaplains Guide

Like many things about being Pagan in the military, when it comes to your interactions with the Chaplain Corps, there's good news, and then there's bad news. The good news is that Wicca is specifically recognized within the Army Chaplains Guide—which is a very helpful thing for Pagans of most traditions, even non-Wiccans. However, the downside to this is the fact that unlike Pagans, most chaplains tend to be a bit more literalistic in their views—both militarily and religiously. So, when you combine these two aspects of life into one handy military guide to religion, your chaplain can often view it as the end-all-be-all in explaining Paganism (especially Wicca).

The Chaplains Guide has been excerpted here for you to review and become familiar with. This is an important document to be fully aware of, since regardless of your individual traditional path, this will be the ultimate source for determining exactly what your chaplain is willing to provide for you in terms of space, resources, materials, and much, much more.

THE U.S. ARMY CHAPLAINS GUIDE TO WICCA[1]

A guide to Wicca for U.S. Military Chaplains

Historical roots: Witchcraft is the ancient Pagan faith of Europe. This nature-oriented, agricultural, magical religion had no central organization, but was passed through families. During the Christian Era, particularly after the beginning of the systematic persecution of Witches in 1484, almost all the public expression of the Craft disappeared. Surviving in hidden and isolated places, Witchcraft has made a comeback in the twentieth century, partially spurred by the repeal of the last of the British Witchcraft Laws in 1951.

Current world leadership: No central authority. Many Witches have, however, affiliated with the American Council of Witches, formed in 1974, to provide a structure for cooperation and mutual sharing.

---

1 Extract from "Religious Requirements and Practices of Certain Selected Groups: A Handbook for Chaplains," U.S. Government Publication No. 008-020-00745-5, April 1978.

Origins in the U.S.: Brought to the U.S. in the 17th century by emigrants from Europe. Since then, many Witches from many ethnic and national traditions have brought their religious practices to the New World. It survived in the isolation of rural settings and the anonymity in the city. The 1960s saw a significant revival of the Craft, and many Witches and "covens" (local groups) became at least partially public. Many discovered others of like mind through the emerging Pagan press. A meeting in Minneapolis formed the American Council of Witches (1974) and a statement entitled "Principles of Wiccan Beliefs" was adopted.

Number of adherents in the U.S.: Unknown: between 10,000 and 100,000.

Organizational structure: The basic structure is the coven (local group) with 5 to 50 members (ideally 12–15) led by a High Priestess or High Priest. The Priest and/or Priestess derives authority from initiation by another Witch. Some covens are tied together in fraternal relationships and acknowledge authority of a Priestess or Priest from whom orders are derived. Many are totally autonomous.

Leadership and role of Priestess and/or Priest: The High Priestess and/or High Priest has authority for the coven. Witches pass through three degrees as they practice the Craft: (1) acknowledges one as a full member of the coven and initiates the process of mastering the skills of a Witch, (2) recognizes growth in ability and admits one to all the inner secrets, and (3) admits one to the priesthood.

Who may conduct worship services? A High Priestess or Priest.

Is group worship required? No, but it is encouraged.

Worship requirements: None, but Witches are expected to practice their faith, which includes mastering magick, ritual, and psychic development and the regular worship of the Wiccan deities.

Minimum requirements for worship: The "athame," or ritual knife; the "pentacle," a metal disc inscribed with magical symbols; a chalice; and a sword. Various traditions will demand other items.

Facilities for worship: Witches worship within a magick circle that is inscribed on the ground or the floor. The circle should be located so as to insure the privacy of the rituals.

Other specific religious requirements other than worship (see above): None.

Dietary laws or restrictions: None.

Special religious holidays: The four great festivals are seasonal:

- Spring Equinox, March 21
- Summer Solstice, or Midsummer, June 21
- Autumn Equinox, September 21
- Yule, or Winter Solstice, December 22

These are joined by four cross festivals related to the agricultural and herd-raising year:

- Candlemas, February 2
- May Eve, or Beltane, April 30
- Lammas, July 31
- Hallowe'en, October 31

Besides these eight, most Wiccan groups meet either weekly or bi-weekly (on the full and new moon).

Funeral and burial requirements: Practices vary widely. In case of death, the coven to which the Witch belongs should be contacted.

Cremation: Many prefer it, but the local coven should be consulted.

Autopsy: Generally no restrictions.

Medical treatment: No restrictions.

Uniform appearance requirements: None are proscribed.

Position on service in the armed forces: No official stance. Many Witches are presently military personnel, while others are conscientious objectors, derived, from the generally pro-life stance of Wicca.

Is a Priest or Priestess required at time of death? No.

Any practices or teaching that may conflict with military directives or practices? None, generally, though individual covens may have some. The local coven should be contacted if specific questions arise.

Basic teachings or beliefs: Underlying agreements are summed up in the "Principles of Wiccan Beliefs" adopted by the American Council of Witches. . . . Specific expressions of beliefs will vary widely, due to the ethnic roots or the traditions of the individual coven.

Creedal statements and/or authoritative literature: (See also "basic beliefs") All Witches use two books, a "grimoire," or book of spells and magical procedures, and a "book of shadows," or book of ritual. Each coven will use a different grimoire and/or book of shadows. . . .

Ethical practices: Wiccan ethics are summed up in the law called the Wiccan Rede, "An Ye Harm None, Do As Ye Will."

How does Witchcraft recruit new members? Witches do not proselytize, but they welcome inquiries from those who hear about the Craft by either word of mouth or the media.

Relationship with other religions: Cooperation with the whole Pagan community is very high. Relations with other religions are cordial, except those groups which have sought to persecute or defame the Craft.

I'm fairly certain that, as you were reading, a great many thoughts crossed through your mind. These most likely included "That's true, but . . ." or "Not necessarily!" or "That doesn't apply to me . . ." Regardless of how outdated the material is, or how limited in its scope, this is the authoritative reference that chaplains will go by when they are determining the needs of Wiccan and Pagan service personnel. This is a fabulous thing, if you'd like to be able to hold rituals for the Wheel of the Year. It's not so great, though, if you'd prefer a Priestess to be summoned if you're dying.

The Chaplains Guide needs to be supplemented with additional information from you, and the other Pagans on your installation, with as much as the chaplain is willing to accept. There is a certain level of diversity within the Pagan community that is very unusual for most mainstream religious denominations, and this diversity is not reflected by the Chaplains Guide. It falls to you, then, to know exactly what the military believes that you need in order to practice your religion and then prove your need for supplemental resources. Anything above and beyond the very narrow scope of the Chaplains Guide will usually require the officers you are interacting with to be persuaded, potentially argued with, and occasionally defended against.

One important thing to note: because Wicca is a faith recognized by the military, personal opinions held by co-workers or officers regarding your religion cannot legally interfere with your right to religious expression. That said, if your religion is not formally recognized by the military (Santeria, for example, or Thelema), then you are going to face an uphill battle in getting formal recognition, especially when your contact is openly hostile toward non-Judeo-Christian paths. The military does not function like the civilian government. Just because you believe something and call it your faith, it does not automatically mean that the military has to accommodate your needs. Your path must first be recognized by the military as a "real" religion that is also in keeping with military standards. For example, many white supremacist groups are legally recognized as 501(c)(3)s and call themselves churches, but they are not recognized by the Department of Defense as legitimate religious organizations. Many religious groups have struggled for years to establish a working relationship with the military that would allow their practitioners to have access to chaplains' support and military resources. In the Pagan community, these often take the form of "umbrella" groups willing to extend their military relationship to encompass many other paths as well. I discuss these groups more both in the next section and in the appendices at the end of the book.

How to Start a Designated Faith Group on Your Base

When my husband and I first moved onto the base where he is stationed, I went with my friend Paula, another military wife and Pagan, to visit the chaplain. We were inquiring about how to go about getting his support to start what is known as a Designated Faith Group on the base. DFGs are basically small, self-regulating meeting groups for faiths whose needs extend beyond the capabilities of your average chaplain. We were well aware of several Pagans on the base and thought that it was appropriate that we be allowed to formally organize, meet, and celebrate together. The chaplain's response was less than enthusiastic. "If I had my way," he said to us, *"you people* wouldn't even exist here. But since you do, I'll do the bare minimum that I am legally obligated to do to help you." Needless to say, he was part of that 60% Evangelical majority within the Chaplain Corps.

So it was, for over a year, that Paula and I worked diligently to jump through every hoop he put before us. Each time we needed something from that particular chaplain, we had to document, over and over, exactly where it was stated that he was obligated to help us with that particular request. To put into perspective how long this process was dragged out, we received our approval in the same week that another group, supported by the same sponsoring body, was granted their approval. Only they'd gotten their DFG up and running in five months . . . in Iraq . . . in the midst of open combat operations. The Besom and Blade Open Circle met together to celebrate a lavish Samhain ritual—the first of its kind ever to be held on this base. A few weeks later, most of our membership PCSed (Permanent Change of Station), and the group fell below the minimum number required to maintain our official status. The plug was pulled immediately—done in by an unsupportive officer who did everything in his power to delay, distract, and deter. Unfortunately, this is life for Pagans in the military. It is my hope that I can help ease some of the burden by compiling a book of suggestions, information, spells, and rituals designed specifically for military Pagans. And by creating an open, positive resource that you can share with your own chaplains, perhaps help create a different outcome for you and your family.

The most important thing to keep in mind is that *you are not alone!* There are other Pagans around, everywhere—definitely on your base, and most likely in your unit. Hopefully, by using the resources presented here, and the networking information contained in the back of this book, you can find one another, support and learn from one another, and create a dramatically different military culture than the one we currently know. In the meantime, I'll give you the basics of forming a Designated Faith Group on your base. Keep in mind that the requirements vary from branch to branch, and occasionally from chaplain to chaplain, so while this is what you may generally expect to comply with, these steps might be more or less complicated depending upon your individual situation.

The first thing you're going to want to do when considering forming a DFG on your installation is to research and contact a sponsoring body that you feel would be the best "fit" both for your needs (since you'll most likely end up as the POC, or point of contact) and the needs of the chaplain. When Paula and I started Besom and Blade, we were fortunate enough to have the Sacred Well Congregation as our sponsoring organization. There are a couple options available to you, including SWC, as well as Circle Sanctuary and the Covenant of the Goddess. Each one will have its own requirements for sponsorship; for example, SWC required that the DFG Leader was also enrolled in its Greencraft-tradition distance learning program. With a little bit of research, you will be able to find the organization that's perfect for your needs.

After you've established your connection with a potential sponsor, it is time to approach your chaplain. Some Pagans have wonderful working relationships with their base chaplains, built on a solid foundation of mutual respect for divergent paths. These are very lucky people indeed. For most of us, however, this initial meeting will be the first extended interaction with the chaplain at all, and it might be the first time he or she is aware of the fact that there are any minority faiths in the unit at all. I strongly suggest that you come prepared with some simple information about Paganism. Paula and I brought a chart we had prepared that featured basic concepts of various Pagan traditions alongside those of more familiar faiths such as Judaism, Islam, and Christianity. Most chaplains don't have the time (or interest) to read anything longer than a few pages, so I don't typically recommend bringing books to share, unless the chaplain requests one for future reading.

Like many people who are wholly unfamiliar with Paganism, the chaplain might ask some intrusive and perhaps even unintentionally rude questions. Our chaplain told us point-blank that the military did not have to accommodate our need for sacrificial animals, which then necessitated a half-hour-long conversation about how Pagans don't typically practice animal sacrifice and thus are perfectly fine with that restriction. Refrain from taking these kinds of incidents as expressions of hostility, and be cautious in how you respond to them. Our goal is to be respectful of the fact that this is both an officer and a clergy member, and to take advantage of opportunities to gently educate, rather than allow a conversation to devolve into acrimony or debate. The chaplain may or may not be immediately receptive to the idea of a Designated Faith Group on your installation. As in the story I recounted earlier, you may be met with outright hostility. However, keep in mind that while we must be respectful of his or her position as an officer, his or her opinion of your religion is irrelevant. The chaplains are required to meet the needs of the service personnel within their unit, and thus—whether they are comfortable with the idea or not—as long as you meet the necessary requirements, they must accommodate your needs through a Designated Faith Group or reasonable alternative.

This term "reasonable alternative" is one of several minefields you'll have to negotiate if you're interested in starting a sanctioned military group. Come prepared with research that demonstrates the extent of the surrounding local Pagan community. Many military bases are in areas that are traditionally more conservative, and a Witchvox search would reveal that it's not uncommon for there to be only one or two open circles within fifty miles of a given base. Being able to demonstrate that you are unable to have your needs met outside of the military community is a powerful asset in making your request. If you happened to be stationed in California, Chicago, or somewhere else with a high-density Pagan population, you can make the argument (as Paula and I did) that civilian groups are unequipped to meet the spiritual needs of military personnel. The military establishment exerts a great deal of time and effort to promote the idea of the military as a culture unto itself and individual units as families. It is difficult to then contradict this idea by forcing a unit member to seek spiritual communion and support from outside the military structure. Another argument against civilian groups is that DFGs are entitled to material support from the base. You can make a reasonable argument that the number of Pagans on your installation would overwhelm the civilian Pagan community and present an unfair burden on them in terms of resources. Regardless of your location (high- or low-density Pagan area), as long as you can present your request logically and effectively, there is no reasonable cause for it to be denied. Once you have demonstrated that a Designated Faith Group is the most logical and accommodating option for your needs, you will be presented with a to-do list by your chaplain. This can vary dramatically, but generally speaking, you'll have to provide the following:

Proof of a Sponsoring Body. Keep in mind that the military decides who is allowed to act as a sponsor. So, a local coven or Pagan organization may be well-established and have an unparalleled reputation, but that doesn't mean that the chaplain will accept it as your group's sponsor. Typically, the chaplain will expect that the sponsor have 501(c)(3) status as a nonprofit organization, an established relationship with the military or Department of Defense, and a protocol to vet the qualifications of the group's leaders. Sacred Well Congregation has a staff member whose sole role is to assist in the establishment of military communities, so even if you're not interested in pursuing the Greencraft tradition, I strongly recommend contacting them for guidance. In some cases, a local Unitarian Universalist church may be willing to act as your sponsor. Contact a local UU minister to discuss what the church might be willing to do to support you.

A Designated Faith Group Leader (DFGL). This would be the person who will be acting as point of contact both for the chaplain and the sponsor. Typically, the DFGL is the public face of the base Pagan community. This means that this individual's contact information is what will be given to those inquiring about the group. It also means that he or she may be called upon to address concerns that arise from within the leadership or community and to act as leader or Priest/ess. Because of this fact, most chaplains like to see documentation that the DFGL is qualified to undertake such a role.

If you are going to be the one to serve as the DFGL, the ideal scenario is for you to be ordained by your sponsoring organization. Keep in mind that the military does not recognize every ordination. Universal Life Church may be good enough for you to make your neighbors' handfasting legal, but it will not cut it for the chaplain. If you are not already ordained, the next best bet is to demonstrate that you are actively pursuing such status (as through SWC's study program) or that you have undertaken professional development courses that would qualify you for the role. These can include counseling or outreach classes, volunteer training, or some other creative solution. Your sponsor should be able to help with this process. The DFGL is lay-minister, public affairs officer, outreach advocate, and community relations director all rolled into one. Keep in mind this is in addition to the tasks that your sponsoring body sets for you that may add seminarian, reporter, accountant, and secretary to your growing DFGL job description. The role of DFGL should not be entered into lightly. Your actions can and will affect the base leadership's perception of the Pagan community for years, possibly forever.

A Plan or Charter. This is usually a document that defines how the group will be organized, what its rules will be, and when and where it will meet. Keep in mind that the military will not allow exclusivity within your group, so you cannot form a Dianic Circle, if that means excluding male participants. The group must be an open circle, welcoming everyone and excluding participation only for very good cause. Besom and Blade was organized in such a way that the only cause for expulsion was intoxication during event participation. The general idea, though, must be compliant with military standards and expectations. You cannot establish rules that contradict existing military protocols. As far as organizational structure, your sponsor will often have input into this aspect of the charter. I strongly suggest avoiding degree-based systems in your planning, in part because the military hates having its personnel ranked by any standard other than its own, and also because most of your members will not be participants long enough to complete a full set of degree requirements. Military life is always transitory, and you must take this high turnover rate into account in your planning.

Proof of Need. No man is an island, and no individual serviceperson may be a Designated Faith Group in and of themselves. You are most likely going to have to provide your chaplain with a list of interested, *qualified* participants. The number of people needed will vary—with our chaplain the magic number was six people—but the qualified part will be constant. In order to count as a verified need, your interested participants must be either military personnel or eligible dependents. This means spouses and children. Retirees with base privileges are absolutely allowed to participate in an on-base DFG, but they do not typically count in proving that the base community has a legitimate need for a Designated Faith Group.

An important thing to keep in mind here is outreach. This concept goes against everything most Pagans believe in. We do not typically "missionary" or seek to convert people to our path, and that's not what I'm advocating for here. But, if your participation numbers fall below that magic threshold required to prove a legitimate need for the group, the chaplains or base leadership do have the right to withdraw support and close the group. So, you need to be proactive in making sure that the base community is aware of your group, that newcomers are informed of activities, and that those who might be interested in participating are approached. Otherwise, and especially if you're dealing with a hostile chaplain, your new group might end as quickly as Besom and Blade. Unlike in the civilian world, where three people make a coven, in the military, numbers matter. The DFGL must be vigilant to make sure that the number of members transferring to new installations is balanced by new participation, thus ensuring that the group is always able to prove that it's serving a legitimate need.

This is just a brief overview of what to expect and how to prepare for the role of DFGL. Your own experience might vary a bit, but the general idea remains the same. I strongly suggest that you establish contact with the Military Pagan Network, as it has staff members who specialize in the regulations pertaining to free worship within each of the branches of the armed forces. If you run into problems or scenarios I was unable to cover here, the MPN is a fantastic resource.

We are living in conservative times, in an already conservative environment. The Southern Baptist Convention, which sponsors more military chaplains than any other religious group, threatened to withdraw its support, and thus decimate the Chaplain Corps, if the chaplains weren't allowed to pray "in Jesus's name" at public military events. The Air Force Deputy Chief of Chaplains, Gen. Cecil Richardson, stated that chaplains "reserve the right to evangelize the unchurched." As more and more Evangelicals join the military, there is a growing backlash against the rights of minority faith personnel to be free from proselytizing and discrimination, both from comrades and commanders. Anti-Pagan comments are not uncommon; my husband has experienced them firsthand for years. The open circle at Fort Hood, Texas, had its ritual space vandalized and nearly destroyed a few years ago. There are a great many who share the sentiment of "if I had my way, you people wouldn't even exist." But the fact remains that we do exist—both within the United States and within its armed forces, and we are blessed enough to have a right to free expression of our faith. Who is more entitled to take advantage of that right than those who are first to fight and die in its defense?

Sexual Freedom in the Military

Generally speaking, Pagans are quite a randy lot, and tend to be comfortable with our sexuality—and everyone else's for that matter! As a rule, we tend to be accepting of sexual differences, such as homosexuality, bisexuality, polyamory, and transsexuality. While we may or may not fall into these categories ourselves, usually we are comfortable embracing those who fall outside the typical sexual lines of our society. We take the statement that "all acts of love and pleasure are Her rituals" at face value.

I firmly believe that a healthy and realistic relationship with our bodies, in both form and function, is one of the greatest blessings of the Pagan faith. Unfortunately, this is not a mindset that is embraced by the military establishment. The dominant military culture is steeped in patriarchal machismo. "Real men" are aggressively heterosexual, dominant in their sexual expressions, and uncomfortable around anything that falls outside of this paradigm. Women in the military often find themselves in a Catch-22, either subjected to harassment and gender-based discrimination for being too feminine for the job, or else viewed as asexual or even homosexual for proving themselves competent in the testosterone-fueled environment.

The military's discomfort with sexuality extends far enough that it attempts a formal regulation of the sexual practices of its personnel. Essentially, the Uniform Code of Military Justice regulates sexual expression to such a degree that, if it were enforced as literally as it is written, married couples could face discharge for engaging in any sexual behavior other than missionary (male on top) style sex. Any other form of sexual activity is prohibited under the sodomy statutes of the UCMJ, including the possession or viewing of adult materials on a military installation, even between consenting, heterosexual, married partners. Thankfully, the letter of the law is not generally enforced to every possible extent. There are some notable exceptions to this benign oversight.

Homosexuals in the Armed Forces

Between 1993, when President Clinton instituted the famous "don't ask, don't tell" policy, and 2003, over 10,000 members of the American military have been separated or discharged from the military because of their sexual orientation.[2] That's a yearly average of 1,000 competent, qualified service personnel released from their enlistment contracts (or else asked to resign their commissions as officers) for no reason other than their orientation. Sadly, these numbers have dramatically increased in recent years. In one recently publicized incident, an Army NCO (noncommis-

---

2 "Gay US Generals Speak Out," BBC News, December 17, 2003, http://news.bbc.co.uk/2/hi/americas/3325335.stm (accessed January 10, 2008).

sioned officer) was discharged because of allegations of his homosexuality, sent anonymously to his commanding officers via e-mail. Additionally, six desperately needed Arabic language specialists have been asked to leave the military because of their homosexuality. This is even as the Pentagon redoubles its efforts to recruit qualified translators.

Part of the problem is a basic lack of understanding about the "don't ask, don't tell" policy itself. Many people, new recruits and civilians alike, assume that it means that as long as you don't discuss your orientation with others in the military, then the military cannot discharge you for being gay. This is not quite accurate. Prior to the implementation of the DADT policy, it was not uncommon for personnel who were discovered to be homosexual to be discharged on a Section 8, a medical discharge due to mental defect and/or disability. This often made finding employment after separation very difficult for the newly discharged serviceperson and attached a lifelong stigma of mental illness. In the mid-70s, homosexuality was removed from the *Diagnostic and Statistical Manual of Mental Disorders*, the guide used by health care professionals to diagnose mental illness, and the status of gays in the military fell into a sort of limbo . . . unwanted, but no longer Section 8 material.[3]

Clinton's policy, implemented as Public Law 103-160, codified at 10 U.S.C. § 654 and commonly known as "don't ask, don't tell, don't pursue," was initially seen as a compromise measure. It intended to give some measure of protection to gays, lesbians, and bisexuals serving in the armed forces. In practice, the "don't pursue" portion was quickly forgotten and the systematic investigation and discharge of suspected homosexuals has continued. This is because, contrary to common perception, DADT did not actually codify an acceptance of homosexual servicepersons, only those willing to pretend that they were not actually gay. The language of the policy is written in such a way as to prohibit anyone who has sexual bodily contact with a person of the same sex from serving in the armed forces of the United States, prohibit any homosexual or bisexual from disclosing his or her sexual orientation, and prohibit them from speaking

---

3 Frank Conahan, "GAO Report on Gays in the Military," June 12, 1992, http://www.ford ham.edu/halsall/pwh/gao_report.html (accessed May 21, 2007).

about any homosexual relationships, including marriages or other familial attributes, while serving in the United States Armed Forces. The policy also states that as long as gay or bisexual men and women in the military do not disclose their sexual orientation, their commanding officers are not allowed to investigate their sexuality. This section of the law is largely ignored, however, and investigations of homosexual conduct, while fewer, still occur with some regularity in the military.

The Pentagon's guidelines on homosexuality are holistic, banning sexual contact, making a statement (i.e., telling someone . . . anyone) that you are gay, lesbian, or bisexual, and marrying or attempting marry someone of the same gender. This is important for Pagans to be aware of, precisely because of that wonderful inclusive sexual spirit discussed earlier. As a member of the military, and especially if you serve as a DFGL, participating in or officiating at a handfasting for a same-sex couple could potentially present grounds for administrative discipline, if not discharge. Likewise, certain followers of traditions that place a great deal of emphasis on sexuality, such as Dianic and Minoan, or those that recognize a fluidity to sexual orientation, such as Faerie, might want to be mindful of how much of their path they share with those on base. Many Pagans that I have known either self-identify as bisexual or else admit a certain level of comfort with same-sex sexuality. It is vital that we, who are typically very comfortable with our sexual natures while at the same time used to a community environment that is welcoming and supportive, are aware of the fact that simply *stating* one's sexual preference—to anyone, not just others in the military—is enough to risk administrative discipline or potential discharge. DADT essentially means that you can be gay . . . as long as you are also celibate and silent.

Your Spouse and You: A Military Guide

Pagan couples are not known for being puritanical in the bedroom, so it may come as some surprise to realize that, in theory at least, the military has the authority to regulate how you express yourself sexually even within the marital bed. Section 925, Article 125, of the Uniform Code of Military Justice addresses the definition of "sodomy" from the legal perspective of the armed forces. When we see the word sodomy today, we assume that the writer is addressing a very specific act (anal penetration) between very specific partners (typically gay men) in a rather outdated and pejorative way. However, from the military's perspective, any act of sexual intercourse that varies from vaginal penetration of a female by her male partner's penis is covered by the term sodomy and is therefore, if only in the strictest sense, illegal.

The UCMJ statute in its entirety reads, "(a) Any person subject to this chapter who engages in unnatural carnal copulation with another person of the same or opposite sex or with an animal is guilty of sodomy. Penetration, however slight, is sufficient to complete the offense. (b) Any person found guilty of sodomy shall be punished as a court-martial may direct."[4] This statute can be (and when it's enforced it *is*) read to include oral sex and anal sex, including digital penetration, no matter how slight.

The flip side of consensual marital sex is forced marital rape. The definition of rape put forth by the UCMJ does *not* acknowledge the existence of marital rape. Section 920, Article 120, of the legal code specifically exempts forcible sexual contact between married partners. The section reads, "Rape and carnal knowledge: (a) Any person subject to this chapter who commits an act of sexual intercourse *with a female not his wife*, by force and without consent, is guilty of rape and shall be punished by death or such other punishment as a court-martial may direct. (b) Any person subject to this chapter, who, under circumstances not amounting to rape, commits an act of sexual intercourse *with a female not his wife* who has not attained the age of sixteen years, is guilty of carnal knowledge and shall be punished as a court-martial may direct. (c) Penetration, however slight, is sufficient to complete either of these offenses." The emphasis above is mine. This is not uncommon, as there are still some individual states that do not acknowledge the existence of marital rape. However, in doing my research I was surprised to discover that the military falls into this category as well. There has been some talk within the military community of updating these statutes to reflect a more inclusive and accurate definition of sexual assault, and I am hopeful that by the time you read this book, the

---

4 *Uniform Code of Military Justice*, Subchapter X, Sec. 925, Art. 125.

injustices highlighted within this section will have been remedied by the Department of Defense.

Until these changes occur, it is my fondest belief that the vast majority of Pagan people do not need to be reminded that all acts of *consensual* love and pleasure are Her rituals. I do not think that many of my readers are going to read this section and say, "Yippee! I can rape my partner!" But I do think that my female readers need to be aware of this "legal loophole" in the UCMJ. It is vitally important that we understand the nature of consent in our marital relations and be willing to accept a "no" from our partners when they are not in the mood. This should go without saying, but unfortunately, often coercion can be subtle and insidious with the coercers failing to recognize the impact of their actions. We must acknowledge our partners' desires and engage in loving, playful exploration of our fantasies with each other when the mood arises. However, pressuring our partners—whether it's refusing to accept that they have a headache or ignoring a request to slow down, ease up, or pull out—is never acceptable and is always a violation of the Rede and the Goddess, if not of the UCMJ.

So what does all of this really mean? Does the Department of Defense install secret cameras in its military quarters, just ready to pounce on a consensual act of marital cunnilingus? Definitely not. However, if you ever end up in the middle of a bitter divorce, or if some other legal trouble arises, you must be aware of the fact that you have technically broken the law, and if someone truly wanted to "throw everything at the wall to see what sticks," charges of sodomy could be added to the petition for divorce or list of charges. I am certainly not advocating a missionary-only marital life and would be a hypocrite if I said that my own husband and I did not break the law several times a week. However, anyone in the military or considering the military needs to be fully aware of the amount of control that is exerted over the most private and intimate aspects of their property: the serviceman and servicewoman.

Extramarital Sexuality in the Armed Forces

It is a common misconception that adultery is a crime covered within the Uniform Code of Military Justice. This is not exactly the case, but under the right circumstances, it can be just as detrimental to a military career. When it is prosecuted, adultery falls under the umbrella of Article 134 of the UCMJ, "General Article," which covers any conduct that brings discredit to the military or otherwise disturbs the order and discipline of a unit. In other words, adultery is not a crime committed against the wronged spouse, but rather against the military itself.

Adultery is covered by Paragraph 62 of Article 134, which specifies three specific criteria that must be met in order to prosecute a charge of adultery. Keep in mind that because this charge is viewed as an offense against the military as an institution, it can potentially be brought regardless of whether or not the other spouse consented to his or her partner's extramarital dalliance. In order to qualify as adultery under Article 134, Paragraph 62, the elements of proof needed are

1. that the accused wrongfully had sexual intercourse with a certain person;

2. that, at the time, the accused or the other person was married to someone else; and

3. that, under the circumstances, the conduct of the accused was to the prejudice of good order and discipline in the armed forces or was of a nature to bring discredit upon the armed forces.

To the dismay of many aggrieved military wives, element one often is so difficult to prove as to preclude most prosecutions. Usually, proving element one requires evidence of the actual act of intercourse, such as photographs of the parties in action, DNA evidence, eyewitness statements, or other verifiable proof. Suspicious activity alone is not enough to warrant court-martial. Element two is notable for the fact that it specifies that service personnel do not need to be married themselves to be charged with adultery. It is sufficient that their partners alone be married to someone else. This is an important consideration for anyone involved in polyamorous relationships, such as triad or quad relationships.

In 2002, changes were authorized by President Bush that resulted in a broadening of the factors to be considered by commanders when deciding appropriate action for personnel charged with adultery. When determining whether or not a crime has been committed, COs must now take the following into consideration:

- The rank, grade, or position of the accused.

- The military status of the accused.

- The rank, grade, position, or relation to the armed forces of the co-actor.

- The military status of the actors' spouses, or their relationship to the armed forces.

- The impact (if any) of the adulterous relationship on the accused, the co-actor, or either of their spouses to perform their duties in support of the armed forces.

- The misuse (if any) of government time or resources in the commission of the adulterous act(s).

- Whether or not the adulterous conduct continued after counseling or orders to desist; the flagrancy of the conduct (i.e., did it cause notoriety on the base?) or if it was accompanied by any other violations of the UCMJ.

- The negative impact of the adulterous conduct on the unit or organization of the units or organization of the accused, the co-actor, or either of their spouses; such as a detrimental effect on the morale, teamwork, or efficiency of their unit(s) or organization(s).

- Whether or not either party was legally separated.

- Whether the adulterous conduct is ongoing, occurred recently, or happened some time in the past.

These standards specify just "how bad" adultery has to be before a serviceperson's commanding officer will get involved. The general rule of thumb is to determine who was screwed more by the adulterous affair— the offender's spouse (was the affair conducted between Marine husband and civilian babysitter at the couple's home while civilian wife was out of town?) or the offender's branch of service (was the affair conducted between members of the same unit, on company time, and on the commander's desk?).

If adultery is such a low-consequence offense and so difficult to prove anyway, why is this subject relevant to Pagans? First of all, many Pagans are polyamorous (involved in a romantic relationship involving more than one partner) in their marital relationships. This can become an issue if commanders or colleagues observe behavior that they consider to be detrimental to the image or efficiency of the unit. For example, while you and your partner have an understanding that "what happens on deployment, stays on deployment," it is possible that someone within the military, observing this extramarital behavior while you are supposed to be "mission-focused," could bring a charge of adultery—even if your partner is not offended by the conduct.

Another important consideration is sacred sexuality. The Great Rite, in my opinion, should always be a symbolic (chalice and blade) ritual when conducted by military personnel. Common sense would (hopefully) lead one to assume that it would be inappropriate for a Designated Faith Group, operating as a supplementary military organization, to *ever* engage in a literal Great Rite ceremony as a part of official group worship. We must always be mindful of how we explain the fertility aspects of our religion to outsiders on base. We may love the fact that a Maypole is symbolic of the sexual union of the Lord and Lady. But I can promise you, if this same information is discussed with random people in line behind you at the commissary, the rumors about the DFG will spread like wildfire . . . and none of them will involve the word "symbolic."

As frustrating as it can be for a religion that sees no shame in sexuality, it is important to be mindful of the perceptions of those non-Pagans around us. Be mindful of your conversations about sex, both in terms of orientation as well as behavior. You never know who will hear you, or how fast your statements will spread. And it's important to note that sexual conduct that is frowned upon by leadership (such as viewing pornography or frequenting strip clubs) might not lead to formal court-martial under Article 134, but it could still result in direct administrative action by your commanders. This can include letters of reprimand or counsel and denial of promotion. The latter is especially treacherous for officers who, if they don't make grade within certain time frames, can face involuntary separation from the service. So yes, all acts of love and pleasure are Her rituals. But discretion is also a virtue, and the reputation and regulations of the armed forces will always come before your right to free expression of sexuality, regardless of orientation, consent, or religious motivation.

Exemptions from Combat

You might be wondering why I've included a section on combat exemptions within a book devoted to explaining military life. Shockingly enough, not everyone in the military is eager (or even willing) to take a life. One of the common dualities within the Pagan community is the Warrior/pacifist dichotomy. Simply put, many Pagans view themselves and each other in one of two extremes: either they are part of Warrior traditions such as Norse or Celtic, Asatru, etc., that view warfare as a noble endeavor and violence as a natural and often reasonable response to conflict, *or* they take the other extreme and declare that violence in any form is never acceptable, that it violates the Wiccan Rede, or that it brings with it energies and karma best left un-messed with. Thankfully, most Pagan servicepersons realize that like most dualities, the truth lies somewhere in the middle.

In my private life, I am a mediator. I work actively to help others resolve their conflicts in a democratic, peaceful way. I believe in consensus. I believe that peace is possible. However, I do not believe that peace is always the best choice, as Neville Chamberlain learned before World War II. Utah Phillips says that to be a pacifist is to recognize our own capability for violence and to struggle against it in much the same way that an alcoholic struggles to stay dry. That's the kind of pacifist I am—the one who recognizes that violence is natural, if not always healthy or good, and seeks to find other ways to cope with life and its struggles. I believe that's the kind of people we aspire to be—those who recognize violence as a last, desperate measure rather than a first step rationalized as being the easier way.

The military is this kind of system. Everyone, from generals to privates, hopes that the governments and diplomats of the world can resolve crises at the negotiation table. But they also recognize that there is evil in the world (however you define evil, be it sin or ignorance) and that sometimes, as in the September 11th attacks, it cannot be negotiated with. For these reasons, the military exists to fulfill the Warrior's role, taking upon itself the physical, mental, and spiritual harm that violence brings with it in order that others might live in peace. Those who truly walk this path between the worlds of peace and warfare sometimes struggle with how to reconcile the need for a military presence with the hope for a potential nonviolent resolution. Many of these choose to serve in noncombat positions within the military, providing material aid and comfort to the fighters, while maintaining their own moral integrity. Others enlist in the military prepared to fight, yet somewhere along the way encounter a crisis of faith or a moral choice that turns their original ambition on its ear. This section is for them.

Conscientious Objector Status

Conscientious objector status, applied for after enlistment, is not something that is easy to obtain on the basis of Pagan faith alone. Unlike religious groups such as the Quakers (Society of Friends), the Mennonites, and the Amish, Pagans do not have an inviolable dogma forbidding military service. In fact, some traditions, such as Asatru and some Celtic strands, actively encourage the pursuit of Warrior standing. These "precedents" can make it difficult to prove that you should be exempted from military duty on the basis of religion. However, one can prove CO status by documenting a long history of anti-war or peace activism. One family I know keeps a scrapbook of their children participating in peace rallies, anti-war demonstrations, and other pacifistic actions. If the draft should ever be reinstated, this can serve to verify their claims that their children are conscientious objectors and have a documented history as such that extends far beyond the "just turned eighteen and got my Selective Service notification" time period.

Odds are good that if you're reading this book, you're not a hardcore pacifist. However, there are times when even those who believe in the value of military service find that the military is being used for a purpose that is contradictory to their moral values. Unfortunately, while it is not impossible, it is extremely difficult to obtain conscientious objector status after joining the military. There are ways to make it happen, but it can be a legal roll of the dice to take such a stand. Once you enlist in the military, it becomes incredibly difficult to show that you oppose military service, and unfortunately there is very little provision for a member of the armed services to object to a specific mission after enlistment.

There have been a number of high-profile cases of military personnel refusing to re-deploy after returning from the front lines. Camilo Mejía served one year in prison after refusing to return to Iraq on moral grounds. Agustin Aguayo was recently sentenced to eight months in prison for missing a troop movement. He also refused to go for reasons of conscience. Perhaps the most famous case has been Lt. Ehren Watada, who offered to serve in Afghanistan rather than deploy to Iraq, which he felt to be a mission that contradicted the oath he took as an officer in the United States Military. His case ended in a mistrial, but will most likely be re-heard in the coming year or so.

These cases serve as an example of the challenge of military service: that one might enlist for the noblest of reasons and yet find oneself compelled to serve in a war, mission, or conflict that is diametrically opposed to one's moral and ethical code. If this happens, you are faced with the difficult decision of weighing your priorities. Do you choose to obey the orders, even if you stridently disagree with them, and fulfill your contractual obligation to the military? Or do you refuse these orders and accept whatever penalty and consequence your command structure imposes? These are the challenges facing more and more members of the military today. As Pagans, we are called to live in accord with the interdependent web of all creation. Our actions ripple far beyond the perimeters of our own consciences. The choices, though difficult, are yours to make. Regardless of your decision, information about your rights and the resources available to you can be found at www.girightshotline.org.

Noncombatant Status

To be honest, many people have asked me why someone would want to join the military if that person were not willing to participate in combat. This is, after all, the primary purpose of military service! However, there are a few specialized roles that allow a serviceperson to serve in the armed forces and yet be considered a noncombatant under the provisions of the Geneva Conventions (Protocol I, Article 43.2). These are primarily chaplains and medics. Unfortunately, the military has yet to recognize a Pagan chaplain. I've provided some statistics regarding chaplains sponsored by "minority" faiths. The inequalities are fairly obvious.

Most recently, Donald Larsen, a highly qualified and very well-respected Army chaplain serving in Afghanistan, decided to leave his Christian faith and pursue ordination and sponsorship through a Wiccan organization (in this case, Sacred Well Congregation) instead. While it has always been accepted courtesy in these situations for the prior sponsoring body to maintain its support for the chaplain until the new sponsorship paperwork has been processed, in this case, the Evangelical group that Larsen previously served through immediately terminated its recognition and support for him. As a result, Larsen lost his position as a chaplain and was relieved of his duty.[5] Soldiers of all faiths and denominations lost a loyal and loving spiritual minister because of anti-Pagan prejudice within the larger ecumenical military community. Until this tremendous barrier has been overcome, the primary way to serve as a Pagan noncombatant in the military is as a medic, nurse, or doctor. Women may serve in any of these capacities, but not in frontline or battlefield positions. Keep in mind, however, that in modern warfare, the front lines are pretty much everywhere, so this regulation is really a protection on paper only.

---

5 Alan Cooperman, "For Gods and Country: The Army Chaplain Who Wanted to Switch to Wicca? Transfer Denied." *Washington Post*, February 19, 2007.

MILITARY CHAPLAINS BY FAITH GROUP[6]

Religion	Military Adherents	Number of Chaplains	Ratio, Chaplains to Followers
Mormonism	17,513	41	1:427
Judaism	4,038	22	1:183
Islam	3,286	11	1:299
Christian Science	636	6	1:106
Buddhism	4,546	1	1:4,546
Paganism/Wicca	1,865*	0	N/A

Note: This figure only reflects statistics from the Air Force and the Marines. The Army and Navy (much larger branches) do not keep statistics on Pagan service personnel.

3. Know Your Basics

Live not as though there were a thousand years ahead of you. Fate is at your elbow; make yourself good while life and power are still yours.

—Marcus Aurelius

What to Expect at Basic Training

Basic training has been described as the systematic breaking down of your civilian personality and a subsequent re-creation into the military model. If this idea disturbs you, then the military most likely is not for you. Mental discipline, attention to detail, and a willingness to follow orders are the primary psychological goals of boot camp. While it can be a time of dramatic personal and spiritual growth, there is a reason why basic training has the pop culture reputation that it does: it's not easy, and it's not fun.

The drill instructors are to indoctrinate you into the ways of the military. They will do this by using every technique at their disposal to make you break your cool, lose your concentration, and react. This is the time to remember the Fourth Law, "To Remain Silent."[1] When confronted with

---

1 For those who may be unfamiliar with mystery and/or occult traditions, many magickal practitioners follow the Four Laws: To Know, To Will, To Dare, and To Remain Silent.

aggression, verbal taunting, or even outright insults directed at everyone from your mother to the puppy you had in kindergarten, quiet your mind, focus your attention, and do not respond unless directly asked a question. Do not argue, do not allow your irritation (or your desire for logic) to control you. A slip of the tongue can earn you extra physical training or work duties.

While you're developing your Fourth Law abilities, refrain from volunteering for additional duties. If your drill instructors believe that you are the right person for a job, they will assign it to you. However, be warned that when leadership responsibility falls into your lap, you will be judged not only by your own performance, but also by the performance of those under your command. If you are thrust into a position of additional responsibility, maintain your discipline, keep your focus, and prioritize your workload carefully. When confronted with 4 a.m. runs and 11 p.m. field exercises, it is understandable that you would begin to want a little downtime. One of the hardest parts of basic training is the lack of time to accomplish basic, required tasks such as laundry, to say nothing of composing an e-mail to home or catching a much needed nap. It is to your benefit to complete the "must do" list before you even think of taking any personal time, no matter how brief. As Stew Smith, a writer for www.military.com, says, "Remember, the military will not make you disciplined, but your Drill Sergeants can make you wish you were."[2]

Each branch of the military publishes a guidebook that enlistees can review for basic military knowledge prior to arriving at basic training. Once you're there, there are only three things you can do with your time: train physically (run, strength-train, calisthenics); train mentally (study, drill facts, listen and learn); and train spiritually (meditate, connect with your body, pray). Pagans as a group tend to be more individualistic and occasionally rebellious. These are not traits that are valued by the military establishment, and they are not mindsets that are likely to serve you well at basic training. The mind games are intense, often confusing, and they can be demoralizing. The indoctrination process is as much about shaping

---

2 Stew Smith, "10 Steps to Joining the Military," http://www.military.com/Recruiting/Content/0,13898,rec_step09_bootcamp_tips,,00.html (accessed January 22, 2008).

your subconscious (the reactive, instinctual mind) as it is about building your physical ability. For this reason, basic training can be a time of intense spiritual transformation. When one is removed from his or her family, faith community, and all the little luxuries that make day-to-day life easier, one can either despair or deepen. Use your boot camp experience to deepen your connection with Deity. The First Law is "To Know," and this is an excellent time to increase your knowledge of your own strengths, fears, abilities, and goals—vital information for any magickal practitioner.

What to Bring with You

The requirements and restrictions vary from branch to branch, and so you can be certain that your recruiter will give you a comprehensive list. However, most of the armed forces require the following:

- Laundry soap

- Blue or black ink ballpoint pens

- Shampoo and conditioner

- Deodorant

- Toothbrush with travel case and toothpaste

- 2 or 3 spiral bound notebooks[3]

- Shoeshine kit with black polish

- Soap with travel case

- Shower shoes and 2 or 3 towels

- Stationery, envelopes, and stamps

- Spray starch and iron

- Small manicure kit

- Sewing kit

---

3 The terminology "spiral bound" was the most common used by the various military websites during my research. Check with your military contact or recruiter to determine what is acceptable.

- Wristwatch
- Phone cards
- Shaving kit
- Birth certificates for yourself and any dependents
- Enlistment contract
- Social Security card
- Approximately $25–50[4]

Bring the following, if applicable:

- Eyeglasses (avoid contacts)[5]
- Vision prescription
- Hair ties (rubber bands, bobby pins)
- Driver's license
- Marriage license or divorce certificate
- Any JROTC, ROTC, CAP certificates
- Immigration papers
- College transcripts
- Acceptable jewelry: wedding band, religious medals (such as a pentacle, Thor's Hammer, etc.) on a chain long enough to be tucked into your T-shirt, and (for women only) small gold ball earrings

DO NOT BRING THE FOLLOWING:

- Any form of weapon (including your athame)
- Any form of playing card (including Tarot)

---

4 Your military contact/recruiter will specify how much money you are allowed to bring with you; however, my research indicated that most branches specified amounts in this range and did not allow credit cards.

5 You will be engaged in vigorous, dirty/messy training maneuvers. Eyeglasses are preferred, since they are less susceptible to getting lost or trapping small particles and causing distractions in the field. Contacts are also prohibited during gas-mask training.

- Any sort of gambling equipment (depending upon interpretation, this may include some forms of divination)

- Any nonreligious literature or other media

- Tobacco products

- Any over-the-counter medications, including vitamins, herbs, and other supplements[6]

- Any form of aerosol

- Any form of pornography (avoid religious materials that may contain nudity or erotic images)

- Electronic devices (everything from iPods to hair dryers)

Warrior Heart Meditation

Note: The best way to undertake any guided visualization is to have a trusted friend or partner read it aloud as you journey into a meditative state. If this is not possible, the next best option is to have someone record it for you on a blank tape, so that you may play it softly. I have found that recording the meditation yourself, while sometimes the only option available, is not necessarily the best one, as we tend to be distracted by the sound of our own voices.

You will need the following:

- Ochre, red body paint, or henna

- Soft blanket and pillow

- Something starchy and sweet to eat

- Cool water

Lie on your back, with your limbs uncrossed and relaxed. Close your eyes. Run your palms over the floor and feel its texture, its temperature.

---

6 This may seem overly strict, but no branch of the military will allow you to bring non-prescription medications or supplements with you to basic training. Check with your recruiter/military contact for more information.

Become aware of your body touching the ground beneath you, your palms, the back of your legs, buttocks, shoulders, and head. Feel the weight of them, supported and cradled by the earth beneath you. Allow yourself to relax a bit more, sink into the earth a bit deeper, feel it rise up to meet and envelop you. The earth is fully a part of you, as you melt your body deeper within. Relax into it. . . .

Relax your hands now, and lie in stillness, aware of your breathing—each inhalation and exhalation filling your body with the light touch of air, within and without. Breathe into consciousness of the air above you, just as you are aware of the earth below. Feel them embrace you, earth supporting you, air caressing you. Both fully present surrounding you. Both fully a part of you. Relax into them. . . .

Now, turn your attention inward, become aware of the flow of blood through your veins, the fluid that sustains you, pushed and pulled by the gravitational tides of moon and earth. Allow your consciousness to ride the current of your bloodstream, absorbing the life-energy you contain within you. Slow your breathing, and feel how air moves the water within you. Allow your body to calm, to slow its racing pace and linger in the moment. Feel the warmth of the energy within you as it rides along on the tide of your blood, guided by the earth, and carrying oxygen, the gift of the air that surrounds you. Earth, air, and water are fully a part of you. Relax into them. . . .

Now, ride the flow of your bloodstream until you reach the center of your being, your heart. This is the seat within where the elements merge, where water carries air into the fiery heart of your earthen body. Focus on your heart, feel it beat and pulse, passionate and strong. Become aware of the heat contained within your core, the warmth of your body, the fire of your heart. Allow this heat to fill you, warming and sustaining you. Feel the hot breath, warmed within you, rush across your lips as you exhale. Feel your heart's energy extend deep through the ground, connecting you to the fiery core at the center of the earth. Feel the smooth and steady pulse of blood through your veins. The heart is the center of your being. Relax into it. . . .

Bring your attention to your heart, and look within it. What does it hold right now? Is it prideful? Is it timid? Is it unsteady? Is it strong? Your heart is the secret place within you, where your deepest fears and greatest powers lie. What does your heart contain right now, at this moment? Search yourself. Place your hands on your heart, comfortably, one over the other, and take a minute to feel the beating. What are you hiding within you that you are ashamed to carry? What would you be rid of? Feel it ride the beats of your heart upward. As you draw it outward, remove it from the darkness and take it into your waiting hands. Now, cast it from you. Push it away, crumple it up, tear it to shreds—but destroy it. You are not bound to carry hidden weaknesses within you. Repeat this as often as necessary. Take your time, and seek out the hidden places within your heart where the shadows linger, where the shame and fear, doubt and worries you've carried within you fester. Then, allow it to rise on the beating of your heart into your waiting hands, and cast it out, away from you, never to return. Your heart is the sacred space within you that bears the glowing light of your soul. Now is your time to cleanse it of all you wish to be rid of. Now is the time to purify the sacred space you carry within you.

When you have completed this task, and you feel ready, relax once again, place your arms at your sides, and become aware of your breath, in and out, and the supportive earth beneath you. It is not easy to examine your heart so thoroughly. You have done battle against the darkness and have reclaimed the treasure within you. Take a few moments to come back to your sacred space, to explore your uncluttered heart-space, and to assess what remains within. When you have returned to center, when your pulse has slowed and you are once again aware of the ebb and flow of breath and blood, place your hands once more on your heart.

Now, turn your focus toward what remains. Find the seat of your sense of justice: that place within your heart that rejects oppression and seeks to serve your brothers and sisters. Imagine what this justice-seat looks like within you . . . is it a royal throne? A smooth rock? A velvet cushion? Within you lies the justice-seat; find it, and dust it off if it needs it. Take a moment to reflect upon this treasure, stored deep within you. If you feel compelled, seat yourself there, and observe the view of your heart from this perspective—that of concern for the rule of law, and of the welfare of others. You carry within you the seat of justice, and no one can deprive you of it. You have only to recognize that it is there. Always.

Next, look around you and find the sword of your Will. Right intention and honorable action, the dual edges of the blade of Will. Take up this sword and feel the weight of it in your hand. Observe it carefully . . . is it sharp or dull? Polished or rusting? Is your Will a broadsword? A battle-ax? A pocketknife? Is it comfortable in your hand? Take a few moments and experiment . . . feel the changes in your body when you are in contact with your Will. And when you are ready, relax and center yourself once again. Become aware of your breathing, your pulse, the earth beneath you. Relax into it, and allow it to support you completely.

Come back to your heart-space, your sacred storeroom, and look next for the shield of your Truth. Where is it kept in relation to your seat of Justice? The sword of your Will? Are they together, or do you keep them separate? When you have discovered the shield of your Truth, observe it carefully . . . how big is it? Is it large enough to protect you? What shape is it? Small and round? As large as you are? Is it polished or dull? Have you taken adequate care of your Truth? Are there repairs that need to be made? Does your Truth serve you well, or is it time to craft a new shield? Take a few moments and observe the shield of your Truth. Look at it with a critical eye . . . are there cracks that leave you unprotected? How well will your Truth serve you when confronting danger? Be honest with yourself, and, if necessary, take a few minutes to begin the repairs. When you are ready, bring yourself back to center, and relax. Notice your breathing, feel your pulse, become aware of the earth beneath you.

Finally, take one last look around you, at the sacred space of your heart. You have removed the negative weight you've carried. You have remembered the armor you carry with you already: Justice, Will, and Truth. What are you missing? Take a few moments to breath, explore, and reflect. Look around your heart. What do you wish were there? What traits or skills do you feel you need? Mercy? Power? Compassion? Confidence? Once again, place your hands on your heart, one over the other, and feel the beating there. Feel the energy of your heart beat outward and upward, reaching toward the stars, extending beyond them, into the realm of infinite possibility. Everything you need is here, accessible. Reach out and take what you need, draw it toward you, and feel it enter your heart. This is the time to build up your reserves and prepare for the trials ahead. Repeat this process as often as you need, until you feel well armed, well prepared, and secure. Then, gently allow your hands to return to your sides, palms downward, touching the ground beneath you.

Feel the ground beneath your hands, your head, your shoulders, buttocks, and legs. Feel its strength and its solidity. Become aware of the places that separate you from the earth . . . the spaces in between, where the air flows through. Focus on these places—the curve of your neck, the backs of your knees, and the base of your spine. Allow these places to expand, gently separating your energy from the earth's, until you are fully returned to a conscious state. Take your time. When you are ready, open your eyes and become aware of your environment. When you feel able, sit up, drink a glass of cool water, and eat to ground yourself. If you so desire, use the red coloring to anoint your sternum, over your heart, with a pentacle or other power symbol. You have fully restored and activated your Warrior's Heart; carry it with honor.

Dedication of Service to Deity

In an ideal world, every Pagan entering the armed forces would have a supportive community capable of carrying out the Rite of Passage ritual described on page 72. Unfortunately, many Pagans still live in isolation, due to either geographic boundaries or personal circumstances that necessitate remaining in the broom closet. This simple ceremony can be conducted at any point during your military career, and in fact should be repeated as often as you feel a need to do so. The words themselves are not new, but are a traditional Wiccan self-blessing that I have re-formed to serve as a simple self-dedication for those who seek to honor the Goddess through armed service.

If possible, take a warm bath, scented with perfume, bath salts, or essential oils that you find pleasing. If you are not using bath salts, be sure to add a pinch of salt to the water as well as about a cup of milk. You may choose to add flower petals as well. Turn off the lights and close your eyes. Imagine the water cleansing you, from the inside out, washing away fear, stress, doubt, anger, and worry. When you are ready (or when the water grows cold, whichever comes first) dry yourself off and make your way toward your altar. (If you are not in an environment conducive to having an altar, use some small image of your patron/matron deity). You will need some saltwater for anointing. Begin by saying the following:

> **Holy Mother/Father _____, I dedicate my every action to your service. By my words and by my deeds, may I ever honor you.**

Anoint your feet and say:

> **Bless my feet, Holy Mother/Father, that I may ever walk in thy ways. May my path be certain and my way sure, as I set forth in your service.**

Anoint your knees and say:

> **Bless my knees, Holy Mother/Father, which kneel in humble adoration before you. Grant me steadfast honor, Holy One, and allow that I might never know submission to my enemy.**

Anoint your pelvis and say:

> **Bless my womb/loins, Holy Mother/Father, which hold the potential to create life, just as you brought forth all creation. May the pleasure I share with others also serve to please you. Grant that I might never seek to dishonor your sacred gift.**

Anoint your belly and say:

> **Bless my belly, Holy Mother/Father, that I might ever hunger to know you better. Allow me to remain full, in spirit and in body, that I might remain strong in your service.**

Anoint your sternum and say:

> Bless my breast/chest, Holy Mother/Father, my heartbeat,
> steady and true. Protect me Holy One, as I set forth into the
> unknown dangers that lie before me.

Anoint your mouth and say:

> Bless my mouth, Holy Mother/Father, and grant that I might
> always speak with truth and dignity. May my words bring you
> honor, as I speak your strength and compassion to those I
> encounter.

Anoint your eyes (careful to avoid getting saltwater in them!) and say:

> Bless my eyes, Holy Mother/Father, that I might have discern-
> ing vision, perceiving danger and deception, aware always of
> the world around me—both the seen and unseen. May I see
> your hands at work in my life, and your face in that of my com-
> rades, and my enemy.

Anoint your forehead and say:

> Bless my mind, Holy Mother/Father, that I might know your
> signs. Grant that I might be clear-headed in combat and healed
> when the battle is done. May I do my duty swiftly, without los-
> ing my humanity, and may I never lose sight of the humanity of
> those around me.

Pour out the remaining saltwater as you say:

> Blessed in body, blessed in soul;
> By the Gods am I made whole.
> One in service, one in faith;
> Strength of a Warrior, Heart of Grace.

Rite of Passage:
Preparation for the Warrior Class

I. The Entrance

The community should be gathered within the circle before the recruit is brought into sacred space. The altar should have pictures of the recruit's ancestors, especially any that served in the military. It should also contain symbols of the branch of service the recruit is being inducted into (e.g., model aircraft, tanks, ships, etc., perhaps toy guns or plastic army men, whatever the group is comfortable with). If there are covenors that are uncomfortable with images of warfare, perhaps the recruit's battle dress uniform (BDU) or a picture of the uniform could be used. If possible, the recruit's mother should be present; if she is not willing or available, then someone chosen by the recruit to act as a foster-mother should be present to assist with the ritual. The recruit should be led into the room by the Summoner, after the circle has been cast. They are met at the Eastern Gate by the Priestess.

Priestess

Who seeks entry into this, our sacred space?

Recruit

It is I, (name), who seeks to enter.

Priest

What purpose have you here?

Recruit

I come to seek the blessings of our community, our guardians, and our Gods.

Priest and Priestess together

How do you enter?

Recruit

In perfect love and perfect trust.

Priest cuts a doorway for the recruit to enter.

Priestess
Enter, then, and blessed be.

Priestess greets the recruit with a kiss and leads him or her to the center of the circle.

II. The Blessings

Priest
Friends, before you stands (name), who has chosen to dedicate himself/herself to (patron or matron deity) through service in the Army/Navy/Air Force/Marines/National Guard/Reserves. S/he has come to seek your blessings on this path. What say you?

Community
We know the heart of our brother/sister (name) and support his/her call to service. We will support him/her and hold sacred space for him/her when s/he cannot be amongst us. We offer our blessings and our protection.

Maiden leads the recruit to the Eastern Gate.

Guardian of the East
Blessings upon you, child of the air. May your thoughts be focused and your mind clear. May the wind be at your back and the sky be your shelter. May your mind ever be your own. May no harm come to you from the east. Blessed be.

Guardian cleanses the recruit with a feather or fan and incense. Maiden leads the recruit to the Southern Gate.

Guardian of the South
Blessings upon you, child of fire. May your heart be bold and your courage true. May the flame be ever before you and the

sun be your shield. May your passion ever be your own. May no harm come to you from the south. Blessed be.

Guardian cleanses the recruit with a flame. Maiden leads the recruit to the Western Gate.

Guardian of the West
Blessings upon you, child of water. May your dreams be clear and your choices just. May the rain cool and soothe you and its waters bring you comfort. May your conscience ever be your own. May no harm come to you from the west. Blessed be.

Guardian cleanses the recruit with saltwater. Maiden leads the recruit to the Northern Gate.

Guardian of the North
Blessings upon you, child of earth. May your body be strong and your movements sure. May the earth rise beneath you and provide you with sure pathways and safe passage. May your body ever be your own. May no harm come to you from the north. Blessed be.

Guardian cleanses the recruit with earth/dust. Maiden leads the recruit back to the altar.

Priest
Who would offer their blessings upon (name), as s/he dedicates himself/herself to the Warrior's Path?

At this time, those gathered can offer their own individual blessings upon the recruit. This may continue for as long as is necessary for everyone to be heard and every spiritual gift to be bestowed by those who would do so.

Priestess
You have received the blessings of the Cardinal Gates and the coven upon your chosen path. May their gifts ever be

within you, whatever your mission, wherever your road. You
stand now before your ancestors, those who have gone into
the Afterworld. What have you to offer them?

Recruit

I bring an offering of (offering) to my ancestors, that they
shall know the honor of their memory.

*Recruit should place the offering either on or under the altar, before the de-
piction of his or her ancestors.*

Recruit

Wise ones, you who have passed beyond the veil, be with me
and guide me. I honor your memory and hear your voices
still within my heart. Guard my path, as I enter into the
service of (deity) as a soldier/sailor/airman/marine/guards-
man/reservist in the (country) military. Protect my path
from danger, and, if my time should come, greet me at my
journey's end. So mote it be.

Community

So mote it be.

III. The Mother's Right

Priest

It is written that a mother has three rights over her children:
to name them, to arm them, and to choose their mate. Who
speaks for this young Warrior?

Mother

I speak for (name), and I would claim my mother's right.

Priestess

What name would you give to your child?

Mother

My beloved, I honor your decision to take up this charge, even as my heart trembles for you. In your childhood, I was your watchful guardian and guide—ever vigilant to keep you from harm. I cannot follow you on this journey, and the time has come for me to release you. I cannot protect your path as I once did, but I can give you my blessing and, with it, a name befitting a Warrior. My child, henceforth, within this space you shall be called (Warrior name). May this name bring you honor, protection, and strength. Blessed be.

Priest

Hail (Warrior name)!

Community

Hail (Warrior name)!

Priestess

Will you arm (Warrior name)?

Mother

I will.

Priest

Kneel, (Warrior name), and receive your mother's gift.

Mother

My child, I cannot see where this path will take you, or what you will encounter when you arrive. My fervent hope is that you may live in peace for all your days. However, it is my mother's right to give you armor, and this I bestow upon you. (She presents her gift.) Take this (gift), and with it, my blessings. May it serve as a protection to you and a connection to your home, your mother, and our Gods. May it bring you strength and honor in the service of your community and (patron/matron deity). And know that we whom you

leave behind will hold space for you for as long as you have
need of it. Blessed be.

Priestess
Would you choose a mate for your child?

Mother
I have taught you all I know of love and companionship, and
you have been a faithful son/daughter to me. You will be
just as loyal and loving to your partner. I relinquish this right
to you, and have faith that you will choose the partner best
suited to your heart and your life. May s/he be brave and
strong, independent and loyal. May you have joy and hap-
piness within yourself, enough to share with the one who
holds your heart. Blessed be.

Priest
Arise, (Warrior name), and blessed be!

Community
Blessed be!

IV. Dedication to Deity

Priestess
(Warrior name), you have come here this night to receive the
blessings of the Warrior. You have journeyed to the Guardian
Gates. You have received the blessings of your ancestors and
the gifts of your mother. Now, you must stand before your
Gods.

Priest
To whom do you dedicate your service? Who stands with
you as patron/matron and as protector/ess?

Recruit

I dedicate myself to (deity) that my service may bring honor to his/her name.

Priestess

Do you swear to serve (deity) with honor and dignity, recognizing that your actions within the Warrior's Realm are a continual offering to him/her?

Recruit

I do swear.

Priest

Do you swear to conduct yourself at all times with the full understanding of your charge as a Warrior and Priest, to cause harm only when necessary and to repair harm as much as is possible?

Recruit

I do swear.

Priestess

Do you swear to honor the presence of divinity within the hearts of those you meet, never losing sight of the humanity of those you encounter in battle?

Recruit

I do swear.

Priest

If blood must be shed, do you swear to do so quickly and with mercy, never engaging in cruelty or wanton violence?

Recruit

I do swear.

Priestess
Will you work to minimize violence, to create peace as much as you are able, and so honor (deity) by exercising restraint in your personal life and on the field of battle?

Recruit
I do swear.

Priest
Take the symbol of (deity) upon you, as a reminder of your oath. May you always seek to embody the Divine Spirit of (deity)—cultivating a heart of peace, yet never afraid to take up arms in defense of justice. Blessed be.

Community
Blessed be!

The ritual may conclude at this time, or the group may decide to add elements of celebration, such as singing, dancing, or the sharing of cakes and wine.

Prayers, Rituals, and Daily Meditations

To my God[s], a heart of flame;
To my fellow man, a heart of love;
To myself, a heart of steel.

—St. Augustine of Hippo

O God, to those who hunger, give bread.
And to us with bread, give the hunger for justice.

—Latin American Prayer

Use me for your service, Gods of my Ancestors,
My hands to your service, my will to your honor.
May my every action carry your justice throughout the world.

—Spiral

II. To Will

*Men acquire a particular quality by constantly
acting a particular way . . .
You become just by performing just actions,
temperate by performing temperate actions,
Brave by performing brave actions.*

— *Aristotle*

4. Willingness to Stand Up

Take courage, friends. The way is often hard, the path is never clear, and the stakes are very high. Take courage. For deep down, there is another truth: you are not alone.

—Wayne B. Arnason

The decision to serve in the military is a decision to stand up for what is best about your country. Typically, these ideals embody the spirit of peace, justice, liberty, and equality. However, while many don the uniform to protect these higher values of civilization, they are often surprised to find that the military community is a microcosm of the larger population and that many of the same problems encountered in the "real" world exist beyond the base fence as well. As Pagans, we have a moral obligation to stand up for injustice, not just on a global scale, as when called to serve overseas, but also in our day-to-day lives—confronting cruelty and bigotry wherever we find it. Even in our barracks, mess halls, and chain of command.

Religious Intolerance
in the Military

Pagans (and Wiccans in particular) have made great strides toward acceptance within the military community. The inclusion of Wicca in the Army
Chaplains Guide was a major achievement in our religious development.
Sadly, however, there is still a great deal of religious intolerance within
the military today, both on an interpersonal and at a command level.
Chaplain (Lt. Col.) Kenneth Bush noted that "in the Protestant community, the number of chaplains is on the rise, as minority faith groups like
the Roman Catholic Church cannot fill the Army's needs. In addition, as
fewer mainline groups support seminarians pursuing a call to the chaplaincy, there has been an increase in the number of chaplains from independent, largely conservative churches and from charismatic and Pen-
tecostal traditions."[1] The rise of the Evangelical community within the
military establishment is nothing new—this has been a group traditionally drawn to military service. The statistical dominance that Evangelicals
present today can create some very specific problems for their minority
faith comrades.

   Mix earnest service personnel, eager to share their faith, with a high-
stress environment such as a combat zone or a military training program,
and you have a recipe for missionary zeal—one that is often impervious
to the reality of "other" paths. One particularly hilarious example of this
fervor to spread the Good News occurred when my husband was serving
on his first tour of Iraq. Several of his comrades purchased pirated copies
of *The Passion of the Christ* to use as a missionary tool. He had to point out
to them the (hysterical) contradiction presented in stealing the life of
Jesus in order to tell people to sin no more.

   There are three ways to handle these situations, and the correct option
will vary depending upon the individual circumstances. The first option is
usually the easiest: thank them for their concern, let them know that you
are "right with God," and move on. You are under no obligation to ex-

---

1 Lt. Col. Kenneth W. Bush, "Military Worship Wars: Blended Worship as a Pastoral Response," *The Army Chaplaincy*, Winter–Spring 2003, http://www.usachcs.army.mil/
TACarchive/ACwinspr03/bush.htm (accessed January 10, 2008).

plain your concept of God, or what it takes to be "right" with him or her. This option usually works well for people you don't know well (such as newcomers to the unit, or visiting guests) and people you don't need to interact with often. However, for those who see you daily, who notice the Thor's Hammer pendant or the triple moon tattoo, you might be tempted to try option two: the discussion. My husband has had fascinating, deep, and respectful conversations about religion, faith, and spirituality with his comrades in arms. These are men he has served with for seventeen years, who know him to be honorable, capable, and decent, and thus respect (and are even intrigued by) his spiritual practice even though it varies from their own. The third solution is the "nuclear option"—one that you don't want to invoke often, but need to know exists. For those personalities who feel compelled to repeatedly offer religious tracts, invite you to worship services, or otherwise witness to you, as well as belittle your practices, insult your spirituality, or compare you to a Satanist or Devil worshipper, it's always handy to mention that you are on excellent terms with the unit's Equal Opportunity Officer, and that you wonder what they would make of the conversation. Generally speaking, I do not advocate this approach, for two reasons. First, it gives the appearance that your spiritual practice is either new to you (and thus mutable) or else so vague (and therefore not a "real religion") that you are incapable of adequately explaining your position. Second, taking a situation like religious discrimination to your EO Officer or to your commander can have serious repercussions, not just for the person engaging in the inappropriate behavior, but for yourself as well. If possible, I always believe it better to resolve these situations on an informal level. However, if you truly feel that you are being discriminated against or harassed, or that your spiritual practice is being inhibited, do not hesitate to report the situation. You have a right to the free expression of your faith.

One technique that I have found works especially well with military Evangelicals as well as with base leadership, is to invoke the words of the Founding Fathers through the course of your discussion. Many Christians today consider themselves to be the spiritual descendents of these leaders, and are often stunned to realize that the Founding Fathers' views might have been more in line with yours than theirs. I have compiled a list of quotes that might come in handy whether you are facing legitimate religious harassment or simply enjoying a late night debate amongst friends.

Influential Americans on Religious Freedom

Note: I have italicized two of my favorite quotes that are very likely to surprise your conversational partners and come in handy when discussing the place religion should hold within the military culture.

History, I believe, furnishes no example of a priest-ridden people maintaining a free civil government. This marks the lowest grade of ignorance, of which their political as well as religious leaders will always avail themselves for their own purpose.

—Thomas Jefferson,
in a 1813 letter to Baron von Humboldt

I never told my religion, nor scrutinized that of another. I never attempted to make a convert, nor wished to change another's creed. I have judged others' religions by their lives, for it is from our lives and not by our words that our religions must be read.

—Attributed to Thomas Jefferson

The authors of the gospels were unlettered and ignorant men and the teachings of Jesus have come to us mutilated, misstated and unintelligible.

—Attributed to Thomas Jefferson

The legitimate powers of government extend to such acts only as are injurious to others. But it does me no injury for my neighbor to say there are twenty gods or no God. It neither picks my pocket nor breaks my leg.

—Thomas Jefferson, 1782

Is uniformity attainable? Millions of innocent men, women and children, since the introduction of Christianity, have been burnt, tortured, fined, imprisoned; yet we have not advanced one inch towards uniformity. What has been the effects of coercion? To make one half the world fools, and the other half hypocrites.

—Thomas Jefferson
"Notes on the State of Virginia," 1781–85

(Note: Thomas Jefferson went on to create the Jeffersonian Bible, an edition that eliminated any reference to "supernatural" events such as the miracles and the resurrection, and focused instead only on what he believed to be the words of Jesus.)

What influence, in fact, have ecclesiastical establishments had on society? In some instances, they have been seen to erect a spiritual tyranny on the ruins of civil authority; on many instances, they have been seen upholding the thrones of political tyranny; in no instance have they been the guardians of the liberties of the people. Rulers who wish to subvert the public liberty may have found an established clergy convenient auxiliaries. A just government, instituted to secure and perpetuate it, needs them not.

—James Madison,
"A Memorial and Remonstrance," 1785

Of all the tyrannies that affect mankind, tyranny of religion is the worst.

—Attributed to Thomas Paine

We should begin by setting conscience free. When all men of all religions . . . shall enjoy equal liberty, property, and an equal chance for honors and power . . . we may expect that improvements will be made in the human character and the state of society.

—John Adams, 1785

I shall have liberty to think for myself without molesting others or being molested myself.

—John Adams,
in a 1756 letter to Richard Cranch

As the government of the United States is not, in any sense, founded on the Christian religion; as it has in itself no character of enmity against the laws, religion or tranquility of Musselmen [Muslims] . . . it is declared . . . that no pretext arising from religious opinion shall ever produce an interruption of the harmony existing between the two countries . . . The United States is not a Christian nation any more than it is a Jewish or a Mohammedan nation.

—The Treaty of Tripoli,
written by John Barlow, approved by unanimous vote
of the Senate and signed into law by John Adams in 1797

When a religion is good, I conceive it will support itself; and when it does not support itself and God does not take care to support it so that its professors are obliged to call for help of the civil power, 'tis a sign, I apprehend, of its being a bad one.

—Benjamin Franklin,
in a 1780 letter to Richard Price

My earlier views of the unsoundness of the Christian scheme of salvation and the human origin of the scriptures, have become clearer and stronger with advancing years and I see no reason for thinking I shall ever change them.

—Abraham Lincoln,
in an 1862 letter to Judge J. S. Wakefield

To discriminate against a thoroughly upright citizen because he belongs to some particular church, or because, like Abraham Lincoln, he has not avowed his allegiance to any church, is an outrage against that liberty of conscience which is one of the foundations of American life.

—Theodore Roosevelt,
in a 1918 letter to J. C. Martin

Every man, conducting himself as a good citizen, and being accountable to God alone for his religious opinions, ought to be protected in worshipping the Deity according to the dictates of his own conscience.

—George Washington,
in a 1789 letter to the United Baptist Chamber

If they are good workmen, they may be of Asia, Africa, or Europe. They may be Mohometans [Muslims], Jews or Christians of any Sect, or they may be Atheists.

—George Washington,
in a 1784 letter to Tench Tilghman

Among many other weighty objections to the Measure, it has been suggested, that it has a tendency to introduce religious disputes into the Army, which above all things should be avoided, and in many instances would compel men to a mode of Worship which they do not profess.

—George Washington,
in a 1777 letter to John Hancock, expressing his opposition to the appointment of military chaplains to the Continental Army

Sexism in the Military

Women have served in the American Armed Forces since the Revolutionary War and in Europe long before that. While not formally allowed to enter the military until World War I, women disguised as men have served honorably and with distinction for over two centuries. However, sexism within the military community is an unfortunate reality even today. While general attitudes have improved recently, there have always been military-specific gender myths, including the following:[2]

• Female POWs face additional risks that their male counterparts do not. *In reality, any POW is a likely candidate for sexual abuse, regardless of gender.*

• Women get pregnant and become undeployable. *In reality, the military loses far more personnel to sexual disease and substance abuse (8%) than to pregnancy (1%).*

• Having women around detracts from male bonding and morale. *In reality, military leaders from several nations have noted that mixed-gender*

---

2 USAF (Ret.) Cpt. Barbara A. Wilson, "Myths, Fallacies, Falderol and Idiotic Rumors about Military Women," http://userpages.aug.com/captbarb/myths.html (accessed May 21, 2007).

units tend to outperform segregated units. American commanders noticed that women work harder to prove their capability to their male colleagues, while the men worked harder not to be outdone.

- The physical standards are different for women and men, making the women less qualified. *In reality, the physical standards upheld by the military vary not only by gender, but by age within the same gender group. The General Accounting Office issued a report stating "there is a widespread perception that the existence of lower physical fitness standards for women amounts to a 'double standard.' However, the physical fitness program is actually intended only to maintain the general fitness and health of military members and fitness testing is not aimed at assessing the ability to perform specific missions or military jobs. Consequently, DOD officials and experts agree that it is appropriate to adjust the standards for physiological differences among service members by age and gender."*

- Women are not provided with weapons training. *In reality, the Army has been requiring individual weapons training for women since 1975, and the Marines since 1985.*

There is also the myth that women can't serve in combat positions. In reality, the conditions of modern conflict put pretty much every service-person within a combat zone into "combat positions." It is true that women cannot serve in specific positions, or in certain divisions such as Infantry, but this by no means precludes their participation in combat maneuvers.

Sadly, these are just a few of the more common gender stereotypes that are still perpetuated within the military. This can often create an environment of hostility or harassment. However, female service personnel now have reporting options available to them (such as the Equal Opportunity Officer) or, if they choose not to press the issue, significant institutional opportunities to thrive within the modern military system. There are two specific issues that I want to address that directly affect women: sexual assault, discussed below, and domestic violence, which will be covered in a later chapter.

Sexual Assault

According to the *Washington Post*, there were approximately 1,700 cases of sexual assault reported by military personnel in the year 2004. These figures include male and female survivors (victims) and encompass the crimes of "sexual assault, which includes rape, nonconsensual sodomy, indecent assault, and attempts to commit those offenses."[3] The vast majority of the survivors (over 1,200) were service members themselves. The Miles Foundation, a nonprofit organization devoted to supporting military personnel who have been victims of sexual assault, states that as many as 41% of female military veterans may have experienced some form of sexual assault during the course of their career. It is a sad fact that sexual assault of sisters at arms is the most underreported crime in the military.

This may have something to do with the fact that, until recently, a military survivor was not afforded the same protections that a civilian rape survivor would have been. The military survivor could potentially face prosecution/court-martial for the very circumstances that enabled the rape to occur. In fact, it was only in January of 2005 that the Department of Defense implemented a policy that allowed survivors to seek medical care, legal information, and advocacy without automatically triggering an investigation. The fear of this investigation process most likely motivated a number of survivors to simply "forget" the assault ever happened. The risk of being accused of fraternization, adultery, or conduct unbecoming prevented the majority of military survivors from coming forward to report their assault, pressing for the prosecution of their assailant, or even (in some cases) receiving basic health and medical attention after the assault. Even today, the anonymity of survivors is not assured, and details of the assault and incidents leading up to the assault will most likely be revealed during the court-martial process, should they decide to pursue prosecution. This risk to reputation and career is often a deciding factor in the choice to pursue a military investigation of the sexual assault.

---

3 Ann Scott Tyson, "Reported Cases of Sexual Assault in Military Increase," *Washington Post*, May 7, 2005, http://www.washingtonpost.com/wp-dyn/content/article/2005/05/06/AR2005050601355.html (accessed January 10, 2008).

Another factor that affects a survivor's decision to press for an investigation is the fact that often the military chain of command handles allegations of sexual assault with administrative rather than criminal action. The *Washington Post* states that within the military, only 2%–3% of cases of alleged sexual assault led to a court-martial.[4] This means that the assailant will be more likely to face a reduction in pay or rank, an Article 15 Citation in his file, or some other nonjudicial punishment than he will court-martial. This also typically means that the rapist/assailant will not be forced to register as a sex offender and that the survivor will most likely continue to interact with and potentially serve under her rapist.

The stigma of being seen as a rape victim is pervasive within our society as a whole, which all too often still assumes that the survivor must have, in some way, encouraged the assault. Survivors are often questioned about their clothing, their behavior, their nighttime activities, or where they socialize. This stigma can be multiplied exponentially in the military community, where a great deal of machismo and misogyny still remain. "It's difficult for any victim of sexual assault to come forward, even in the best of circumstances. Women in the military do not feel safe to say this happened to them, especially if it means the information is going to their commander,"[5] says Christine Hansen, the executive director of the Miles Foundation. Hansen also points out that there is a conflict of interest in the military, where the decision to prosecute an alleged assailant is made by leadership within the chain of command. The balance between maintaining a secure environment for female service personnel and prosecuting their assailants, while also maintaining morale and protecting personnel with valuable training and skills, can make the decision to seriously pursue claims of sexual assault difficult for commanders.

Women in the military need to understand what their rights are, what they can expect if they pursue prosecution and what other options they may have. First and foremost, anyone, regardless of their rank, has the

---

4 Ibid.

5 Marie Tessier, "Sexual Assault Pervasive in Military, Experts Say," *Women's eNews*, March 30, 2003, http://www.womensenews.org/article.cfm?aid=1273 (accessed January 22, 2008).

right to say *NO* to unwanted sexual advances. It does not matter if the survivor is a private and the assailant a colonel, superior rank does *NOT* give the assailant the right to demand sexual favors or intimate activity, or to make inappropriate comments. It can be difficult for survivors to say no to someone that they've spent their entire career being trained to obey without question. Coercion is one of the most common sexual assault techniques, used by high-school date rapists and three-star generals alike. The socialization of women in a patriarchal society makes it difficult to stand up to coercion under the best of circumstances. This same technique, applied by someone in uniform, can be devastating. However, coercion is not the only technique available to the rapist. Forcible sexual assault is on the rise as well, especially overseas and in combat zones, where military women are more isolated from support networks and civilian resources. The stresses of combat have been correlated to increases both in domestic violence (to be covered next) and to sexual assault. Many bases overseas, especially in areas like Iraq and Afghanistan, post signs near the women's showers reminding them of the importance of a "battle buddy" and suggesting that they avoid using facilities after nightfall. Violent assaults, repeated assaults, and even gang rapes are not uncommon for female service personnel overseas.

Many survivors of military sexual trauma, or MST (the most commonly used term within the VA system), are unaware that they are able to request a Military Protective Order, or MPO, from their chain of command. An MPO may be verbal or written, and it "may direct servicemembers to stay away from victims or designated places; refrain from doing certain things; require the servicemember to move into government quarters."[6] MPOs are enforced by the command issuing the order, though arrest is not mandated for violations of an MPO, so they are helpful to a point, but they will not stop the determined assailant.

The military is increasing its awareness of military sexual crime and it is my hope that with an increased awareness of the number of assaults, coupled with a larger voice for victims' advocacy groups, the Department

---

6 Information obtained from the Miles Foundation at http://members.aol.com/_ht_a/
   milesfdn/myhomepage/.

of Defense will begin to move its personnel in a direction that is more protective of survivors. Until that time, though, it is vital that military personnel realize that they do have resources outside of the base community. Many counties within the United States have nonprofit agencies that provide emergency shelter, legal advocacy, and increasingly forensic nursing programs for assault survivors. Having an awareness of your local resources, even if you think that you don't need the information, will come in very handy should you ever be faced with the aftermath of sexual assault. Knowing that you may, if you choose, receive medical treatment and counseling from outside of the military system might mean the difference between seeking treatment or not—and it is vital that survivors of sexual violence seek treatment for injury, pregnancy, and disease. Whether or not these separate agencies will report an assault to the military command will vary from state to state and agency to agency—but regardless of this fact, the women's shelters and forensic nursing programs they run can provide a nonjudgmental, woman-centered, advocacy-based model of care that you are unlikely to find at the base medical clinic. Know who they are, even if you never need their support; you might know someone who does.

More Information and Resources on this Topic

The Miles Foundation: http://members.aol.com/_ht_a/milesfdn/ myhomepage/

Women Veterans Homepage: http://www1.va.gov/womenvet/

National Guard Sexual Assault Progam and Policy: http://www.ngb.army.mil/jointstaff/j1/sapr/default.aspx

Sexual Assault Information (General): http://www.militaryonesource.com

Suzanne Swift (MST Survivor Refusing Redeployment) Case: http://www.suzanneswift.org

To find civilian legal advocacy, counseling, or forensic nursing program: http://www.rainn.org

Homophobia in the Military

According to *The Advocate*, a third of women serving in the military and over a quarter of men have directly experienced acts of homophobia.[7] While there is no statistical data regarding the prevalence of biases within the military community, it is a common belief that homophobia is the most prevalent and accepted form of discrimination in the military today. Sexism and racism are still existent, and are covered by this book, but homophobia presents some very specific problems for those experiencing its touch. Homosexuals, by definition, are not allowed the protections extended to other minorities and, in fact, open themselves up to discharge (or worse) for reporting abuse at the hands of their comrades, since to do so requires them to violate the "don't ask, don't tell" policy.

The official ban on homosexuals in the military was implemented during World War II. Since this time, persons who were openly gay, or who were discovered to be homosexual, were released from service. In fact, I have heard some accounts (perhaps urban legend, perhaps oral tradition) that part of why San Francisco became the seat of GLBT culture was because of the numbers being discharged from the Navy and left off in that city. This explanation, while intriguing, is not one I've been able to verify. In recent years, a quiet, honorable discharge was arranged and that was the end of things; however, the *Washington Post* reports that while there has been a dramatic drop in "homosexual separations" since September 11th, traditionally there has always been a spike in such discharges at the conclusion of wartime hostilities. Such was the case after the Persian Gulf War, and it is anticipated to occur again when we have concluded the current missions in Afghanistan and Iraq.[8]

So where does that leave someone who is either currently in the military or else considering enlisting, who also happens to be gay, lesbian, or bisexual? I have known several military members who have had successful, lengthy careers, even though they were homosexual. Sadly, I've also known a handful who have faced harassment or discrimination because

---

7 David Kirby, "Serving Out Loud," *The Advocate*, October 26, 1999.

8 Evelyn Nieves and Ann Scott Tyson, "Fewer Gays Being Discharged Since 9/11," *Washington Post*, February 12, 2005.

of their orientation. I have not been able to identify a pattern of behavior (other than being completely closeted) that will assure one type of treatment over another. To a large extent, the reception that homosexual service personnel will receive depends on their branch of service, their duty station, and their command structure.

There are a few organizations that are outspoken advocates for the rights of homosexual service personnel. The most recognized is the Servicemembers Legal Defense Network, which has an established mission of overturning the "don't ask, don't tell" policy and advocating for equal treatment of all military members. Its website is www.sldn.org, and it has a wealth of information and resources available to those seeking more information or support.

Racism in the Military

The military, like most of America, has a history of racial segregation and discrimination that it is still working hard to overcome. Thankfully, I do believe that like most of our culture, progress has been and continues to be made in the struggle for full enfranchisement and equality for all persons, regardless of race. In recent years, the military has worked diligently to establish an open line of communication within the chain of command to address issues of racial discrimination and harassment when they occur. Likewise, the Department of Defense has created a policy that mandates the presence of an Equal Opportunity Office and staff on each military base around the world so that issues that are not resolved within the command structure can be addressed from a more advocacy-based system. The Department of Defense also has an active affirmative action policy in place for consideration in hiring and promotion decisions. So, there has been a vast improvement since the time of the Buffalo Soldiers. My husband's unit is honored and proud to be a part of what was the famous Tuskegee Airmen's unit back in World War II; and they all, to a person, carry that legacy of heroism forward with them through their service. However, work still remains to be done.

One point of contention that has been widely debated in recent years is the fact that the military itself disproportionately targets black and Hispanic youth in its recruiting efforts. The idea behind this (from a military perspective) is that those groups are more often low-income, raised in single-parent homes, and have less access to higher education. This makes them more likely to be responsive to the recruitment incentives of money for college and career training. Some minority activists call this "economic conscription," meaning that those with more money and more resources do not elect to go into the military, choosing instead to pursue college and other career endeavors; the lower-income, mostly minority youth view the armed forces as one of their only options out of poverty. Hence, the decision to enlist is not so much a freely made choice to serve the ideals of American patriotism, as it is an option of last resort for those seeking to escape inner-city economic conditions. The end of the draft was the ending of the "great equalizer" in military service, where everyone over a certain age knew that they were just as likely to be called for duty as anyone else. Now, the military is viewed by many (especially upper class) young adults as being beneath their dignity, or something for those of the "lower spectrum peoples" (to use the words of one college student I interviewed) to pursue.

Due to recruiting shortages in recent years, the standards that potential enlistees are required to meet have been modified—some would say lowered—in order to bring in the number of new servicepersons that our military requires. One of these new standards allows those with a past history of involvement in neo-Nazi, white supremacist, or other racist organizations to be eligible for service in the military, whereas in years past, there had been a prohibition against such conduct. I do not believe that the membership of these groups is large enough to make a significant impact on the military culture as a whole, but it is fair to mention that one is far more likely to encounter a virulent racist in uniform today than one would have been five or ten years ago.

Sadly, although unsurprisingly, some of the most common racist views within the military today are negative perceptions of Arabic persons. This is mostly directed at foreign populations, which is not surprising given the hostilities we are currently engaged in and the experiences of the past few years. But it is also directed inward—toward those Americans of Arab descent who are serving with loyalty and honor within the military. Manifesting as hostile conduct such as insults, jokes, and racial epithets, or taking the other extreme as isolation and exclusion, there is a pervasive aura of negativity directed at these persons by those who serve in uniform. Some would argue that one's experiences in combat and in interacting with foreign populations have a legitimate impact on one's perception of those peoples and races. To be honest, there is some psychological (if not ethical/moral) truth to that. But when it comes to those serving beside us, growing up in the same neighborhoods, and wearing the same uniform in the same military, there is no excuse for racist ideologies.

Does racism exist in the military establishment today? Many would answer yes—and I can say that I have spoken firsthand with those who have witnessed incidents of command abuse or interpersonal hostilities that they would attribute to racial factors. Is this a common occurrence? It is my opinion that it is not, although that does not mean that we do not have an obligation to address the incidents as we see them and work actively to create a more tolerant, diverse military population.

MINORITY MEMBERSHIP: U.S. MILITARY[9]

Race	Army	Navy	USMC	USAF	DOD Total
Black	101,931 (24.6%)	65,465 (20.9%)	19,818 (12.5%)	51,007 (17.1%)	238,221 (20.1%)
Hispanic	46,759 (11.3%)	28,855 (9.2%)	23,039 (14.5%)	17,757 (6%)	116,410 (9.8%)
Asian	14,287 (3.5%)	21,290 (6.8%)	4,298 (2.7%)	9,987 (3.3%)	49,862 (4.2%)
Pacific Islander	0 (0%)	870 (.3%)	503 (.3%)	1,041 (.3%)	2,414 (.2%)
Native American	4,109 (1%)	9,892 (3.2%)	4,140 (2.6%)	2,345 (.8%)	20,486 (1.7%)
Multiracial	0 (0%)	1,851 (.6%)	812 (.3%)	2,312 (.8%)	4,975 (.4%)
Other	9,620 (2.3%)	3,867 (1.2%)	6,075 (3.8%)	6,230 (2.1%)	25,792 (2.2%)

9 Department of Defense, "Population Representation in the Military Services," http://www.defenselink.mil/prhome/poprep2001/chapter2/c2_raceth.htm (accessed May 21, 2007).

Daily Self-Blessing

This is a simple blessing you can incorporate into your daily routine, whether at home or abroad, as you prepare to start your day. It requires no special tools or equipment and can be said on your way out the door, as you drive, or whenever it is most convenient to fit into your day.

Mother Goddess, gracious Lord,
Bless my path this day;
May my every word and deed,
Serve as an example of your love,
Your kindness and your way.
I am a Witch*
May my actions be worthy of the name.

Pagan/Druid/something else may be substituted

5. Willingness to Serve

Let your soul lend its ear to every cry of pain . . . let not the fierce sun dry one tear of pain before you yourself have wiped it from the suffering eye.

—Traditional Vedic Prayer

Stateside Service

Much of the attention that the military has received in recent years has focused quite naturally on its work overseas. Many countries are engaged in combat operations within the Middle East, and it is not surprising that the attention of the world is mostly centered upon the places with the most conflict. However, the vast majority of a career soldier's time will not typically be spent in the combat theatre. The military is used for any number of purposes including research, routine maintenance of military assets, and providing emergency assistance at home in times of crisis. Earlier I spoke briefly about recruits who join the military and find themselves disappointed to realize that it will not necessarily provide the training they expected to receive for the outside world. Those who view the military as a broadcasting school or conservatory are usually disappointed. The flip side to that situation, however, is the enlistee who wants desperately to serve in the elite units of the armed forces: Special Forces, pilot or space training, rescue, etc. Obviously, the supply of interested candidates for these programs vastly outpaces the demand. This means that many service personnel are just as disappointed to find that their military service can be, surprisingly, rather dull.

So what does day-to-day life look like in the military today? For my husband, it means repairing wheels for F-16s, teaching first aid and CPR courses, and preparing training reports ten hours a day. For many others, a typical day of military service might include aircraft or vehicle maintenance, vast amounts of paperwork for logistical tasks such as human resources, data management, or accounting, or even eight-plus hours spent staring at a radar or sonar screen that seldom, if ever, changes. The commercials that air on television show the military as one adventure after another: rappelling, parachuting, diving, rock climbing, combat. While there is a very good chance that those entering the military today will see combat, the years they spend *outside* the zone of operations are much longer and very seldom so exciting. There are a few exceptions to this rule, but I've never met the serviceperson alive who hopes for one of the following scenarios to arise, no matter how great the need for adrenaline can be.

Disaster Relief

Many of the people who go into the armed forces enter with the goal of providing immediate, emergency assistance to their country and fellow citizens. In the United States, the branches of the military that are most frequently charged with duties of disaster response and civil assistance are the National Guard (Army and Air) and the Coast Guard. In recent years, these heroes have guarded airports against the threat of future terrorist activity, rescued whole families stranded by Hurricanes Katrina and Rita, protected homes and lives by fighting wildfires in the Western states, and even thrown hay bales to horses stranded in dangerous snowstorms. All of this is in addition to their regular training and job duties as well as possible overseas deployments to combat zones.

The National Guard is particularly unique in that they are the philosophical descendents of the Minutemen, who fought for American independence during the Revolutionary War. Today, they serve as state-run militias and their missions are directed in tandem by the governors of their states as well as the president and Department of Defense. This unique role means that Guard units are often utilized for missions that directly benefit their state populations. In times of crisis, a state governor or the president may deploy one state's Guard to assist another state in disaster relief or rescue. Additionally, a National Guard unit may be federalized in order to serve a national agenda such as in Iraq or Afghanistan today.

One factor to keep in mind is the standard line of the National Guard, "one weekend a month, two weeks a year," which has led to the belittling nickname "weekend warriors." I will say that based on my experience as a Guard wife, those parameters are not entirely accurate. In the eight years I've been married to a member of the Air National Guard, there has never been a year when my husband has been activated for *only* one weekend a month and two weeks a year. Depending upon your career field, you may find yourself as a highly deployable member of the Guard. For instance, those who belong to Air National Guard Combat Search and Rescue or Army National Guard military police units are involved in either directly supporting combat operations (like finding and picking up downed pilots) or serving in various capacities as security, such as was mentioned above. The National Guard is traditionally the unit of first response on the home front, and if your focus is on national, domestic service, it is worthy of your consideration.

The other branch primarily charged with homeland defense is the Coast Guard. The Coasties come under the command of the Department of Homeland Security rather than the Department of Defense, but they are nonetheless considered a vital part of our American Armed Forces. The Coast Guard is tasked with three primary duties: search and rescue, maritime law enforcement (including intercepting drug runners), and port security. The Coast Guard is deployable to overseas conflicts, but this is rarely exercised since it performs an integral service to our home defense.

Coasties are primarily stationed on ships, which can mean that you are separated from your family for extended lengths of time, even if you are technically stateside.

The Coast Guard also works as a law enforcement agency and is responsible for intercepting criminal activity in U.S. waters. It actively pursues drug boats and those who smuggle illegal immigrants into the United States. Coasties assist boaters by guiding the lost through waterways and inspecting watercraft to ensure that they are seaworthy. If you are concerned with environmental defense, the Coast Guard is one of the leaders in environmental cleanup and safety enforcement. In air and on sea, it truly is on the edge of homeland security.

Terrorism and/or Domestic Warfare

The primal imagery is consistent in the minds of nearly every American, and nearly everyone else around the world: a plane, flying into one of the biggest landmarks in New York City, even as word breaks on the news that there are other planes, other targets, including the Pentagon. September 11, 2001, left an indelible mark on the hearts of people around the world and became a catalyst for dramatic changes in American life, both good and ill. Many Pagans especially mourned the loss of many civil liberties along with the human casualties of the attack. Not surprisingly, military recruitment skyrocketed in the weeks afterward. Today, there is a whole generation of military personnel who can trace the lineage of their service back to that one terrifying morning.

Every branch of the military today is actively engaged in what has been termed the "war on terror." Indeed, many countries around the world have joined with us in trying to eliminate the use of terrorist tactics against civilian populations in many different contexts. Recent examples of terrorist acts include the bombings of passenger trains by Basque separatists in Spain, plots of mass murder such as September 11th by Islamic extremists under Osama bin Laden, chemical and insurgent attacks against military and civilian populations in the Middle East, and suicide bombings around the world. This means that intelligence and communications specialists are in demand now more than ever, especially those with foreign-language abilities. Anyone in the military today is familiar with the single-minded determination never to allow such atrocities to occur again.

If the focus of your military service is a desire to actively assist in the fight against terrorism, then the Army or Marines is most likely the place for you to be. These are the frontline fighters, actively engaged in combat operations against those who seek to cause further harm. This is not an easy path to choose, since the enemy is well-hidden in plain sight. One of the most common themes I hear from those returning from overseas is "you can't tell who they are." This same concern manifests itself here in the states, as anyone who's ever seen an elderly woman in a wheelchair being frisked by airport security can attest. The enemies are insidious and invisible, and fear is their greatest weapon. We who find holiness in balance must be ever mindful of the words of Benjamin Franklin: "He who would trade essential liberty for temporary security deserves neither." It is a sacred charge to protect and defend our people not only from outside harm, but also from the harm that arises from trying to overprotect, or overcompensate out of fear.

The Wiccan Rede says, "An it harm none, do as ye will," and this is often interpreted to mean passive harm as well. In other words, we can harm other people by trying too hard to act *for* them, instead of *with* them. Pagans in the military, especially those who serve in career fields such as military intelligence and policing, have the opportunity to create that balance organically, seeking always to protect without causing additional harm in the process. May justice be done, may peace prevail, may balance be restored.

Overseas Deployments

One of the best opportunities presented by military service is the chance to explore the world around us by living in and around other cultures. Currently, the United States has bases in Europe, Asia, the Middle East, the Pacific Rim and Australia, and even Antarctica. I can't even begin to count the number of those who have told me they enlisted in order to see the world. If your spiritual practice is based in Western culture, there are many opportunities to explore the birthplaces of your spiritual practice.

Depending upon your branch (usually active-duty Army or Air Force) you could be stationed in Italy, Germany, Iraq, or Britain, to name just a few of the "birthplaces" of many modern Pagan traditions. It should go without saying that the military is not a travel agent and that you may be expected to engage in dangerous duties while stationed overseas, but the opportunity to delve deeper into your spiritual practice is a decided advantage to military life. Keep in mind that there are stations that will not allow you to bring your family with you, such as South Korea, and you do not get to decide where you will be sent, but for those with an open mind and a sense of adventure, the military presents many opportunities for cultural dialogue.

In today's political climate, one should not enter into the military with the expectation of being sent to Europe or remaining stateside. Most likely, those who join the military today are assured of serving in combat operations at some point in their career; depending upon your branch and career field, it may come sooner rather than later. Iraq, while incredibly dangerous, is the seat of ancient civilization. This is the birthplace of Lilit and Marduk, Enki and Inanna, and while those who are sent to this region on military orders are unlikely to be able to explore the anthropological resources of the region, they may very well be able to tap into ancient energies as a part of their private spiritual practice. Likewise, those who are fortunate to be stationed near some of the most sacred Pagan sites—Glastonbury and Stonehenge; the living temples to Amaterasu, Kwan Yin, and Buddha; Chartres Cathedral; the ancient temples of Italy and Greece—might be able to enhance their connection with Deity by working intimately with the spirits of the land.

The alternative scenario, of course, involves those who work closely with the energies of their native soil: shamans and Native American derivatives, who may find it very difficult to be separated from their homeland. These persons, if they desire to do so, can build relationships and ties to the specific energies of their new duty stations and work to recreate their private practices as much as possible in the new environment. If you feel that you are unwilling or unable to do this, I have also seen military personnel bring boxes of their home soil and vials of nearby sacred streams or bodies of water with them to their new duty stations; carrying with them a physical tie to the beloved land they've left behind. This may (depending upon the customs regulations you are subject to) be something you wish to incorporate into your practice regardless of tradition. Reclaiming Witches have practiced the collection of "waters of the world" and use them, mingled together for earth healing and water blessing. Likewise, you may choose to collect small containers of soil from each of the places you are stationed and each of the lands you have worked magickally within. If you choose to save such energetic souvenirs, I strongly suggest making your collection small, so as to leave the least imprint upon the soil you have departed. Small dram vials, typically used for essential oils, work quite nicely.

6. Willingness to Sacrifice

The first quality of a soldier is constancy in enduring fatigue and hardship. Courage is only the second. Poverty, privation, and want are the school of the good soldier.

—Napoleon Bonaparte

The hallmark of military life is sacrifice. Everyone, regardless of their motivations, understands this fact when they enlist. Whether the sacrifice you are called to make is the simple act of shaving your head at basic training or laying down your life on the field of battle, the acceptance of military service as a sacrificial act is imperative. This understanding is a part of why I believe that Pagans are ideal military personnel. We have an intimate understanding of the nature of sacrifice, as a spiritual and ritual act,[1] which brings a sense of mindfulness to our military service. This is true both for those wearing the uniform, and for the families they leave behind. When you marry into the military culture, you must

---

1 For those who are not familiar with Paganism, please understand that I do not mean animal/human sacrifice, but rather tangibles such as offering coins, milk, and honey or undertaking fasts and other material sacrifices.

be willing to accept a certain level of loss—loss of time with your partner, loss of stability in your day-to-day life, and possibly the loss of life that comes with military service. Spend some time in meditation, look at your decision to live the military life as a conscious act of perpetual sacrifice, and evaluate your spiritual practice from that place. What do you see?

Relocation/PCS

The average active-duty serviceperson is relocated approximately every two to three years. For some, this is a key motivation for joining the military—they look forward to the opportunity to see the world and experience new cultures. For others, especially those with families, the PCS (Permanent Change of Station) process can be stressful and overwhelming. It is important to take this constant moving process into account when determining which branch of the military one elects to enter. Some, such as the Army and Air National Guards, do not PCS their members, but rather assign them to one base where they remain throughout their career, unless they elect to move elsewhere. However, if you are active duty, you *will* be moved, and frequently.

It becomes necessary, then, to cultivate a sense of internal balance, since military personnel (and their families) must often carry their sense of home with them. You may not always have access to your family, your personal belongings, or a strong spiritual community. I believe that this has the potential to create an extremely close bond within military families, as well as some unique challenges to their spiritual practice. Many service members develop an ability to forge strong psychic bonds with others—usually coven members who are separated by great distances. Those on shamanic paths find that these situations encourage dream walking or other astral visits. The flip side of this, of course, is that the majority of military Pagans are solitary, unwilling, or unable (due to distance or location) to form a supportive religious community or coven.

Often, the mundane tasks involved in a move (such as packing, hiring a mover, etc.) are taken care of by your branch of service. However, this does not necessarily mean less stress, since you must still go through the heartache of severing relationships, finding new homes for beloved pets and familiars (in the case of some international moves), preparing children for the transition, and coping with the unknowns of moving to a new city, state, or even country. Moving is one of the most stressful experiences in life (after death and divorce), and yet military personnel will go through this process approximately seven to ten times over the course of their career. Developing a habit of continual grounding and centering, taking a moment out of your day to locate and connect with your sense of center, will go a long ways toward coping with the PCS moves.

PCSs can be especially difficult for dependents (children and spouses), since they must essentially give up their whole lives for the sake of one family member's career. It is very important that this sacrifice is acknowledged and honored, because it is all too easily overlooked in the shuffle. Spouses are often asked to give up their jobs (putting their own economic self-determination into question) as well as social networks and support systems they've developed. I strongly suggest that dependent spouses contact a headhunting or recruiting firm in the new location as soon as possible, even prior to the move, in order to submit their resumé and begin the interview process as soon as they arrive at the new duty station. This can help smooth over any financial bumps that they may encounter due to the job loss, as well as hopefully prevent a buildup of feelings of resentment that can arise when they arrive at their new location and sit home alone while they watch their partner go off to his or her first day of work. If you are a stay-at-home parent, or if you choose to live on one income, then research volunteer and social opportunities that will be available to you at your new station. Getting involved in the community around you prevents depression and helps you to make friends and rebuild social connections. The Witches' Voice (www.witchvox.com) is an excellent resource for learning about the local Pagan community, including open circles, covens, stores, and events. It offers international listings, which is a wonderful thing for military personnel to have access to; however, keep in mind that none of its listings are investigated or vetted, and so some groups may not be appropriate for your circumstances.

Children present a different dilemma for military parents, since the cycle of relocation often means that they are PCSing at intervals that roughly correspond to just about every developmental stage. Communication is the most important aspect of preparing your children for the move—allow them to express their feelings, both positive and negative, and involve them in the planning process as much as possible. Use the Internet to show them your new base and the surrounding attractions. If your children are little (under six years old), try not to get rid of many of their belongings. What grown-ups view as "paring down" for the move can be profoundly distressing to little ones. Along the same lines, explain to your children what you're doing when you pack their toys and furniture. Many kids see their possessions going into boxes and assume they are being thrown away. Explain to your children what is going on—using a storybook or some toys as visual aids can be extremely helpful. Regardless of their age, avoid making any other big changes, such as potty training, or changing sleep patterns or household routines. Older children may express resentment or anger during the moving process. This is to be expected and, honestly, is not unfounded. Teens often take moving the hardest. They have more emotionally invested, especially once high school starts, and you may want to consider allowing them to stay with friends or relatives if they are close to graduation or deeply involved in their social community. Be patient with your children, do what you can to meet their needs, and understand that this will most likely continue until your family is reestablished in your new environment.

When you arrive in your new location, set up your altar as soon as possible, because this is the spiritual center of the home. This will provide a sense of continuity for everyone in the household as well as an energetic anchor amidst the uncertainty of life in a new place. Magickal tools should be carried with you when you travel, since military movers are notorious for packing in a haphazard manner. You do not want to get to your new duty station and realize that you cannot find your athame, or that your child's favorite Goddess statue was shattered in the move.

Ritual Blessing for Military Housing

The experience of living in military quarters can be quite exhausting when you are sensitive to energies in the surrounding environment. Military quarters seem to contain more of the residual energy of those who have lived there beforehand, most likely because of the exceptional circumstances military families endure. The stress, fear, and joy that accompany deployments, especially those in times of war, linger within an environment. If you are moving into older quarters (some bases have housing dating back to World War II), you might be surprised at the amount of "vibration" you'll feel upon entering your housing for the first time. I always recommend a thorough cleansing prior to moving your belongings into new housing. If this is not possible (if, for example, military movers will be there with your possessions prior to your arrival), the spell is still workable—it's just much easier when you are not maneuvering around furniture. This might seem like overkill, but the accumulation of decades of military life can be overpowering to those who are extremely sensitive to psychic energy.

The first thing you will need to do is sweep the floors thoroughly, beginning on the second floor, if you have one, and sweeping down the stairs. Working from the front of the house to the back, finally sweep the debris out the back door. Take a bucket of clean, cool water and throw it out after the sweepings to wash away any remaining dirt. After the sweeping you will need to refill the bucket with clean, cool water. To this, add a handful of sea salt, a few drops of High John the Conqueror, frankincense, and myrrh oils. If you have a purification oil that you'd prefer to use, feel free to substitute this for the other three. Proceed to wash or mop the floors with this water, again working from top to bottom and front to back.

After the sweeping and mopping has been done, turn your attention to the air. Smudge the whole house, top to bottom, front to back, with either sage or sweetgrass, or a combination of the two. Then, using the same mixture of water, sea salt, and purification oils, draw pentacles on the inside and outside of your front, back, and basement (if you have one) doors, as well as on the thresholds outside of your home. Finally, take a container of sea salt and walk the perimeter of the house, sprinkling the salt as you go, to create a circle of salt around your quarters. This completes the cleansing and blessing of your new housing and can be repeated as often as you feel necessary. Typically, I recommend making an annual routine of it, as my own family does on Beltaine Eve (April 30).

Dealing with Financial Hardship

Nobody joins the military intending to become the next Bill Gates. For most, financial considerations, other than the fact that there is some degree of job security, do not enter into the equation. It is a sad reality that many military families struggle to make ends meet, especially when a partner or parent has been deployed. For active-duty servicepersons, military housing or housing allowances can go a long way toward alleviating some of the burden. For National Guard and Reserve families without access to many of the resources available to active-duty personnel, the situation can be dire. I remember one specific incident my husband and I encountered. We had a string of unexpected bills pop up that left us shorthanded and in need of financial assistance. We went to the Financial Readiness Office on our base and spent three hours completing the paperwork they required. At the end of this process, the worker reviewed it for about thirty seconds, then looked up and said, "Oh no . . . no . . . I'm sorry . . . you're National Guard. You're not eligible for this. This program is only for *real military.*" My husband, due to be deployed to the Middle East the very next week, stormed out angry and hurt. Sadly, this response is all too common for the so-called weekend warriors and their families.

For some in this situation, the financial hardship arises after they've been activated. There are quite a number of Guard members and Reservists whose civilian jobs pay them significantly more than the military does. This means that when they go on active-duty orders, or are deployed overseas for any length of time, their income actually drops, sometimes causing catastrophic financial hardship for families already dealing with a great deal of stress. There are programs set up to assist military families (active duty, National Guard, and Reserve), although many require you to be on active-duty status at the time. Among those that I have worked with and know to be fast, efficient, and courteous are U.S.A Cares, which has an online application at www.usacares.us, and Operation Homefront. U.S.A. Cares might take awhile to contact you after you've completed the application, but once contact is established it makes a very fast decision regarding your request for assistance, and it typically processes the request within a day or two. Operation Homefront is a national program; however, not every state has a branch. Each branch has its own budget, so its ability to help is contingent upon the funds available at the time. Staff are very easy to contact (you can locate your local chapter through its website at www.operationhomefront.org), and they will reply quickly to explain requirements and discuss how they are able to assist you.

Prosperity Spell: The Money Pot

This is a very simple magickal technique that my family has used for years with great success—both energetic and material. You will need an earthenware bowl, jug, or other container. In theory, any container will work, but I prefer to use something made of clay for that extra bit of earth energy. When you find the right container, wash it with cool, clear water and leave it outside in the sun and moonlight for three days and nights. At the end of this time, bring your container back inside and hold it while saying:

> Jar of Earth and Bowl of Clay
> Never emptied, always stay
> Abundant with prosperity,
> And as I will, so mote it be.

Repeat this simple chant as many times as you feel you need in order to fully charge the pot or jar. If you are not comfortable with chanting, you can skip this step. The important part is the intention you imbue the container with—in this case abundance—rather than the method used to do so.

All magick requires practical work as well, so keep your newly consecrated container near the front door, where you will see it first thing upon leaving the home and returning again. Empty your pocket change into the pot, to have on hand for those times when cash resources run low. Feel free to take coins as needed (sometimes our money pot has been the difference between eating or not!), but always remember to return at least a penny or two to the container so that it is never truly empty. This simple spell serves as a microcosm of your household bank account. As long as you keep a coin or two within the container, it serves as a sort of prosperity magnet, drawing in what you need to keep your family safe and comfortable—lottery wins or other instant riches not guaranteed.

Dealing with Absences

Shellie Vandevoorde, in her book *Separated by Duty, United in Love,* defines several stages that military families go through mentally and emotionally when experiencing the deployment process. I have found her insights to be extremely accurate when compared to my own family's experiences, as well as those our friends have shared with me. I believe that she has identified something very important, especially since Pagans tend to be very sensitive to energetic changes in our environment and our relationships.

Vandevoorde calls the first phase "Mind Games." This is the period two to four weeks prior to the deployment date, when all of us (both military personnel and their family members) are mentally preparing for the separation. As I write this chapter, my own husband is preparing for a deployment in a few weeks. We are experiencing everything that Ms. Vandevoorde describes, including petty disagreements that escalate until someone finally reaches a "just leave and get it over with" breaking point. In the past, I have noticed that minor flaws, personality quirks, and misunderstandings are blown (often deliberately and quite wildly) out of proportion. We are trying to mentally separate from one another in order to make the day of physical parting a tiny bit easier. It's a classic example of "thought making form," and is a subtle, insidious form of mental magick that is all too easy to fall into. Vandevoorde points out that close friends preparing for a Permanent Change of Station will often go through a similar process. I know that when the time came for Paula (my covenmate and co-founder of our base's Designated Faith Group) and her family to move to their next duty station, our families slowly stopped gathering for our weekly card nights, Paula and I spoke on the phone far less than before, and we began to ease ourselves out of the intricate, intimate friendship we had built over the years. This Mind Games phase, which can manifest as either bitter fighting or a slow drifting apart, is difficult emotionally for everyone involved. It comes hand in hand with feelings of resentment, loneliness, and isolation, all of which may seem less threatening to feel when confronting the unknown dangers of deployment.

Approximately two weeks before the deployment, the Mind Games change a bit. At this point, we are no longer pushing our loved ones away, finding it easier to hate them than to see them leave. Now, we begin to cherish our military family members, becoming more romantic and, in some relationships, more clingy. Vandevoorde calls this the "I've Got to Love You While I Can" game. This is a far better way to manage our stress and fear about the separation, but it is still a coping mechanism/ game. It was during this phase prior to my husband's 2001 deployment to Saudi Arabia that I insisted upon, at the last minute, our family sitting for a very expensive set of professional portraits just days before he left. I was terrified that something would happen to him while he was away and we wouldn't have any photos of the whole family together. It turned out that my fears were not entirely unfounded, since after many delays in his departure, he arrived in country on September 10, 2001.

Vandevoorde's second phase of separation is called simply "Depression." It has been my experience that our whole family endures a certain level of depression immediately after the departure of my husband, which lasts up to two weeks after he leaves. Once again, our experiences correspond with her theory. In this phase, military families (especially spouses) tend to isolate themselves. Often I find myself making excuses to decline social invitations or skip out on Sabbats and other religious obligations. Usually I am busy making random home improvements or putting the children to bed at seven thirty in the evening. It is easier, mentally, to simply stay home. Those who know my partner is away want to ask questions: "Is he safe?" "Was he involved in (insert last CNN televised assault here)?" "Where is he stationed?" and other things that I most likely don't know the answer to and certainly wouldn't answer if I did. The alternative means interacting with people who have no idea your partner is away and therefore can be incredibly insensitive or oblivious in their comments. Sometimes, the latter group does nothing that you can put your finger on, but just the fact that they don't have to worry the way you do is enough to make you want to scream.

The depression, isolation, and irritation are all perfectly normal responses. However, I have learned that this is not an easy or healthy phase to get stuck in and have worked hard to push through it as fast as possible. Redecorating and making home improvements is my most common coping mechanism, and so I have learned to work through the depression while staying within my comfort zone. Rather than avoid attending ritual because I'm busy repainting my kitchen, I offer to host the Sabbat feast and get my friends to help clear the room afterward. If I don't feel up to attending the girls' night out with friends, I invite them over for a painting party instead. The key is to keep moving forward through the negative, without actually stepping outside the carefully constructed "safe zones" we build during deployments.

Phase three (occurring two or more weeks after departure) brings "The Resentment." These feelings occur within both the deployed partner and the home-front spouse. Those in the field often wish they could be at home. Those with children resent the "lucky" partner's ability to be at home for those once-in-a-lifetime milestones: births, first steps, senior proms. The home-front spouses, meanwhile, are angry that all the household responsibility falls on them. I know that I get so angry with my husband whenever I am "forced by the military" to have to shovel snow. The resentments build and are shared with our partners during those rare, cherished phone calls home. The partners at home spend time venting about the bills, the unruly children, and the snow shoveling while their deployed spouses grow more and more frustrated with the triviality of the frustrations expressed while they are dodging IEDs or working eighteen-hour shifts. The resentment grows exponentially, and it is vital that both partners recognize their own relationship patterns and develop habits to ground and center the negative energy that arises and overflows if not properly addressed. As Pagans, we have access to skills and techniques that make these habits easier to incorporate into our daily routines. A suggestions that other military families have shared with me include keeping a pentacle paten on their Deployment Altar and, when they feel it is needed, taking up the paten and mentally "pushing" all of their resentment into the pentacle, allowing it to be reabsorbed by the earth. Another idea involved keeping salt and lemons on hand. Whenever the spouse at home felt especially resentful, she would dip a wedge of lemon into the salt and then taste it. Maybe just once, maybe quite a few times. She found that being able to physically manifest the bitterness she felt inside went a long way in reminding her just how distasteful those feelings were to hold on to.

Stage four can overlap a bit with the other stages, although I have found that by this point, which Vandevoorde calls "Getting into the Routine," I have usually moved beyond the negative feelings experienced earlier in the separation. The hardest part of establishing the routine, for my family, is always the hours between 4:30 and 6:00 p.m. We only have one vehicle, so this is the time when I am usually packing up our boy and heading off to the base to pick up my husband. By six, we are back home selecting dinner. During deployments, my schedule is no longer bound up with his and I go through a period of drifting each day. I am not really sure what to do with all the time. What works well for my family is a trip to the dollar-show movies. We catch a late matinee, and by the time we're home, we're back on "schedule" and wondering what's for dinner. Establishing a daily routine is vital to surviving a lengthy deployment. Each family will have its own rough times. For some it is weekends, when the children are used to having their parent home from work and ready to spend time with them. For us, it's the rush hour. I have come to the conclusion that there is nothing unhealthy about distraction. Distraction can be built into your long-term routine. This is the time when enrichment classes, yoga, or meditation all become activities that we actually have time to do!

The final stage, which Vandevoorde calls "Living on Love," is the "acceptance" phase of the deployment process. By the time we reach stage five, the deployed spouses are acclimated to their new environment and their partners at home have established a workable routine for themselves and their children. This doesn't mean that we stop missing one another, or that we're never lonely. It does indicate that we have all reached a point where we are functioning well within our changed circumstances. This is the more enjoyable part of the deployment, for me. I realize that I can eat out and always choose the restaurant. I can eat off of paper plates for ninety straight days without anyone complaining. We have not only established our routines, but we have become comfortable within them and are able to look forward toward homecoming, and with it all of the new joys and stresses that come with our loved ones' return.

Spell: Home Away from Home Mojo

This little charm serves as a sort of energetic "tether" to connect individuals to their homes. We made our first one prior to my husband's deployment to Saudi Arabia. We found it to be a very fortuitous bit of magick, since he ended up arriving there on September 10, 2001! His mojo bag was carried with him on every deployment (including into three combat zones) until recently, when it went missing. Thankfully, it was found again a few months later and taken to a Build-a-Bear Workshop, where it was tucked within the body of a stuffed cat, which was blessed and dressed by our son to be carried with Daddy on his next deployment. You can choose to omit any step involving a stuffed animal—although putting it inside of something similar does make it harder to lose your mojo!

You will need the following:

- A small bag or pouch that can be carried in a pocket or around your neck

- 2 small plastic containers (contact lens cases or ¼-dram bottles work very well)

- A charm or picture of Deity

- Household dust (if you happen to be a neatnik, try looking on top of your ceiling fan blades or door jambs)

- One hair from each member of the household, rolled together into a knot or ball

- A small pebble or pinch of dirt from near your front door
- A picture of the whole household together

Place the dust and hair each into its own container. Add the pebble or dirt from near your front door and the images of your family and Deity. You may choose to include whatever other small items you feel will serve to connect you to home; some mojos I've seen have included dram bottles of breast milk, a drop of blood from a spouse, dried plants from a family garden, even baby teeth and pet hair! Include whatever you're most comfortable carrying with you—as long as it's freely given and causes no harm—that will connect you to your home. When you have completed the mojo assembly process, sit together in a circle as a family and pass the pouch from person to person. Ask everyone to breathe upon the mojo, so that it can collect a bit of energy from each family member. Carry it with you whenever you travel, so that you'll always have a bit of home and family with you, wherever you happen to find yourself.

The Military Wife

Magickal Name: Grey Ghost

Primary Duty Station: Geilenkirchen/NATO AWACS Air Base, Germany

Branch of Service: United States Air Force

Status: Dependent Spouse & Veteran

Tradition/Path: Celtic Warrior

How long have you been in the military? How long have you followed your spiritual path? Do you feel that one influenced the other? Why or why not?

I was in the military on active duty AF from 1984 to 1987. I have been a military spouse since 1985, and a dependent since 1987. This means my military affiliation spans twenty-three-plus years.

I have followed my spiritual path since 1991, or approximately sixteen years. Since the two events did not overlap during my active-duty status, there really was no influence on either side.

How does your spirituality affect your role as a serviceperson? Which do you feel holds you to a higher ethical/moral standard, your religious path or your military path?

Although no longer active duty, I still feel that my spirituality affects my role as a military dependent because I know there is a great need for more equitable service from chaplains and commanders in dealing with Pagan/Wiccan followers. As the spouse of a field-grade officer, I think my ethical/moral standards are equally affected by both the military and my path. I use both to gauge responses and actions I must make when called upon to address an issue.

Have you developed any spiritual practices or magickal techniques that you incorporate into your military service?

I would say my biggest change to dealing with a military lifestyle, where moving every two to three years is the norm, is the use of protection devices when we move, cleansing homes, and creating easily portable altars. Because I am primarily a solitary practitioner, most other physical aspects do not change. The other difference is in learning to sense the different energies and entities each new location presents to me.

What have your experiences interacting with fellow service personnel, officers, and/or chaplains been like? Are you in the "broom closet" or open about your faith?

Because I am a field-grade officer's wife, I have many instances to interact with all ranks of service members and their spouses. I do not hide my chosen path, openly wearing my pentacle to most functions, both formal and informal. If asked, I do not hesitate to explain I am a "practicing witch." Sometimes this is greeted with hesitancy, occasionally with a look of shock and fear, but mostly with curiosity and even a little interest. This is mostly from the active-duty members and their spouses. Many chaplains I have met, while not outright hostile, usually will not speak to me. In fact, one chaplain at one overseas duty station took this to an extreme. If he saw me at a function, he made sure he stayed as far away from me as he could without trying to appear too obvious about it. If I even started to move his way while speaking with others, he made sure he moved as well. The irony of the whole situation was, his wife, while she didn't seek me out, had no trouble conversing with me on any subject that came up, without affectation.

Do you feel that there is such a thing as a "Warrior's" spiritual path?
Do you find that military Pagans have a different relationship with or
perspective on Deity than civilians?

Since I follow a Celtic warrior path, I do believe in such a path. In fact, history reveals that many Pagan paths had warrior credos as part of their path. Because I have spent most of my time with military Pagans/Wiccans, my perspective concerning differences of Deity between military and civilian persons is somewhat skewed. However, those civilians I have met have similar perspectives as most of my military acquaintances, with one difference. Military Pagans/Wiccans, for the most part, seem to consider more often the consequences of their actions against the Wiccan Rede—whether consciously or subconsciously—than civilians. I think this is because they live every day and every hour of their lives with the knowledge that this day they may be called upon to do harm in the line of duty.

Which facet of your personality has elicited a strong reaction from the
community around you: your Pagan faith or your military service? Please
explain.

This particular question doesn't really apply much at the current time, since the military is my community. This is true of most military members and their families. Non-military people have a hard time with this concept. Because we live apart from family and friends from our hometowns, we usually "adopt" those living around us at each assignment as family and friends. We rely on them just like we would rely on those we leave behind each time we move. When you consider this, then military service would normally elicit the strongest reaction from the community around any military Pagan/Wiccan or their family. And, because most military members, on a personal but not necessarily professional level, are usually more open-minded than their civilian counterparts, it has been my experience that Pagan/Wiccan paths do not elicit as strong a response from the neighbors as when they find out whether you are an SP, OSI agent, or pilot.

Do you believe that Paganism is essentially a religion of pacifism? What do you say to those who believe that a military career goes against the Rede?

While I do feel that Pagan/Wiccan paths strive to promote peace and harmony in the world, I do not consider it essentially a religion of pacifism. When I think of pacifism, I think of Jesus's teaching of "turn the other cheek," very much like the lifestyles adhered to by the Quakers, Amish, and Mennonites. While the Wiccan Rede advises us, "An it harm none, do as thou wilt," it does not tell us we cannot defend ourselves, our family, our homes, or our country. In fact, it implies that we are tasked with ensuring many of the freedoms provided by the U.S. Constitution, by implying that we are spiritually bound to honor what is right and just within our world, including others' rights to follow their own religious paths.

I have never had to defend my military career as being against the Wiccan Rede, yet. I have considered this issue and would probably simply refer to the very ideas I mentioned in the preceding paragraph. These would be the reasons for my belief, and then I would ask my "accuser" what they would do if it was their life or their family's lives, or how they would handle it if a foreign power invaded their city.

In some Pagan traditions, the spirits of fallen Warriors are taken to a separate afterlife from civilians (such as Valhalla). What do you believe happens to your soul when you die?

Since I believe in reincarnation (most Pagans/Wiccans I know do), I feel my soul would rest in Summerland/Tir nan Og until it was time for it to be reborn and try again to attain spiritual wholeness and unity with the Creator (Wakan Tanka).

Knowing what you know now, what advice would you give to someone considering joining the military?

Because I've seen the military go from being men and women who truly felt called to defend their country even if it meant their life, to an organization more akin to a business run by those who have never experienced military life, full of individuals who think their duty is a nine-to-five, five-day-a-week job with all holidays off, I would point out what it really means to be a military member. Then I would ask them to really consider if they are willing to give up family, friends, holidays, weekends, vacations, and various other "civilian" benefits, including the ability to openly follow their chosen religious path. Most civilians have no idea what it means to be truly active-duty military, or even a military spouse/family, and they should be given the unvarnished truth of the military world before committing themselves, even for a short time, to such a lifestyle. It is even harder on Pagan/Wiccan military members, since there is such misinformation about our religion.

How have your family's spiritual practices been shaped by your military experience?

Because each member of my family follows their own very different paths, we are primarily solitary practitioners, so are not impacted by our military lifestyle. The military is not conducive to covens, though I have known some individuals who have tried that path, even with only family members. Deployments and separations are major detriments to regular coven work. I have found it much better to develop a group of Pagan/Wiccan friends who meet regularly to decide if they wish to hold open rituals and circles, or simply work as solitaries and simply meet to share experiences and knowledge.

Has your religion or spirituality had an impact on your relationships with other military spouses/families? How or why not?

My spirituality's primary impact on relationships mostly occurs in forming (or not forming) relationships with others at my duty stations. For most of my relationships it's just something others know about me, but it doesn't necessarily become an issue. It has helped me deal better with those people who simply cannot get past my chosen path. I simply remind myself that, if they were my "friend" before knowing, they are the worse off by not remembering this and any good times we might have shared. I do not force my presence on people like that, but I also do not go out of my way to avoid them, since I'm not the one who seems to have a problem with my religion.

In what ways (if any) do you feel that your Pagan beliefs present challenges to the military culture?

The biggest challenge to military culture from my beliefs is the ability to hold rituals on base because of lack of free base facilities. While there are a few chaplain's offices that are actually trying to provide such places, there are usually so many "requirements" to be met in order to use these facilities that it sometimes is not worth the effort when other locations off base may be found. This is very much a challenge at overseas bases, where going off base means learning the local country's culture and customs as to open fires, etc. Also, the majority of chaplains aren't comfortable with Pagans/Wiccans doing ritual in chapel facilities, considering it somehow sacrilegious (I've actually been told this before). Picnic areas on base usually have a fee, and also usually must be reserved months in advance of an event, so there is no chance for spontaneity or short-notice rituals. There also are no open fires allowed, only those used in grills, which can be worked around, if it's a portable grill, but not if it's a brick BBQ pit.

Another challenge is one that's been in the media lately, the penchant for chaplains to have prayer at public functions such as dining-outs, parties, etc. I haven't met a chaplain yet who, though they may try to keep the prayer generic, doesn't always end it with "In Jesus's name we pray," which of course comes right back to being prejudiced towards Christianity.

What advice would you give to other Pagans considering "marrying into the military"? Is there anything you wish that you had known?

For those marrying into the military, I would pose the very same questions as I did to those wishing to enlist. I would also point out that the spouse who is left behind must be prepared to act as a single parent/individual, and as their military member's legal representative in all matters, for long stretches of time. They must also be prepared to accept and deal with attitude changes that can occur during separations (based on the reasons for the deployment). There is also the problem of spouses wearing rank, knowing how to deal with emergencies on your own with little support many times from the base community. While there is supposed to be a good support system for deployed spouses, it has been my personal experience not to have this support system work when it was needed the majority of the time.

Is there anything else you'd like to add?

One last thing I would add is a request of our leaders—both civilian and military—to be more diligent in abiding by their own laws and regulations as they regard to working with Pagans/Wiccans/alternative religions. We are, by the U.S. Constitution, allowed the right of freedom of worship—which means we are constitutionally guaranteed the right to follow our own religious path no matter what it is. Department of Defense regulations (as well as each individual branch of the DOD) mandate that followers of any and all religious paths are to be accommodated. This is *not* happening. I have known military members to be bounced out of the service for simply not meeting physical fitness requirements no matter what they do to meet them, and yet discrimination of Pagans/Wiccans and several other alternative religions is still being practiced through much of our military. Many instances are started by our own generals and congressmen, such as [former Representative] Barr. I wonder how they would feel if they were on the receiving end of their own prejudices? There are many "Christians" who commit hate crimes and other crimes against those who do not believe as they do, yet they are never prosecuted. But let one Pagan or Wiccan so much as profess to their religion in some workplaces or communities and their bosses and neighbors are finding any little problem in order to have them fired or forced to move. This was *not* what our Founding Fathers wanted for our country. And I firmly believe that not even the Judeo-Christian concept of God or Jesus would condone such behavior, so why is our own government condoning it?

Pagans/Wiccans try to abide by the laws of our country, and many are losing their lives in order to protect those laws. Yet those who claim to uphold the laws of our country are most likely to be the ones who break those very same laws and have so little respect for them that they won't even acknowledge the sacrifice of those Pagans/Wiccans who give their lives to protect their right to break rights provided by the U.S. Constitution.

* * *

7. Willingness to Kill

The sword of murder is not the balance of justice! Blood does not wipe out dishonor, nor violence indicate possession.

—Julia Ward Howe

"Killology"

Lt. Col. Dave Grossman is pioneering the study of what he has termed *killology*, "the scholarly study of the destructive act, just as sexology is the scholarly study of the procreative act. In particular, killology focuses on the reactions of healthy people in killing circumstances (such as police and military in combat) and the factors that enable and restrain killing in these situations."[1] His Killology Research Group is conducting ongoing studies of the cultural phenomena of killing, its causes, effects, and implications. No discussion of military service would be complete without an examination of just this subject, since regardless of branch of service or chosen career field, each and every member of the military is ultimately engaged in or supporting the act

---

1 Lt. Col. Dave Grossman, *On Killing: The Psychological Cost of Learning to Kill in War and Society* (Boston: Little, Brown & Co., 1995).

of killing. This is not a value-based statement, but rather a simple fact. Therefore, it is only responsible for us to take a look at the implications of this fact.

My husband often says that he believes there would be fewer wars if we still used the weaponry of era's past: catapults, battle-axes, and the like. Much of modern military technology is focused on distancing the weapons, and thus the warriors, from their targets. This has a twofold effect. On one hand, it protects the lives of our service personnel, by keeping them well outside the heart of battle even as they engage the enemy. This is undoubtedly a positive trait. The physical distance, however, also enables the military to psychologically and emotionally distance itself from the act of killing. Unlike the days when in order to stop an enemy you had to step in front of him and plunge your sword into his body, the enemy is now a blip on a television monitor or radar screen—no more human than the pixilated characters in a video game. This causes the relationship between combat opponents to change from the honored enemy of chivalric times to the "ragheads, camel jockeys, and sand n---ers" of today.

The dehumanization of both shooter and target begins during the training process. One of the "greatest" accomplishments of social evolution in the past thousand years has been the modern military's systematic retraining of its members to overcome their aversion to killing. One example given by Lt. Col. Grossman is the simple change of rifle-range targets from abstract bull's-eye designs to human silhouettes that fall when struck. This process, consistently applied in ways subtle and overt throughout the military training process, has had tremendous results. By conditioning personnel to react reflexively regardless of environmental conditions or personal feelings, the military has dramatically increased the rate of kill among its members—from about 20% in World War II to approximately 90% today.[2] This is a good thing, if you are taking hostile fire and need to react quickly. The problems arise when the soldier returns home and can't turn off these aggressive reflexes.

---

2 Ibid. See also Lt. Col. Grossman's article "A Resistance to Killing," available online at http://www.killology.com/art_onkilling_resistance.htm.

Without a proper recognition of the change in realities (from combat theatre to home front) that the military personnel experience, the risk of posttraumatic stress disorder, depression, and addiction is high. Lt. Col. Grossman points out that "Every warrior society has a 'purification ritual' to help the returning warrior deal with his 'blood guilt' and to reassure him that what he did in combat was 'good.' In primitive tribes this generally involves ritual bathing, ritual separation (which serves as a cooling-off and 'group therapy' session), and a ceremony embracing the warrior back into the tribe."[3] The Disarmament Ritual later on in this book is one attempt to create such a ceremony for returning serviceper-sons. However, without this validation, support, and ceremonial release (even secular society has its ceremonies, often in the form of Memorial and Veterans Day activities, homecoming parades, etc.), the soldier does not receive the mental triggers that signal an end to the combat "mode" and a return to the peace/safety "mode." As Pagans and Witches, we are in a wonderful position to recognize this need and seek to provide it for those returning home from combat.

Sometimes, killing is necessary. The willingness to pull a trigger or re-lease a missile may be an act that saves dozens, if not thousands of lives. The problems arise when we dehumanize our opponents and thus reduce our own human capacity. As people of magick, we must be mindful of the implications that come with being trained to kill—quickly and with mini-mal reflection. We must be willing to act with speed, awareness, and com-passion—even when called to take a life. And perhaps most importantly, we must be willing to forgive each other (and ourselves) upon return.

Preparing for Combat

The task of mentally and spiritually preparing for deployment is one that you begin long before you set foot on that ship or plane. Many friends report that they or their loved ones become distant, "itchy," eager to get there and get it over with. This can be difficult for their children and part-ners, since they grow more and more distant even as their families want

---

3 David Grossman and Bruce K. Siddle, "Psychological Effects of Combat," in *Encyclopedia of Violence, Peace, and Conflict* (San Diego: Academic Press, 2000).

to hold them the closest. I have yet to meet anyone who has overcome this mental "girding" process, but it is possible to minimize the impact on those around you. Prior to his recent deployment to Iraq, my husband and I basically came to a tacit agreement that he would resist the urge to pull away, or spend time in the company of his comrades or at work, until the trip began, and I, likewise, would resist the urge to be clingy, to demand a great deal of physical affection or outward displays of emotion. This gentle agreement, which allows us to spend time with each other prior to departure without putting any additional demands on the changing psyche of the deploying warrior, worked wonders in helping us both cope with the impending departure. Well, that and Xanax.

Warrior Poppet

The Warrior Poppet is a simple charm that my husband and I created six years ago, and still use today—although to say "use" is overstating it a bit, since the general idea is that the poppet should sit in a place where it is visible to the family members at home, yet safe and unlikely to fall, get lost, or get damaged.

You will need the following:

• One piece of well-worn BDU material (taken from old trousers or an overblouse)

• Needle and thread

• Quartz crystal, hematite, amethyst, and rose quartz

• Embroidery floss

Cut two basic human shapes out of the worn BDUs. You might want to draw this out on paper first so that the pieces are identical. This will make the stitching easier. If you choose to do so, use the embroidery floss to add facial features and hair to one of the shapes. Sew the two shapes together (remember to put the embroidered face on the inside!) and stitch all the way along the edges, leaving a 1.5-inch opening near the head. Cut the remaining BDU material into small pieces and use these to stuff the empty poppet, being sure to get scraps into the arms and legs to thoroughly shape it. When it has reached the desired "stuffiness," take the rose quartz into your hands (if working this spell with your partner, hold it together) and charge it with love and heart-energy. You might wish to recite the following:

Heart of Rose, warmed in my palm,
May love and comfort flow from thee;
From our hearts to his/hers afar,
And as I/we will, so mote it be.

When the rose quartz has been thoroughly charged, place it within the poppet roughly where the heart would be. Next, take up the hematite. Holding it between your hands, charge it with strength and muscular energy. You might wish to recite the following:

Stone of Iron, Stone of Earth,
Grant him/her honor, grant him/her mirth;
May Strength of Will radiate from thee,
And as I/we will, so mote it be.

Place the hematite within one of the arms of the poppet, and take up the amethyst. Hold it between your hands and visualize it connecting with Deity. Allow the energy of the Goddess to flow through you and charge the stone. You might wish to recite:

Queen of Heaven, Maiden Moon,
Grant your child a simple boon;
Lend your arrow, swift and sure,
Guard your son/daughter, keep him/her secure.

The amethyst should be placed in the opposite arm from the hematite. The final stone is the clear quartz. This is an all-purpose stone that you will charge together with your partner, so that it is thoroughly charged with the energy of your relationship, be it passionate, devotional, or familial. You might consider passing this particular stone to children or familiars if you have them. The idea is to mingle the energy of all who live with the departing serviceperson into a single stone. This is placed in the poppet's head, with the following words:

> Our spell has been wrought,
> linking hearth and far field;
> Our magick is consecrated,
> our connection is sealed.
>
> By the Will of our spirits,
> by the Goddess's kiss;
> The poppet is you/me,
> and your/this essence is this.

The final steps in the creation of the poppet involve stitching up the little section that was left open and connecting the individual person to the poppet. I suggest adding one of his or her hairs before closing it up, and then having the serviceperson breathe upon the poppet. Depending upon your tradition or path and your level of squeamishness, you might decide to add saliva or other secretions/fluids to the poppet. This poppet should be kept on or near the home altar, where it is visible. It is the energetic personification of the serviceperson it was created to represent and serves as a psychic connection linking him or her to home—much like the mojo bag we created earlier for the individual to carry. *One important note: It is NOT a "voodoo doll," and it cannot be used to control the serviceperson or for any other malicious intent. Seriously, do I really need to tell you that?*

Armoring Ritual

If you are a serviceperson facing upcoming deployment, you may find this ritual useful for extra protection.

You will need the following:

- Your helmet

- Your battle dress uniform (BDU)

- Your body armor, flak jacket, or Kevlar

- Your boots

- A large mirror (full length preferable)

- Salt

- Water

- Incense

- Charcoal

Before you begin this ritual, spend some time in a ritual bath. With the lights off, light a few candles and fill a warm tub with Epsom salts and (if you'd like) an essential oil such as High John the Conqueror or dragon's blood. Spend this time in meditation, clearing your mind of worry, planning, anticipation. Allow yourself to be fully in the moment. When you are centered, dry off and continue with the ritual. It is best performed in the nude (or in your undergarments) in the beginning. If it is your tradition to do so, cast a circle and call the quarters. If you don't feel a need to do so, you may skip this step. Place your uniform pieces on your altar (if you keep one) or lay them out on the floor in front of you.

Casting the Circle

Close your eyes and visualize your energy-field (or aura) expanding around you. Take your time, and allow it to expand until it encompasses your body, the altar if you're using one, and your uniform. Take three deep breaths—with the first, align yourself with the energy you've expanded; with the second, open yourself up to Deity and take a moment to honor this connection; finally, with the third, seal the circle and open your eyes. Stomp your right foot to bring yourself to center.

Calling the Quarters

Hail to the East and the powers of air. I call you to this circle to witness this Rite. Hail and welcome!

Hail to the South and the powers of fire. I call you to this circle to witness this Rite. Hail and welcome!

Hail to the West and the powers of water. I call you to this
circle to witness this Rite. Hail and welcome!
Hail to the North and the powers of earth. I call you to this
circle to witness this Rite. Hail and welcome!
Hail to the Center, the power that is spirit. I call you to this
circle to witness this Rite. Hail and welcome!

Cleansing

Place three pinches of salt into a small cup of water. Stir it three times
counterclockwise and say:

> Water and Salt, where thou art cast, no spell nor adverse pur-
> pose last not in complete accord with me and as I will, so mote
> it be.

Then, using your fingers, sprinkle saltwater over your uniform pieces. Say:

> Elements of the Divine Feminine, Water and Earth, cleanse and
> consecrate these tools in the name of the Mother Goddess.

Place three pinches of incense onto the lit charcoal. Stir the air above
three times counterclockwise and say:

> Fire and Air, where thou are cast, no spell nor adverse purpose
> last not in complete accord with me and as I will, so mote it be.

Then, using your fingers, fan the incense over the pieces of your uniform
and say:

> Elements of the Divine Male, Fire and Air, cleanse and conse-
> crate these tools in the name of the Father God.

Working the Spell

Take up your BDUs and put them on. When you have them on, stand before the mirror and extend your arms and legs so that your body forms a pentacle. Look yourself in the eyes and say:

> I am the air, the strong eastern wind.
> My breath, quiet as whispers through the trees,
> My voice, sure as the tornado's roar.
> I am the air itself, and I carry its power within me.

Close your eyes and visualize your body filling up with air, swirling inside you and inflating your lungs. Take a few deep breaths to push this air into each of your limbs. When you feel the element within every part of you, open your eyes.

Put on your boots, and lace them in the usual manner. When you have completed this task, resume the pentacle position before the mirror and say:

> I am the earth; its bedrock, my bones,
> My muscles are carved from the mountain tops,
> My body as sure and as certain as the fertile soil.
> I am the earth itself, and I carry its power within me.

Close your eyes and visualize your body filling up with earth, soft, yielding, and strong. Feel yourself strengthen and harden. Run your hands along your body and take a moment to recognize the solidity of it. When you feel the element within every part of you, open your eyes.

Take up your body armor and put it on. Stand before the mirror in the pentacle position and say:

> I am fire, the heat of the southern sun,
> My will blazes with a yearning for justice;
> My heart burns with a passion for my fellow man,
> I am the flame itself, and I carry its power within me.

Close your eyes and imagine a flame burning in your heart chakra. Feel it expand until it fills every inch of your body, burning with a flame that does not hurt but rather fuels your physical self. Allow yourself a few minutes to embrace this sensation. When you feel the element within every part of your body, open your eyes.

Take up your helmet and place it on your head. Stand once again before your mirror in the pentacle position and say:

> I am water, the western stream of peace.
> Within my blood flows the gentle, nourishing rain
> And the awesome force of the flood.
> I am the water itself, and I carry its power within me.

Close your eyes and visualize water gently filling your body. Recognize how the sensation varies from point to point within yourself. When you feel the element within every part of yourself, open your eyes.

When you are fully dressed (as you should be by this point) stand before the mirror in the pentacle position. Look yourself square in the eyes and say:

> I am Spirit, the embodiment of the All,
> I am the culmination of creation:
> Earth, air, fire, and water are merged within me.
> Within my spirit lies the power to create,
> Within my spirit lies the will to act,
> Within my spirit lies the desire to serve.
> I am Spirit itself, and I carry its power within me.

Assume the Goddess position, arms extended upward and gently curving. Take a moment to feel the presence of the Mother. If you have dedicated yourself to a particular aspect of the Goddess, you may wish to invoke her now. Then say:

> I am a child of the Great Mother,
> She who is gentle and loving,
> Yet never hesitant to protect her young.

I am beloved of the Mother Goddess,
Whose gift is both action and restraint.
I am a part of the Mother, and I carry her power within me.

Kiss your fingertips and offer a salute to the Goddess.

Next, assume the God position, arms crossed over your chest. Take a moment to feel your connection to the Father. If you have dedicated yourself to a particular aspect of the God, you may wish to invoke him. Then say:

I am a child of the Wild God,
He who is both Father and Hunter.
He does not hesitate to take life,
when doing so is necessary.
He does not hesitate to lay his life down,
When doing so is necessary.
I am beloved of the Wild God,
The Stag and the Spear, the Corn and the Scythe.
I am a part of the God, and I carry his power within me.

Kiss your fingertips and offer a salute to the God.

Releasing the Quarters

Hail to the Center, the power of spirit. I carry you within me as I depart from this place. Thank you for your presence, now and always. Hail and farewell!

Hail to the North, the power of earth. I carry you within me as I depart from this place. Thank you for your presence, now and always. Hail and farewell!

Hail to the West, the power of water. I carry you within me as I depart from this place. Thank you for your presence, now and always. Hail and farewell!

Hail to the South, the power of fire. I carry you within me as I depart from this place. Thank you for your presence, now and always. Hail and farewell!

Hail to the East, the power of air. I carry you within me as I depart from this place. Thank you for your presence, now and always. Hail and farewell!

Close your eyes and remember the energy you first expanded outward. Slowly, draw the energy back to you with each steady intake of breath. When the energy has returned to its usual place just outside and surrounding your body, open your eyes and stomp your right foot. The ritual is ended.

Battlefield Meditation: The Karmic Web

This is one of those magickal techniques that you should practice well in advance of actually needing to use it, since the ideal scenario is to have established a familiarity with the skill that will allow you to tap into it immediately, without much conscious thought or effort. The Karmic Web is a Buddhist concept that can be incorporated into your meditation or magickal practice and utilized in a myriad of ways. However, for our purposes, we are going to look at how the Karmic Web can be used as a form of protection in battle.

Buddhists (and many others) believe that we are all connected. Each of us is creating our own reality, through our thoughts and actions. Also, through our thoughts and actions, we are nurturing the seeds of what our experience will be in the next lifetime. When one thinks good thoughts, sends out positive energy, and does good works, one is creating "good karma," and on the physical plane, one is creating a better experienced reality. However, individuals do not create their realities and experiences in a vacuum. We encounter other people, and beings, who are each in turn creating their own realities. Each of these individually created realities meld into what some Buddhists collectively call the Karmic Web.

By calling upon the Karmic Web, you are invoking an interesting and rich protector. In my interpretation, you are stating two things. First, you might be promising to work, in this lifetime—and possibly your next lifetimes—to promote the greater good, therefore, to karmically "draw" protection to yourself, so that you may be able to do this good work. Second, you are drawing on the created reality of not just your friends, allies, and the people for whom you are fighting. By invoking the Karmic Web as a whole, you are also trusting the created reality of your enemies, those people who are shooting at you, to wrap you in protection.[4]

Many Pagan traditions have similar concepts, most likely derived from Buddhist or Native American origins. The web of life, the Akasha, the Ether, the Astral Plane—Pagans have many ideas that encompass the same general concept. I think that the language of the Karmic Web is a powerful imagery to invoke on the battlefield, however, since it reminds us that we are connected not only to those we ally ourselves with but also to those we are called upon to actively oppose. The Buddhists acknowledge the fact that no human being is devoid of hope, of love, or of a desire for peace. Perhaps we only seek these things under our own specific terms, but the facts remain that each of us here on earth contributes our desire for a positive reality to the universal Karmic Web and that this energy remains accessible to anyone who chooses to connect to it.

---

4 Thanks very much to my friend Carrie for the wonderful explanation!

PAGAN
PERSPECTIVES
* * *

The Coalition Partner

Name: Oliver Peltier

Magickal Name: Offi Dvalinson/Spanglemaker

Primary Duty Station: RAF Leeming, UK

Current Location: Kandahar, Afghanistan

Branch of Service: Royal Air Force

Tradition/Path: Asatru

How long have you been in the military? How long have you followed your spiritual path? Do you feel that one influenced the other? Why or why not?

I have been in the military since 1991; currently I have served fifteen years. I have followed a spiritual path for twenty-four years, and have been dedicated to the Goddess Freyja since I was eighteen. During my youth I held an affinity for Pallas Athena, the Grey-Eyed Goddess of Wisdom and War. My father served in the Army until I was eight, so I had early contact with a military lifestyle. My view is that I was meant to serve in the armed forces; it was my wyrd or my destiny.

How does your spirituality affect your role as a serviceperson? Which do you feel holds you to a higher ethical/moral standard, your religious path or your military path?

My spirituality confirms and supports my role as a serviceman as the values of Asatru are close to the values of the military. I have always followed the call of my soul and have found that the moral standards of the military have evolved into a modern nonbigoted but certainly not politically correct philosophy. This means that military personnel can appear to behave in certain ways but are open to change through a shared worldview of comradeship.

Have you developed any spiritual practices or magickal techniques that you incorporate into your military service?

I have internalized much of my spirituality, making it a part of my being. The path of the Mage and the Mystic is cyclic in nature and my worldview is a rather mystical one. When I express my spiritual practice I tend to fuse my experiences of contemplation, meditation, Reiki, the Craft, and the Runes into a synergistic whole. I suppose I have made the expression of magic an act of the soul. Some effects useful in a military context that I have worked are creating wards of protection, sending healing to problem areas in the world, and countering magical and psychic intelligence gathering.

What have your experiences interacting with fellow service personnel, officers, and/or chaplains been like? Are you in the "broom closet" or open about your faith?

Most people in the military in my experience may not understand a Pagan or heathen's path, but they are supportive and it's relatively easy to explain the absolute basics of a Pagan path to the majority of service personnel. Generally people within the military tend to view differences as weird, but are accepting and tolerant of differences, especially within the corps or regiment. I have had several good professional relationships with some chaplains and have found them accepting and supportive generally. I am and have been out of the broom closet for several years now.

*Do you feel that there is such a thing as a "Warrior's" spiritual path?
Do you find that military Pagans have a different relationship with or
perspective on Deity than civilians?*

I do feel that there is such a thing as a "Warrior's Path"; it is related to the path of the Visionary or Leader and to the Path of the Guardian. Within a military context, a definition of leadership is being able to express your vision and bring others to your viewpoint or to the fulfillment of the objective envisioned. I feel that not all Pagans or heathens serving in the military are necessarily on the Warrior's Path. It is a personal choice and a calling of the heart and of the soul. I have found that service personnel tend to generally hold a grim or fatalistic view of the universe. It seems a common folk belief that when you are called, or when it's your turn to die, then and only then will it happen. There is plenty of lore about people who missed death by a hairsbreadth in military legend. I feel that it's only the view of the universe which differs between civilians and military personnel and not perceptions of Deity(s).

*Which facet of your personality has elicited a strong reaction from the
community around you: your Pagan faith or your military service? Please
explain.*

I have found that it is what is known about a person that elicits a response within the community. My neighbors are aware of me as a serviceman and are supportive of me and my kin. My friends and those who are aware of my spirituality are more affected by that same spirituality. Probably one of the most interesting anecdotes I can give is about my soul brother, who was originally not a Pagan. I met him in Germany and we were neighbors in our single accommodation. Our friendship was and is very strong, and he started finding that aspects of my spirituality impinged on his life. He is aware of Freyja, as she tends to take an active interest in him. He follows a Warrior Path, is now Pagan, but has taken the view of not worshipping any deity. I know that was the influence of the Goddess rather than my efforts that led my soul brother to his current path.

Do you believe that Paganism is essentially a religion of pacifism? What do you say to those who believe that a military career goes against the Rede?

I view Paganism as a federation of religions, some of which are pacifistic, some martial, and most being rooted in the sheer blood, sweat, and tears of everyday life. In Buddhism it is expressed that all is suffering, and only by being free from desire can one transcend or escape pain. There is suffering in the world, but there is no need to escape the world; we can be fluffy or genuine and send love and healing to the world. It is our intentions that color our worldview, as we are co-creators with Spirit and we are part of Nature. The Rede states, "An it harm none, do as thou Wilt, Love is the Law, Love under Will"; the channel for that phrase originally was most probably a supporter of the military, at least in principle. On one level the Rede applies absolutely to all and everyone, regardless of belief. Those who chose to do as they want, rather than what they Will, are the ones who initiate conflict. A soldier's task is to follow the orders of her officer or noncommissioned officer (NCO). They must trust their superior rank's experience and integrity. An NCO's task is to lead her subordinates and to follow the orders of her officer. An NCO must also be able to challenge the orders of her superior through sound reasoning, personal discipline, and duty of care to her subordinates and moral courage, but loyalty to the team, the corps, and the chain of command is paramount. An officer's role is to be a source of inspiration, leadership, and integrity. They must know within their heart the results of any command decision that they make and be able to live up to the consequences of action or inaction. The soldier does and is Action, the NCO is Love and the Law, but the officer is Will. The officer acts as True Will and is inspired, the NCO acts with Love and is tempered with their knowledge and experience of Law. The soldier acts totally within the Rede. Well apart from when he's what's called a squaddy in England, and then he gets drunk and may act violently—the cost of too much testosterone and alcohol. Not all military personnel are squaddies, but a minority tends to tarnish the image of the majority. Ultimately the service man or woman is there to perform a duty to serve and protect their homeland, their people, and also to preserve life, even that of their opponent. We are not judges, but defenders of all. In England it is the duty of service personnel to be a force for good.

In some Pagan traditions, the spirits of fallen Warriors are taken to a separate afterlife from civilians (such as Valhalla). What do you believe happens to your soul when you die?

I believe that people's souls go where they are destined to go. The saying "birds of a feather flock together" I feel relates very well to this view. I personally feel that I will go to Asgard, in particular to Folkvang, where I will be with my Goddess until Ragnarok and then afterwards in the new worlds.

What charms or spells have you developed to carry with you during a deployment?

If necessary I conjure Karmic Webs to constrain or restrict hostility. I also utilize other warding effects and spells; one of my oldest I call the Twilight Elk, is a simple astral bind rune made from Elhaz/Algis, Isa, Dagaz. It can freeze time and space to create a distraction, create a ward of invisibility, or illuminate the soul to banish negativity and invoke the energies of Asgard, Alfheim, and Vanaheim. It can also be used to communicate with your Fetch/Fylgia, which can be viewed as an aspect of your higher self.

Knowing what you know now, what advice would you give to someone considering joining the military?

Look at your options. What do you hope to gain and what do you hope to give? The military is really a path of service, as you may be called upon to perform tasks in service of others, whose nature you may dislike intensely or be comfortable with. Are you able to follow orders? If not, then still think about it. But a true understanding of military discipline reveals that it's about care, duty, and about inspiration. If the appearance is smart and well kept, it is likely that the person takes personal pride in doing a fine job and will care for others in a similar vein and ultimately inspire others to follow their lead. Are you prepared to follow a legitimate order with good conscience, even if you disagree with it or find the source disagreeable? Can you handle having limited freedoms, so that others can be truly free? If so, then it's the decision of which military part of service you take, as all are valid and true.

Has your religion or spirituality had an impact on your relationships with other military spouses/families? How or why not?

During my first day of duty in Cyprus, I was in my unit's administration office and saw an advert for a personal awareness course. This course was offering healing, aura, and energy work, things that I have been involved in for years. I knew that I had been guided here by the Goddess, as there were too many meaningful events involved in my posting alone. The people I met on my course were wonderful, and we had three years of working together, the group changing as military life dictated. I was not the only military person involved, but was at the core of the group, which was led by a wonderful spiritual medium called Claire; she was a service wife and is a fellow Reiki master.

In what ways (if any) do you feel that your Pagan beliefs present challenges to the military culture?

Military culture really dislikes change; it's based on tradition. But things change and the world keeps turning. As a gay, mixed-race heathen, I stand between the worlds. What I have found is that the majorities of military personnel are not religious and tend to view religious people as weird. They also have difficulty in comprehending why I as a Pagan could feel uncomfortable about "church parades" and the use of Christian prayer at certain military ceremonies. In England, religious diversity is a poor cousin to sexual diversity; from an English perspective it's reversed in America, where religious freedom is supported within the military, but sexuality is not really spoken about.

How has your spiritual practice been shaped by your combat experience, if at all?

For me, my spirituality has always been there and the military life is something that has slotted into my life. It's an oddity that I have always had an affinity for rather martial goddesses; my forename is Oliver and one of my many nicknames is Owl, which is my fetch or totem animal spirit. As far as my experience of combat goes, I have found that the Goddess protects her own and provides succor to where it's needed.

Knowing what you know now, what advice would you offer to someone considering enlistment in the military?

Follow your heart; speak to others. Make sure that you are choosing to serve for the right reasons and those reasons are your own.

* * *

8. Conjuring Peace in a Culture of War

One day we must come to see that peace is not merely a distant goal that we seek, but a means by which we arrive at that goal . . . we shall hew out of the mountain of despair, a stone of hope.
—Martin Luther King Jr.

Working for Peace While Serving in the Military

I don't believe that there is anyone who desires peace more deeply than those who know firsthand the ravages of war. It is the natural state of soldiers to hope that the missions they undertake, the losses they endure, and the evil they encounter might be the last. Warriors suffer and struggle in order that their children and their compatriots will not have to do so. In order to honor this aspect of the Warrior, I'd like to discuss for a few minutes the ways in which military personnel can work actively for peace, even as they are called to fight.

The simplest and most basic way that servicepersons can work for peace is by encouraging peaceful prayer and by incorporating this practice into their own spiritual routine.

Prayer, spoken or silent, is one of the most basic forms of energy raising, and it can contribute to the collective unconscious and lend its power to the universal call for peace. A friend of mine, Jason, wrote this prayer litany in response to a description of the military experience. I believe that his words eloquently refine the hopes of every Pagan veteran I've known. With his permission, I include it here as an example of a beautiful prayer for peace.

> I pray for healing and cleansing for the men and women I serve under and beside. I pray that we can put aside the wars of ancestors and make peace for our descendents. I pray that men would be willing step into their power as teachers, musicians, healers, engineers, plumbers, workers and any other trade or skill, but that they do not lightly enter into the skill of killing. I pray for an end of the glorification of violence and for all people to have the strength to handle conflict in the slower, harder way of diplomacy and negotiation. I pray for forgiveness from and healing for those whom my government have hurt, killed or wronged in my name. And I pray for forgiveness from and healing for those whom I have hurt, killed or wronged in my government's name. I pray that our brothers and sisters in the military come home whole in mind, body and soul. I pray that those in Iraq, Afghanistan and all countries around the world (including my own) will have peace, healing and prosperity. I pray for an end to war and an end to the need for all institutions that support and enable war. I pray for justice and peace for us all.

Truly, the act of lending your spiritual energy in common prayer with others is one of the most magickal actions a Pagan can undertake.

I've known many Pagans who either don't feel called to pray, or who see prayer as one part of their peacework—a beginning step, not a final action. There are many questions about what military personnel are allowed to do, when it comes to speaking their minds about matters of political policy and governmental action. Upon speaking with many service personnel, I have noticed that very few are fully aware of how their civil rights are affected by their military service. Many misconceptions abound, such as the ideas that members of the armed forces can't sign petitions, write letters to Congress, or speak out against aspects of the government with which they disagree. These facts are important to know, because one's voice as a citizen is something that must never be given away easily nor exercised lightly. Each person—soldier and civilian—has an obligation to fully undertake the rights and responsibilities of citizenship; and when those who are charged with defending these rights are not clear about their own, then we as a nation and as a military have a problem.

It is not my place to advocate for any one political perspective. In fact, the armed forces community holds as many varied political positions as the civilian population. However, civilians, in my experience, are more confident in their right to voice these opinions than are military personnel. And so, I believe that this is an appropriate place to explain (generally) the rights and restrictions placed upon members of the armed forces, in the hopes that you will take this information and use it to speak truth to power in whatever way your conscience dictates.

You Have the Right to Protest. Department of Defense Directive 1325.6 ("Guidelines for Handling Dissident and Protest Activities Among Members of the Armed Forces") states that you can pass out literature critical of the government or its policies, as long as it is done *off base and out of uniform.* Likewise, service personnel can attend protests within the United States, as long as they are off base, off duty, and in civilian attire.

You Have the Right to Be Politically Involved. Department of Defense Directive 1344.10 ("Political Activities by Members of the Armed Forces on Active Duty") states that military personnel are allowed to do the following:

- Contribute financially to a political campaign

- Express their political opinions regarding issues and candidates, as long as they are speaking as citizens and *not* as members of the armed forces

- Attend partisan and nonpartisan political rallies and events, as long as they do so out of uniform

- Run for elected, nonpartisan offices such as school board, notary public, neighborhood commission, etc.

Military personnel are forbidden to participate in the following activities:

- Soliciting votes or financial contributions for any particular candidate or issue

- Using their authority or influence to interfere with or affect the outcome of an election

- Run for an elected partisan position (i.e., governor, senator, mayor)

The action of last resort for military personnel who feel called to speak out for or against a particular issue related to the armed forces is a little-known right called an "Appeal for Redress." The appeal process, covered under section 3.5.7 of the DOD Directive 1325.6 (the first directive we discussed) allows members of the military to file complaints with their member of Congress to object to and request redress for actions taken by their commanding officers. For one example of the Appeal for Redress in action, you may view www.appealforredress.org, where hundreds of active-duty personnel are seeking an Appeal for Redress to end the War in Iraq. Regardless of whether or not you agree with their objective, the organizers have compiled a very informative website that will help you understand your own legal rights when it comes to issues and concerns that matter to you.

For those who don't feel called toward political involvement or activism, there are still ways that you can work for peace. My husband volunteers as a community mediator, assisting litigants in resolving their conflicts together collaboratively rather than going to court. Acting as a mentor, serving as a Big Brother or Big Sister, or sponsoring a SpiralScouts hearth are all ways that you can promote peaceful choices in young people. I truly believe that our best hope for the future is to create a future generation that understands that war is the action of last resort and that possesses the skills to resolve its conflicts diplomatically and, in most cases, nonviolently. I don't think that there is anyone better able to teach the importance of peace than those who have experienced warfare.

It is my hope that every member of the military works to maintain balance in the energy they put into the universe. The armed forces are a noble and necessary path, in order to ensure a strong protective ward around our nation and its citizens. However, those who spend vast amounts of their lives pursuing the Warrior's Path have an obligation to restore the balance by emphasizing the value of peace. In this way, the careful line between action and restraint will be honored and upheld.

Lobbying Congress and the Senate

There is no regulation prohibiting military personnel from meeting with their elected officials, provided they go as individual citizens and not as representatives of the armed forces. For those who want to actively engage in dialogue about world affairs and military policy, this is one very effective way to do so. If you have not met with your congresspeople or senators before, it can be shocking how easy it is to make an appointment. Odds are good that you will not be able to meet directly with the politicians, but they have many issue-specific legislative aides who are quite influential not only in how their bosses vote but often in the writing of legislation. Each member of Congress should have a military affairs aide, who will typically be willing to meet with you and discuss your concerns (anything from increased Veterans Administration funding to military housing to foreign policy) and take them back to the congressperson or senator.

My own family has lobbied Congress frequently on behalf of veterans' issues and military family concerns. I am always surprised by the reception we receive. Sometimes, the aide who was so rude to us on our last trip will be absolutely delighted to tell us about his or her change of heart. Often, the most conservative, yellow-ribbon-wearing politicians were the first to dismiss our concerns with a shrug and an offhand, "You volunteered for the military—why are you complaining now?" Usually the response falls somewhere in the middle, although I can say that I have experienced both extremes. I have walked out of meetings elated by the response I received, and I have sat down in the halls of Congress and sobbed into my arms.

If you are interested in visiting your elected officials, to lobby for support for Sacred Well's Wiccan chaplaincy candidate, for example, here's the short version of what you need to know: First, wear a business suit or professional attire. Depending upon his or her schedule, the staff person you are meeting with may be dressed in khakis and a polo shirt, but you must convey an image of both professionalism and respect for the office in how you present yourself. Second, bring your notes with you. Prepare for the meeting in advance and bring statistics, relevant articles, and other helpful "cheat sheets" along. The experience of walking into these offices can sometimes be rather intimidating, and it is always better to come prepared than to have your passionate eloquence get lost somewhere on the way to the meeting. If you are worried about coming across as amateurish or unprepared, then carry multiple copies of your notes with you and leave them for review at the end of your appointment. Nothing says prepared like coming with handouts! Third, use your manners: make an appointment, show up on time, and clearly identify who you are and what you wish to discuss. During the meeting, use simple, respectful language, do not engage in technical jargon or verbal hostilities, and afterward, be sure to follow up with a thank-you note that gently reinforces your key points.

Interaction with the Media

Most military personnel, outside of the Public Affairs and Information Office, will have little need to speak with the media. Sometimes, however, situations can arise wherein you are asked for comment or an interview. These can occur at political "photo ops" such as presidential speeches or during military operations by embedded journalists. If you are politically active, you may be approached for comments on specific issues. This can be tricky, since the military is essentially a politically neutral organization. Members of the armed forces are limited in their rights to free speech, and the rules can often seem contradictory. For example, you are not prohibited from giving your opinion on the administration, but you are not allowed to criticize the president. If your comments are positive, you are able to speak freely. If your views are negative, that may present some difficulties for you if you choose to give such a statement to the press or while wearing your uniform.

Your freedom of speech is directly related to your rank and branch of service. National Guard members and Reservists have more rights than do active-duty personnel, and enlisted servicepersons are granted more freedom than officers in any branch. It is not uncommon, however, to give media interviews as a part of an organized public affairs event or promotion. Under these circumstances, you are allowed to speak with members of the press in order to give statements or interviews, but there will typically be a public affairs officer present to act as a military censor. That officer will not hesitate to jump into the conversation in order to tell the journalist that the answer you just gave cannot be published or to dismiss a question as one that you are not allowed to answer.

Likewise, you may be surprised to see that the finished product is never used, especially if you tend to be one of the more "subversive" Pagans—like me. A few years ago, my family and I were selected to be a Pledge of Allegiance family for a local TV station. At the time, in a spurt of pre-war patriotism, this particular channel was featuring video clips of various all-American (most white, all straight and with children) families reciting the pledge. We arrived at the studio, where they filmed us several times over the course of an hour. In the end, it never aired . . . because we were both wearing our pentacles that day! For the most part, though, the military does not force its personnel into these scenarios, so if you are uncomfortable interacting with the media or enduring censorship (self-censorship or that imposed upon you), it should be fairly easy to tell Public Affairs to find someone else to act as poster child.

Keep in mind that while we sometimes feel a personal moral obligation to speak out against something with which we stridently disagree, or see as overt oppression, such speech can have potential consequences to your military career. My husband was invited to speak as a Gold Star family member and recently returned veteran to a peace rally held in a city about an hour away from our base. It was a small crowd of less than two hundred, and he spoke to them of his experiences in war, what he had seen, how it had affected him, and the loss of his cousin, killed just one year before. It was an emotional speech and he wept through parts of it. His words were met with cheers of "Welcome home!" and "We support you!" and his words, while vehemently opposed to what he had recently experienced, were patriotic and fully within the bounds of the law. He advocated for self-awareness, military enlistment, and participation within the democratic process. We were shocked, upon our return home, to hear rumors that he would be "investigated" by his commanding officers and was facing possible disciplinary action. After a few terrifying days spent wondering if he was trading his career for his voice, we were reassured that no action would be taken against him. However, there are those who serve beside him who stridently disagree with his decision to speak publicly about his experiences; some have expressed a loss of camaraderie. The choice to speak out has been incredibly difficult but also vitally important to our family.

Paganism, and magickal practice, recognizes the power of words and the importance of right action. There may be times when, like my husband, you feel called upon to dissent, to speak up, to cry out. Recognize the limitations that the military places upon these actions, and decide according to your own conscience how far you are willing to go. It is never wrong to demand justice. But you must be willing to bear the cost.

III. To Dare

Patriotism is not short, frenzied outbursts of emotion,
But the tranquil and steady dedication of a lifetime.

—*Adlai E. Stevenson*

9. Daring to Deploy

I am only one,
But I am still one.
I cannot do everything,
But I can do something.
And because I cannot do everything
I will not refuse to do the
Something I can do.

—Edward Everett Hale

Preparing for Deployment

It is imperative that, prior to deploying, you prepare your-self adequately for the change, both mentally and spiritu-ally. We've been discussing some techniques for spiritual preparation throughout the book, but I would like to take a few pages to discuss how Pagan servicepersons can pre-pare themselves mentally for combat. War is an environment unlike any other, and no amount of exposure to "aspects" of war can prepare one for the real experience. There is no movie you can watch, no first-person shooter you can play, no book you can read that will ever equip you for the experi-ence of direct combat, whether in the frontline infantry or in a rear-support capacity. Mental preparation is the key.

You will notice that throughout this book there have been no images of Pagan symbols or other overtly occult imagery. This is because I have designed this book as a resource that can be carried into the field, and it is my hope to create a volume that will be easily carried through customs inspections in any nation, regardless of its cultural background. I would like to take a moment and have you imagine a pentacle. This five-pointed star, enclosed within a circle, forms the base design for many military medals, among them the Congressional Medal of Honor. Many traditions ascribe various concepts and images to the pentacle. I would like to discuss what I call the Warrior's Heart. It was created as a meditation tool for my husband and his friends prior to their deployment, in the hopes of establishing a strong spiritual and emotional center within them that would hold firm in the chaos of battle and attack. Spending time meditating and working magick around the Warrior's Heart will reaffirm the ethics of a Pagan Warrior. It can create a spiritual anchor that will serve one well when confronted with the split-second decisions and life-altering experiences that come about so often in warfare.

THE WARRIOR'S HEART

HONOR

WILL   WISDOM

ACTION   RESTRAINT

Honor holds the place of Spirit, because without honor, the spirit cannot be truly whole. As Pagans, we must strive always to act in accordance with the ethics and morals of our path, and never engage in behavior that would bring dishonor to our Gods.

Wisdom comes from the air, where logic and rational thought are born. All action must come from wise thought, even if it takes place in a fraction of a heartbeat. This is a gift for a blessed few, and a skill to be cultivated for the rest of us. Training our minds to take action from a place of wisdom is a task that can take a lifetime to master. We are each much improved for beginning the attempt.

From the earth, we draw restraint. Restraining ourselves from wrong action, or from rash action, is an absolute for the Pagan Warrior. Making a decision to serve, to fight, does not mean blindly rushing into any battle. The ability to pause, for that same fraction of a heartbeat, can mean the difference between life and death, honor and disgrace. Restraint is the gift of Mother Earth.

Out of fire arises action, the burning within that compels us to move, to duck, to fire, to run. The quicksilver energy of flame burns within the Warrior, overcoming petrifying fear, burning away momentary panic, and spurring the soldier forward across the battlefield. Action is the core of the military mission. It must be in harmony with the other aspects of the Warrior's Heart, or else one is likely to slip into the Berserker mindset, and engage in behavior that is foolhardy, dangerous to the mission, or deadly both to the serviceperson and those around them.

Finally, from water arises Will. Those who have a strong foundation in elemental correspondences may be surprised that I place Will in the domain of water. It is an apt placement for the Warrior's Heart. Water can be channeled, it can be focused in its flow, but it can never be truly stopped. It will overflow the dam, it will wear away the stone that blocks its path. Like the heart of a Warrior, the water's course may be directed, but it cannot truly be moved. Water is flexible in its movements, but constant in its composition.

The soldier may change strategies, or even enemies, over the course of a career. The personal mission of honorable service to country and Deity cannot be moved. The Warrior's Will is the will of water, which will overflow, erode, or drown whatever stands in its path. It is firm but not fixed. It is unmovable yet ever flowing.

Spend as much time as you can working with the Warrior's Heart. Take a few days, or a few weeks, and meditate on each of the five aspects.

You may want to spend some time engaged in free association, automatic writing or drawing, or some other method of deep-consciousness access. Integrating the Warrior's Heart into your own code of practice and belief will validate your intentions, strengthen your mental resolve, and enable you to react to any situation you find yourself in with honor and skill.

Cleansing and Blessing
Before a Deployment

My husband and I have developed a routine that works well for us to cleanse and bless him prior to a deployment. We don't use any particular words; however, you might decide to incorporate some songs or chants that speak to you. While this is something that my partner and I do together, it is not a specifically marital act, and it can be performed by anyone willing to undertake this serious and lovely task for a serviceperson.

You will need the following:

- A sweetgrass or sage smudge stick
- A bowl of saltwater
- A candle
- A bell or singing bowl
- Blessing Oil (my blend or your own)

Begin by having the service member take a ritual bath or shower. This should be done in silent contemplation, focusing on allowing any fear, worry, last-minute stress, and other negative energies to be absorbed into the water and drained away. Using pure castile soap, wash hair and body thoroughly. After the ritual bath, the individual should dry off and enter into the altar area. There, the service member should stand with arms and legs extended in the classical "Vitruvian Man" or pentacle stance. Maintaining silence the entire time, take up the burning sweetgrass and smudge the service member thoroughly, taking care to get the top of the person's head, front half, back half, and all the way around his or her body. Repeat this process with the candle (we have a special rainbow-colored candle we reserve exclusively for this purpose), bell ot singing bowl, and saltwater.

Finally, take up the Blessing Oil and anoint the top of the head, the forehead, lips, chest/heart, hands, groin, knees, and feet. Seal the blessing with a kiss.

Blessing Oil
1 dram of sweet almond oil

3 drops of lavender oil

2 drops of orange oil

1 drop of High John the Conqueror oil

1 drop of dragon's blood oil

Magickal Tools in the Combat Theatre

Most Pagans I know have a strong connection to one or more of their religious tools—usually their athame—and tend to feel disconnected or out-of-sorts when they are away from these repositories of personal energy for any length of time. Unfortunately, as much as they might want to pack up their altar and all its accoutrements and carry it with them in country, this is not a very wise decision.

There are several factors to consider here. On a practical level, you must consider the fact that carrying edged weapons in your luggage is frowned upon by pretty much every airport security program in the world. Confiscation, if not outright personal detention, is a best-case scenario in this situation. There is a very high likelihood that your religious books and paraphernalia could be confiscated by authorities of the country you are traveling into. This is especially true in the Middle East, where diplomatic relations give our allied nations the right to enforce their own laws upon visiting service personnel.

Your rights as a U.S. citizen to practice the religion of your choice may not be enforced while in some Islamic countries, for example, which may forbid the practice of other religions. The fact that you are a representative of the U.S. Military will not change this fact. Frankly, in the grand scheme of things, maintaining a positive atmosphere of mutual cooperation between nations in a time of war supersedes your right to carry Silver RavenWolf's latest tome into battle. My husband has had firsthand experience with these policies. When he was deployed to Saudi Arabia for Operation Southern Watch, he brought with him several fiction novels intended for young teens called the Circle of Three series. I had suggested that he might want to read them before we passed them along to his daughter, who was nine at the time. The cover art was innocuous: three teenage girls standing against backdrops of various colors and elemental design. The entire collection was confiscated by Saudi authorities upon his arrival into the country and never returned.

The lesson I'm trying to make is simple but very important: you must prepare for spiritual practice overseas in a way that assumes that you may have literally nothing to work with. This means that you should not pack anything you couldn't bear to see confiscated or destroyed. It also means that you must prepare yourself mentally, emotionally, and most importantly spiritually to connect with Deity without any of the usual props that we in the Pagan community so often rely on. This is a skill that all magickal practitioners should develop, regardless of their military affiliation. Service personnel are just fortunate enough that they are put in a situation where might be forced to develop this technique a little sooner than the average magickal practitioner.

An alternative scenario, if you are unwilling to put forth the effort required to develop a strong mental/energetic practice exclusively, is to create new working tools while in country, using materials that you can easily access and that you are not in danger of being separated from. This is a viable option for those who packed their magickal gear and were caught off-guard by host-country confiscation, luggage losses, or some other "catastrophic" occurrence. In this case, you might be able to substitute items for your usual ritual implements, such as using a bayonet for an athame, or a canteen for a chalice. I personally find this to be unnecessary. The magick lies within your soul, not the beloved pentacle paten left behind. If you truly feel that you must have some sort of device by which to focus and direct your energy, the options are endless. I've been told of one particularly effective ritual held in Baghdad, where the pentacle was drawn in the dust of the ground, the athame was one participant's utility knife, the wand was a piece of wooden debris, and the chalice was a CamelBak of water passed amongst the participants. Truly, the Goddess was present—even without the pretty objects that so many Pagans love to collect.

In the meantime, if you have time to prepare before your deployment, I strongly suggest that you spend some time in meditation. Learn to work the ritual process without relying on magickal tools. One technique that I've used in the past is laying comfortably with my eyes closed and mentally walking through a ritual, saying every word aloud while imagining myself carrying out the physical gestures. Instead of literally circling the altar with my besom, I mentally picture myself carrying out this simple task. Instead of casting the circle with my athame, the same process, from the drawing and focusing of energy to the directing of the same through my blade, is carried out within my mind only. The end result (after the "imaginary" ritual was complete) was the same: the results intended were accomplished, and the movement and direction of energy was completed without ever moving from my spot on the bed or even being in the same room as my usual ritual tools. Visualization is a powerful form of magickal practice. Diligently developed and correctly used, it can reduce or eliminate your reliance on items you may not have access to when your boots are on the ground.

Portable Altar

Another way to carry your altar with you, now that we've determined that literally packing it up probably isn't the best idea, is to create a small shrine or altar that can be carried with you in a pocket or duffle. This should not be a large project. It is intended as a sort of mini-chapel, a source of spiritual comfort and a focus for meditation and prayer, rather than as a full-scale working altar. I suggest using an Altoids tin, travel soap dish, or something of a comparable size.

You will need the following:

• A small metal box (I do not advise using cardboard or plastic. The materials should be able to withstand exposure to the elements and rough handling.)

- Wrapping, scrapbooking, or craft paper in a pattern, color, or texture that you find appealing

- Small statuary or images of your patron/matron deity

- Any small items you would like to decorate the interior of the box with, such as silk flowers, glitter, charms, magazine cuttings, etc.

- Either several small containers (such as dram bottles or contact lens cases) *or*

- Several small silver charms representing the usual altar tools (I have found that a wonderful source for these items is www .bluemud.com, a charm-bracelet wholesaler that carries small silver charms shaped like pentacles, swords, and chalices.)

What to do:

I suggest leaving the exterior of the box as it is, for two reasons. First, any decoration you apply to the outside will inevitably get faded, torn, or otherwise destroyed by wear and tear, and it is my belief that a shrine should be kept in a condition that is as pristine as possible. Second, a simple exterior, especially that of a mint tin or other food-related product, will not be likely to draw attention. This means that those hostile to your spiritual practice within the military community around you are less likely to make comments while the representatives of foreign governments are less likely to confiscate the box of mints in your pocket than the full-sized wand in your duffle.

That said, embellish the interior of the tin as much as you desire. Line the lid and base with patterned fabric, rice paper, or fur. Place your images of Deity (the best way to do this is probably to find appealing graphics online, shrink them to the size you need, and then have them laminated) inside and then decorate the space around them. There are two ways to place the images: side by side in the lid (so that the tin rests in its normal fashion, with the lid opened to reveal the Goddess and God above a small container-space) or one placed in the lid and one in the base. You then turn the tin sideways so that it opens like a book. This style is similar to Russian iconography.

Within the altar box, you can place the tiny ritual tools you've gathered. Keep in mind, these should be symbolic focuses for your energy, not actual working tools. Imagine how ridiculous it would be trying to cast a circle with a ¾-inch blade or using a chalice that holds less than a thimble! Alternatively, you can use small containers and place within them dirt or salt for earth, water (from home perhaps, but don't be disappointed when it evaporates!), and other elemental substances. One of the greatest inventions I've found are small matchbooks that burn matchsticks of incense rather than flame. If you can find one or more of these, they would be ideal for your portable altar. I've even created altar bracelets, using charms from www.bluemud.com to represent the elements and Gods.

The finished project should be capable of being carried with you without interfering with routine operations or the fit of your protective equipment. If you don't want to carry it with you, an altar-box of this size stores in a duffle or footlocker and takes up minimal space. One final item you might wish to add: the Lady Liberty League at Circle Sanctuary (www.circle sanctuary.org) offers small laminated prayer cards free to servicepeople. With an image of the flag on one side and a simple prayer on the other, these make a lovely addition to your deployment-sized shrine.

The Wheel of the Year in Foreign Locales

One of the biggest challenges in the practice of any military Pagan is how to best honor the Wheel of the Year in a way that is fulfilling and practical, when your career might take you from Alaska to Iraq to California to the middle of the Mediterranean in the span of a few years or less. How does one follow the tides and the seasons when they are ever changing? Where do you place the watchtowers when the ocean is all around you? For those with shamanic hearts and strong ties to their land, the constant reorganization can be disorienting and frustrating.

Pagan traditions can be divided into two variations: the fertility traditions and the ecstatic traditions. The former is most concerned with keeping a ritual year in sync with the natural year, including an assumption of specific traits that are either "God" or "Goddess," either "man" or "woman," either in season or not. The latter, while still nature-based, is less concerned with agricultural timing and the planting and harvesting gender roles that arise out of an agricultural focus and more with the celebration of the natural world and its daily rhythms. T. Thorn Coyle does a wonderful job of explaining the philosophical variants in her book, *Evolutionary Witchcraft*:

> Fertility traditions in Witchcraft tend to look for sexual polarity outside of the individual person, developing ways to work with sex and gender by seeing men and women as representatives of specific qualities that are masculine and feminine . . . (ecstatic traditions) do not do this, feeling that each person can balance sex qualities within themselves, both energetically and physically. All Gods and humans, whether male or female in form, hold the energy of God Herself, the energy of creation, lust, love, and a connection to beginnings. All women hold the male within them and all men hold the female, along the myriad ways of being that are beyond and between genders. Not one thing or another, we are human in all its forms.[1]

For my part, I hold the view that fertility traditions honor the cycles of life and time their practices to the planting and harvesting. Ecstatic traditions celebrate life itself and its wonders—daily practice becomes a ritual, each breath a prayer. Fertility traditions place their emphasis on the ways in which the human body mirrors the natural world, whereas ecstatic paths concentrate on the ways in which the human soul cries out for connection with God/dess.

For the military Pagan, ecstatic practice tends to be most effective, since it eliminates many of the contradictions or dichotomies that come from trying to practice a fertility-faith in an environment that is at odds with what your seasonal worship should be. Many Pagans in the military have expressed to me the sadness and feelings of disconnect that arise when the Sabbats roll around in a foreign environment. How best to celebrate Yule in Alaska, where the growing light is completely hidden

---

1 T. Thorn Coyle, *Evolutionary Witchcraft* (New York: Tarcher Penguin Publishing, 2005), 98–99.

by the twenty-plus hours of darkness a day? How to soothe feelings of homesickness when you know your children are spinning rune-decorated eggs and hunting for crocuses while you are sitting in 100-degree heat, surrounded by sand? The seasonal and the environmental are not mutually exclusive, and there are a great many resources available for practitioners who want to evolve their form of worship. Below, you will find a simple myth that my own family uses when celebrating the Sabbats. It is based on the traditional Wheel of the Year, and can be incorporated into standard fertility-based rituals. However, it is flexible enough to allow my husband to work with its imagery even when he is far away from our hearth. It can be a great source of comfort and a morale boost to know that you are united with loved ones halfway around the world through a common practice. This mythology was designed to supersede differences in space, culture, and climate, to allow families stateside and their loved ones overseas to honor the same holy times.

The Story of Dea and Jack: A Wheel Tale

Once, long ago, there was a woman of radiant beauty. So beautiful was she that each person who chanced to gaze upon her saw something different. To those who found the pale, Nordic features beautiful, she appeared as a milk-white woman with long blonde hair and eyes the same blue as snow at twilight. To those who longed after the ebony perfection of the savanna, she appeared with wild, woolly hair and skin and eyes the same dark mahogany as their own. It was said that she could not be mortal, for no human woman could ever be as lovely as she. Her name was Dea.

Dea was a healer, known far and wide as much for her knowledge of herbs and skill in midwifery as she was for her beauty. All day and all night, those in need of her assistance would come to her cottage and find her sitting at her loom beside the hearth, or else drawing water from the well or tending her small garden. They would come to her with their sicknesses, their worries, their hopes. And Dea would hear and help them all. But Dea herself was lonely.

Dea longed for a husband—someone to share her cabin and help her tend to the people who sought her aid. She wanted a lover, a helper, a friend. So Dea sat by her hearth, and whispered to the fire, "Bring me my husband to love and to aid me. And for a sign that he is to be mine, may he wear a crown when I first see him." As the smoke rose up into the night, a shepherd walking by noticed that it did not rise straight into the sky, as smoke was wont to do, but rather floated sideways and drifted off out of the village, and into the nearby woods. "I have been too long in the fields," said the shepherd to himself, "for my eyes begin to play tricks on me in their boredom."

The next day, Dea set off for the woods to gather some nettle, for as a midwife, she knew that nettle was a soothing tonic for women carrying babies. Dea wrapped her shawl around her shoulders, took up her willow-basket and walked into the forrest. Dea was as much a part of the forest as the deer and the owl—there was no tree that she did not recognize, no animal that she feared. But not long after leaving the well-marked path, she came across something that she had never noticed before—the footprints of a man.

Curious, Dea followed the tracks, until she came into a hidden meadow clearing that she had never seen before. There stood a man, unlike any other. He was very tall, with shaggy brown hair that curled around his shoulders. His eyes were green and twinkling, and his smile was pleasant. He was bare chested and well muscled with strong arms. His pants were made out of what looked like goatskin, still furry, and rather comical in appearance. But what Dea could not take her eyes away from was the wreath of oak leaves that he wore upon his head. It looked like a crown made entirely of growing things. Then the man spoke: "What brings you to my meadow?"

"My prayers," responded Dea, "for I believe that you are the person I am meant to marry."

"If that be the case, then perhaps we should know each other's names, lady. My name is Jack."

"I am Dea."

Dea's basket remained empty as the pair spent the day in the meadow, gathering wildflowers and learning all that there was to know about each other.

When the sun had near finished setting, Dea told Jack that it was time for her to return home. "I will come to you soon, my love, and you shall become my bride." With that, Jack and Dea kissed, and she walked up the path to her cottage, as he watched from the edge of the wood.

At the time of the spring equinox, Dea was busy delivering the babies that were being born to the village women and had no time to return to the wood. Her thoughts were often of Jack, and when she returned home after delivering a set of triplet girls into the arms of their mother, Dea was surprised to see someone sitting on her front step. "Jack!" she cried, and ran into his outstretched arms.

They were married on May Day, and the whole village came to dance the Maypole and feast in their honor. Jack took his place at Dea's hearth. Now, when the villagers came to ask assistance, they turned to Jack for his advice as well. Together Jack and Dea were known far and wide as healers and keepers of the secrets of the stars and of the earth.

'Twas not long after May Day that Dea turned to Jack and said, "Bring me water from the well, for your child is thirsty." It was in this way that Jack understood that his seed had taken root in Dea and that she would bear a child.

It was at this same time that famine came to the land. Dea and Jack noticed that more and more people were coming to them, asking for help not with laboring women, or uneasy hearts, but with fear for their crops. The field that grew around the village provided food for the people for the entire year. If the crops failed, the people would starve.

Jack and Dea went out and walked among the corn and wheat, and they saw that the plants were too short and were pale in color. "This is not right," said Dea. "What can we do?" Jack was silent for some time, and when he at last spoke, his eyes were heavy, and his voice sad. "The land is dying and will continue to die unless something can be found to take its place."

Dea and the people of the village wept when they heard this, for they knew that kindly Jack would never expect anyone else to accept this burden. They knew that in order for the crops to grow, and for the people to live to see another year, Jack was willing to give up his very life.

The people of the village came to Dea when she was alone, and begged her not to allow Jack to make such a sacrifice for them. "We are not worthy, that such a man should die for us!" they cried. But Dea knew better than they what was required, and so she said nothing when Jack was with her, and wept when she was alone.

At last the appointed day came, and Jack cloaked himself in the green wool cape that Dea had woven for him. He placed his crown of leaves upon his head, and kissed his wife goodbye. Jack placed a hand upon Dea's still-flat stomach and blessed the child within her. Then he walked alone into the fields.

That night, the men of the village went out to the place where Jack had told them to go, and there, in the furrows between the rows of corn, lay Jack in his green cape. The crown of leaves had disappeared, and most mysteriously of all, it looked to the men as if a battle had been fought in the cornfield. For all around there were broken stalks and fallen corn. Jack himself had not a mark or scratch upon him, but he was no less dead.

A great wailing went up in the village, as the men carried Jack back to Dea's cottage. She stood by the well and waited for them, as they placed Jack in the bed that she had shared with him for so short a time. The women came to her, and comforted her, and helped prepare Jack's body for the pyre. They anointed him with oils, and placed in his hand coins to pay the fare into the Underworld.

The next day was the funeral day. A great pyre of nine different woods was built, and Jack's lifeless form was placed upon the top. Dea's face was calm even as tears ran down her cheeks. Taking an ember from their own hearth, she lit the flames that would carry her beloved into the next world. The people, trying to comfort Dea, did not mourn, but rather danced and sang songs of Jack's bravery and kindness, and gentle heart. Only when the last ash had cooled did they all return to their homes. And Dea was alone again.

"I cannot live without him," Dea said to herself. "He is a part of me. And if he is dead, then I must go to the land of the dead likewise." But she did not know how to get there. Dea went to her well, and drew up enough water to fill her cauldron, where she brewed her teas and tinctures and other potions. Then she stoked the fire until it roared. Taking up her place at the hearth, Dea took out her spindle, and a piece of the same green wool that she had made Jack's cloak from. She watched as the wool spun, spun, spun into a slender thread. Growing dizzy, Dea looked up, and happened to glance into the steam that was rising from her cauldron. There within the mist she saw an apple.

Reaching out her hand, Dea said to herself, "I must be overcome with heat, for the apple looks real enough for me to touch," and surely enough, she was able to grasp the apple and pull it from the clouds.

Dea hesitated not a moment before she bit into the sweet, reddish-gold fruit. Then she gasped! Her eyes began to see visions that she knew could not be real. Outside of her window, she no longer saw the small garden and far-off well. Instead she saw a moor at twilight, heavy with fog and quite barren.

Dea rose and opened her front door. Surely enough, she was no longer standing in her own cottage yard, but rather in the Underworld, where all the honorable dead reside. Looking behind her, she expected to see her cauldron and hearth and the spindle she had dropped in her surprise. But there was nothing behind her but fog.

At last she heard a voice, although where it was coming from she could not say.

"Who dares to enter my kingdom without the proper tribute?"

"It is I, Dea, and I have no coins to offer, because I fear I am not dead."

"How, then, have you come into my land?"

"I have come through the power of a broken heart and the authority of undying love."

"Undying love? Do you not understand that nothing in nature can exist without death? For the dying are what make room for the babies that you deliver into your world."

"This is true, and I have no fear of death. I understand that life has a need for death. They are two halves of the same coin. Likewise, my love and I are two halves of the same, and I cannot live without him."

"You are either very foolish or very brave to have come on this journey. I do not know whether to reward your bravery or punish your foolishness."

"Do neither then, and let me return with no more than myself, for my husband and I are as one."

Surprised by the resolve he heard in Dea's voice, the ruler of the Underworld (for if you haven't guessed by now, that is whose voice Dea was hearing) said to her, "You are wise, and your logic is sound. I have enjoyed our conversation, and so will release your beloved. But there is an obstacle you must overcome first: those who come to me have left their mortal bodies behind in the world of the living. When your husband returns to your home, he shall be no more than a spirit or ghost, unless you can find a living body for him to inhabit."

Dea was shocked. She had never considered the fact that Jack's body had gone on the pyre, and she herself had given him up to smoke and ash. But then she smiled, for an idea had come to her.

"Give me my husband, and I assure you, all will be well."

And so, the fog parted, and there before her was Jack. Dea gasped, because she had no way of knowing if he had just appeared, or if her true love had been so close to her the whole time long. Jack and Dea embraced, for in the Underworld, spirit is as weighty as flesh, and Jack kissed her passionately. Then Dea took his hand, and led him along the path that had appeared at her feet.

"How?" asked Jack. "How can I return to you without a mortal body?"

"Ask me nothing, love, but trust me completely," was all that Dea would say.

The longer they walked along the path leading back to the world of the living, the heavier Dea began to feel. Likewise, when she would look at Jack, he seemed to be growing paler and paler, until eventually she could see right through him. Dea looked down and saw that as Jack grew paler and more transparent, her stomach grew larger and rounder. For indeed, as her husband faded away, her child grew stronger within her.

At last she reached the door to her own cottage, and as she reached out to grasp the knob, she was struck by the first of her labor pains, and cried out. She turned behind her, to ask Jack to open the door, but he had completely disappeared.

Dea went into her cabin and lay down in the bed that she had shared with Jack. Not long later her child was born, and as she reached between her legs to bring the child to her breast, she saw that she had borne a son—with hair the same brown as an oak trunk, and twinkling green eyes.

———————

We have found that this works well for our family. It might not make sense (biologically) to celebrate the winter solstice when you are serving aboard an aircraft carrier somewhere near the equator. But one can venerate the Maiden Goddess, rebirthing her own true love regardless of whether you see snow or sand outside your windows. This is just one example of working a spiritual tradition within the military life. I am not saying that all military Pagans should use this (or any) particular mythology. It is presented as one option that bridges many divides and makes life within the military system a bit easier for our military family. As always, follow your heart and heed its calls.

There are ways to find balance in your ritual life, regardless of whether you consider your practice to be one of fertility or ecstasy, and wherever you happen to find yourself. Often, by thinking creatively about the energies of each Sabbat, we can create meaningful seasonal rituals without either relying on or contradicting the natural environment we are situated in. I have created a list of suggested ritual focuses that can enhance your military service and honor the Warrior's nature. I chose not to include fully scripted Sabbat rituals, since it is especially difficult to write for the myriad of situations, practitioners, groups, and environments that might call upon this book as a reference. Instead, I have provided a general idea, based on ecstatic practice, along with an explanation of how it can be incorporated into a more fertility-based mindset. I have also included a simple and elegant Esbat ritual that should be easily adaptable to nearly any circumstance. It is my hope that they will provide some inspiration to you as you work within your unique situation to create a practice both practical and magickal.

Imbolc
Blessing the Tools

Imbolc or Candlemas is traditionally the Sabbat of new beginnings. Many covens accept new members or undertake initiations during this time of the year. Sacred to Brigid, the Celtic goddess of the midwifery, art, and smithcraft, it is a time to gather together the necessary tools and supplies you will need for the coming year's magickal and ritual workings. One traditional activity at this time is candle making, and some families will work together to craft enough tapers and pillars to last the rest of the year. For those in the military, this is a time to examine the tools of your trade: body armor, weapons, and other equipment. Spend time carefully organizing, cleaning, and making any necessary repairs so that each tool of your Warrior's trade is in optimal working condition. If you have access to milk, consecrate it to Brigid and sprinkle some over your tools to bless them. Acknowledge this most important goddess and ask her to keep watch over your equipment in the days ahead, ensuring that they work when called upon to work and rest when allowed to rest.

Ostara
Acknowledging the Enemy

The spring equinox is the regenerative time, the promise of coming warmth and growing light. It is a happy and hopeful time, often celebrated as the season of youth and rebirth. It might seem a little silly to have grown men and women in uniform rejoicing in the return of an egg-bearing rabbit from the north, but this is a perfect time to engage in the ancient practice of acknowledging the existence of life and light, even in the darkest of places. This may be one of the more difficult ritual intentions for the soldier to wrap his or her mind around, but it is one that is vitally important. We must take time out to recognize and honor the human spirit within those who oppose us and so pay homage to the divine spark within us all. This is a wonderful time to work with Kwan Yin or the Buddha and to embrace the knowledge that many of our perspectives are based on our cultural upbringing and experiences, and that we are not nearly as different from our enemies as we would imagine ourselves to be.

Beltaine
Connecting with Home

Beltaine is one of the Pagan community's favorite holidays! Who doesn't look forward to the wild celebration of spring and romantic love? Traditionally, Beltaine is the marriage of the Goddess and her consort, the time when fields are fertilized and conjugal bliss is rhapsodized about in poetry, song, and often practice. How does one join in to the mid-spring revels when stationed far away from family or partner? By using this time as a chance to harness these energies to connect with home and those we love best! This is a great time to combine sex magick with astral travel or meditation. Spend some time nurturing your erotic nature, and send that energy to your partner far away. If you are blessed enough to be stationed at home, or on leave at the time of Beltaine, make time to be alone with your partner and reconnect physically. If you two so choose, you may direct any energy raised by your play toward a common cause such as strengthening your energetic connection for an upcoming deployment or else for a greater cause such as peace, de-escalation, or general safety.

Litha
Toasting Liberty

Litha, or the summer solstice, is in my tradition the time when the Dark (or Holly) King battles the Light (or Oak) King for dominion of the second half of the year. Summer solstice is the longest day of the year—from this point forward, the nights will gain strength and lengthen until the light times are short and wan. This is not a tragedy, for we recognize the nobility in both Warriors: the fallen king, willing to sacrifice himself for the benefit of his people (or quite literally the crops giving themselves up to nourish the bodies of those who will consume them) and the triumphant one—who fights fairly and defeats the foe with honor and swiftness. We in the military community can embrace both, for both are represented in our essential natures. This is the perfect time to celebrate the good things that arise out of military service—especially those of the past year, raising a glass (or canteen) in honor of catastrophes averted, comrades rescued or restored to health, humanitarian aid delivered, and other positive products of military labor. If you would like, you can invoke Lady Liberty and Uncle Sam as cultural icons and proto-deities.

Lughnassadh
Reaffirming the Warrior

Lughnassadh, in my tradition, is the funeral rite for the fallen Light King. We celebrate and honor the willing sacrifice of the noble warrior, the brave soldier who enters into battle knowing he may not (or perhaps *will not*) return alive. This is the point of the year wherein it may be beneficial to reaffirm your own place within the military community, spend time reflecting on the role you play within the greater society around you, and reflect on the challenges, ambitions, and honors that come part and parcel with the uniform you wear. For those who serve voluntarily, this is an opportunity to reaffirm or reevaluate that decision, rededicate yourself to Deity and duty, and meditate on how the experience has changed you. Funerals in the Pagan tradition are tragic and joyous: tragic to those who are left behind alone to grieve, but joyous for the one transformed and recreated. How do you view this time in relation to your military service? Do you need time to grieve the loss of your civilian identity or the physical distance between you and your loved ones? Or can you spend the Sabbat in celebration, honoring the new life and new identity you took on for yourself when you raised your right hand and uttered the oath of enlistment?

Mabon
Giving Thanks for Victories

Mabon, the autumnal equinox, is the second harvest: that of the fruit that comes after the granaries have been filled. The energy of the second harvest is different from that of the first. In the grain harvest, the killing is active, although necessary: we must physically put scythe to stalk and make the cut that takes life from the plant. The fruit harvest is different—most orchard fruits, if left untended, will fall on their own—and the taking of them, even directly from the plant, does not kill the body of the flora. Fruit is the symbol of life's gift—easily retrieved instead of forcefully taken. Now is a time of rest for the military Pagan—a period of reflection and thanksgiving for the victories of the past year. Every day we live is a fallen apple, a gift from the Goddess to sustain us for a few hours more. Those in the military know intimately how vital a few hours or even a few moments can be. Use the energies of the equinox to offer thanks for that gift of time. Time is the end result of every victory in battle: to survive another day, to gain advantage in the ongoing war, to create an oasis of calm after a period of intense fear and stress. In the heat of battle, each soldier prays for the same thing—another day. Another taste of the fruit of life. Share an apple with your loved ones or comrades today and share the tales of victories won. Raise some energy together and bless the time you have together for ritual and rest.

Samhain
Honoring the Fallen

Samhain, Halloween, is the third and final harvest—the harvest of blood. In ancestral days of Western culture, this was the time of year when the animals were culled and meat cured in preparation for the coming winter. In many parts of the world, this harvest is carried out on a daily basis— we in the industrialized world are the rare few who are able to separate the bloody reality of death from our day-to-day lives. This is not always the case for the military serviceperson. For many, the spilling of blood is a common occurrence; unfortunately, rather than being confronted with the loss of simply a chicken for dinner or a cow to feed the family through winter, they are confronted with the cold truth of human death. The military's business is the spilling of blood, and few who wear the uniform lose sight of this fact for long. Samhain is traditionally a time when the veil between the living and the dead is thin and divination or channeling is practiced to connect with departed loved ones. There is no reason why these practices can't also be incorporated into your spiritual practice at home or abroad. Samhain is the ideal time, seasonally and spiritually, to hold remembrances, spirit masses, or memorial services for those brothers and sisters in arms who have fallen in battle. To recognize and honor our own sense of sorrow and loss in order to heal ourselves is a worthy endeavor but one that many in the military are unwilling to recognize a need for. We must take the time to reach through the veil and remind ourselves that they are not truly gone, just in another, not-so-distant place.

Yule
Praying for Peace

Yule, the winter solstice, honors the Light King, who returns from the Otherworld and defeats his twin, the Dark King, in order to assume the throne of the next six months. This is the longest night of the year, and it is viewed as the most hopeful of holidays, since we have once again survived the darkest of times and will see the light grow stronger once again. Where there is light, there is hope, it has been said; and Yule is a time to sing out our hopes and bless the world with them. As I've said previously, I do not believe there's a soldier alive who does not pray for peace. The winter solstice is the perfect time to work magickally to manifest peace in our hearts and in our world. As the sunlight waxes and grows stronger, we can call peace into the world accordingly.

This is just a brief overview of how the Wheel of the Year can be adapted and focused on the issues and concerns of military personnel. Feel free to incorporate these ideas into your own practice, or ignore them completely as you desire. Regardless, spend time in meditation and reflect on how the energies of the year best support and serve your own spiritual needs as you complete your time of service (however long or short it may be) in a spirit of peace, magick, and honor.

Esbats
Restoring the Spirit

I. Grounding and Centering

Extend your spirit through the soles of your feet and into the earth, as if it were tree roots. Close your eyes and imagine these soul-roots descending through the soil, past the bones of our ancestors, through the water table and the bedrock, deep into the earth. Push further, until you reach the hot, molten core at the center of the planet. Feel the heat, and the spinning, swirling vortex of liquid iron. Now, slowly let that energy flow upward, through your roots. Back past the bedrock and the water table, past the ancient burial grounds and the loamy soil, up through the soles of your feet. Feel the hot, swirling energy flow up your calves, past your knees, and through your thighs; feel it pulse through your root chakra and settle into the space between your naval and your diaphragm.

Now, draw the energy upward toward the crown of your head and feel it reach out into the sky above you, expanding like tree branches to provide a sheltering cover even as it expands ever upward, through the atmosphere, through the ozone, and into the black of space. Gently relax and allow this energy to expand until it connects with the stars and the comets, and draws this pulsing white light into itself. Feel the energy course down through the branches of your soul, running like falling water back through space, through the ozone, through the atmosphere, through the sheltering branches of your spirit's reach, into your crown, down through your head and arms, shoulders and neck, into your chest, and through your diaphragm.

Feel this white, running, pulsing astral energy meet and blend with the flowing, swirling red energy of the earth's core. Allow them to merge and mix and expand to fill your entire physical being. Gently draw in the roots below you and the branches above until they have once again become contained within you. Take a few moments and breathe, experiencing the energy within you. Inhale deeply and exhale through your nose. When you are ready, open your eyes.

II. Casting the Circle

East:

Hail to the Ancestral Dwellers of the East, philosophers and logicians, we welcome you! Be with us here and join in our rites. Hail and welcome!

South:

Hail to the Ancestral Dwellers of the South, warriors and lovers, we welcome you! Be with us here and join in our rites. Hail and welcome!

West:

Hail to the Ancestral Dwellers of the West, poets and dreamers, we welcome you! Be with us here and join in our rites. Hail and welcome!

North:

Hail to the Ancestral Dwellers of the North, caretakers and curators, we welcome you! Be with us here and join in our rites. Hail and welcome!

Center:

Hail to the Center, the Spirit, the Core, all that which is greater than ourselves. Above and below, within and without, be with us here and join in our rites. Hail and welcome!

At this time, cast your circle in the manner that is most comfortable for you. If you are working in limited space, or if movement would prove dangerous, you may cast the circle accordingly: Hold your dominant hand out in front of you, palm upward and approximately at the level of your heart. Close your eyes and breathe deliberately, focusing your attention on the palm of your hand. Visualize a silver spark of energy sparkling in your hand, like a star. Breathe into this energy and see it flatten and spread, forming the shape of a silver disc approximately the size of a coin. Breathe into it, and feel it expand until it is the size of a saucer. With your next breath, set the silver disc spinning gently in a clockwise (or deosil) direction. When you are ready, take a deep breath and on the exhalation, toss the disc upward. As it rises above you, see it expand until it encompasses the space above you and your sacred space. Breathe in, and feel the silver disc expand to fill the entire space around you; exhale and feel it settle, surrounding and covering you in a peaceful, mercury-colored bubble. Stomp your foot or clap your hands to seal the circle. It is cast and you may say:

> **The circle is cast and we are between the worlds. What happens between the worlds affects all the worlds. So mote it be.**

III. The Working

This is the place to work any magickal spell, Sabbat ritual, or Esbat celebration, depending upon your intention. The ritual below is a simple Full Moon Esbat and can be substituted for the working of your choice.

You will need the following:

• A bowl of water, preferably metal or glass

Fill the bowl with water and place it where you can see the reflection of the full moon upon the surface. If you are working in a group, take each other's hands and slowly circle the bowl in a clockwise (or deosil) direction. If you choose to do so, you may sing a traditional chant such as "Isis, Astarte, Diana, Hecate, Demeter, Kali, Innana" or "The ocean is the beginning of the earth/All life comes from the sea." If you're feeling especially talented, you may choose to combine the two into a gentle round, raising energy as you allow the moonlight to charge the water.

When you are content, sit together around the bowl and, holding hands, invoke the Goddess. If you wish to do so out loud, you may choose to say:

> **Silver Mistress of the Fertile Moon,**
> **We gather in darkness to honor you;**
> **Beloved Mother, whose light draws the tides,**
> **The stars raise their voices in praise.**

Enter here, Goddess, and witness our Rite,
Accept our homage, loving and true;
Bless us this evening as we kneel at your feet,
And be with us through all of our days.

Spend several moments in stillness, scrying into the moonlight water for visions or messages from the Goddess. If you wish, and if you feel it would enhance your divination, you may hum, tone, or chant during this time. When you are done, rise and join hands once again, this time circling the bowl counterclockwise (or widdershins) as you chant: "We all come from the Goddess/and to her we shall return/Like a drop of rain/flowing to the ocean."

I do not believe that we need to bid farewell to the Goddess, since she is with us at all times. If it is your practice to do so, you may simply say:

Holy Mother, Light in Darkness,
We are thankful for your presence in our lives;
Be with us now and ever after,
Hail and farewell!

Finally, take up the bowl of water and dip either your hand or a chalice into it and drink. This water has been charged and consecrated and carries the simple energy of Moon and Mother.

IV. Releasing the Quarters

Center:

Our thanks to the Spirit, the Center, the Core, to all which is greater than ourselves. Above and below, within and without, we thank you for your presence. Hail and farewell!

North:

Our thanks to the Ancestral Dwellers of the North, caretakers and curators! We are humbled by your presence here and carry your blessings away with us. Hail and farewell!

West:

Our thanks to the Ancestral Dwellers of the West, poets and dreamers! We are humbled by your presence here and carry your blessings away with us. Hail and farewell!

South:

Our thanks to the Ancestral Dwellers of the South, warriors and lovers! We are humbled by your presence here and carry your blessings away with us. Hail and farewell!

East:

Our thanks to the Ancestral Dwellers of the East, philosophers and logicians! We are humbled by your presence here and carry your blessings away with us. Hail and farewell!

You may now release the circle in the manner most comfortable to you. If you cast the circle using the silver disc method described above, simply close your eyes, breathe three times, and visualize the silver bubble being absorbed into the earth or, if you prefer, floating away to the Astral.

Blessing the Transport

If possible, you can walk around the vehicle and cast a circle or sphere of protection to enclose it and ward it. The easiest way to accomplish this is to walk around the transport and scratch a circle in the earth/dust. Then, imagine it rising up and sinking below, until the two halves meet above it and below to form a complete "bubble." Now, imbue this energy with protective visualization, by seeing it as being iron, flame, or a protective elemental. After you've cast this protective circle, recite the following prayer:

Ares, you drove your chariot fearlessly into battle,
To ward what needed warding, to defend who needed defense
And to slay those who must be slain, that goodness may prevail.
Ride with me this day as I journey forth from this place.

May your spear protect me—
May your shield protect me—
May my vehicle be your chariot—
And my battles be at your side.
Let no harm come to those within this vehicle.
May our way be safe, may our path be smooth, may our journey
See us returned at the conclusion of the day.

If you have more time and access to the supplies, you might want to bless your vehicle with water, earth, light or flame, and air. The simplest way to access these is to acknowledge the sun as flame, the ground as earth, your breath as air, and either the contents of your canteen or simple saliva as water. My husband always draws a quick pentacle with his fingers on the side of any aircraft as he's boarding. These are just a few ways to ward your transportation, and are just as appropriate at home or driving from the base to your house as they are in the combat theatre. The magick is in the intent . . . not the elaborate ritual.

Prayer for the Combat Theatre

I call the spirit of my home to me,
I call the spirit of my land to me,
I call the spirits of my ancestors to me,
I call the spirits of the wise ones to me.
Be my allies, in this strange and foreign place,
Be my guardians, before and behind my every step.
And grant me rest, and grant me peace.

The Combat Veteran

Name: Robert Barner Jr.

Deployed to: Kirkuk, Iraq (2004) and Balad, Iraq (2007)

Primary Duty Station: Selfridge ANG Base, Detroit, Michigan

Branch of Service: Michigan Air National Guard

Status: Two-tour Iraq War Veteran, Gold Star Family Member

Tradition/Path: Unitarian Universalist Pagan

How long have you been in the military? How long have you followed your spiritual path? Do you feel that one influenced the other? Why or why not?

I've been in the military for seventeen years now, but I've been a Pagan for only about eight of those. I think that Paganism has influenced my military service because I look at it a lot differently than I did when I was a Christian. I take a more critical view of it and find myself questioning more and more my actions and the policies we serve under. It has helped me to be a more challenging person, not accepting things at face value anymore. I don't take things (information, etc.) for granted anymore.

How does your spirituality affect your role as a serviceperson? Which do you feel holds you to a higher ethical/moral standard, your religious path or your military path?

I find that the Wiccan Rede, although simple, helps me hold myself to a higher standard. It informs my decisions and my conscience and influences the actions I choose to undertake. I feel that my spirituality holds me to a higher standard of morality than even the military ethical code dictates.

What have your experiences interacting with fellow service personnel, officers, and/or chaplains been like? Are you in the "broom closet" or open about your faith?

I'm very open about my faith. The chaplaincy in our wing has treated me mostly with what I would call benign indifference. There was one Catholic chaplain who used to ask me about my religious beliefs, and we would discuss the beliefs that are bridges between Wicca and Catholicism. Once, in a war zone, I was approached by the same individual nearly every day for three weeks about my "need to find Jesus," and one other individual has made fun of me—calling me a Satan worshipper, etc. But after being politely confronted about their behavior, they backed off, and it has been basically a nonissue at work. Interestingly enough, one of them described their grandmother in such a way that it leads me to believe she may have been a Strega. Most of the time, though, people aren't concerned either way. When it comes up, I speak openly about my beliefs and practices. Otherwise, I do my work just like everyone else.

Do you feel that there is such a thing as a "Warrior's" spiritual path? Do you find that military Pagans have a different relationship with or perspective on Deity than civilians?

I think that we have a different view of Deity, especially when we're involved in war, because when you're in a combat zone you have to pretty much accept the fact that you're already dead or else you go nuts worrying about living. The only way to keep sane in this acceptance is by recognizing that it allows you to be closer to Deity. In essence, that's one portion of the Warrior's Path. The other is acting not as a mere soldier but undertaking conscience action, holding yourself up to a higher standard than the one you are made to uphold: working the military world from within a space of mindfulness, keeping on a right moral track, and being able and willing to address orders or policies that you feel are wrong in light of the expectations of your country and your Gods.

Which facet of your personality has elicited a strong reaction from the community around you: your Pagan faith or your military service? Please explain.

My military service, because it seems like that's the thing that people care about most. Most people in the public just treat Paganism with an indifferent eye, by and large. Your military uniform is more visible than your pentacle, and my service elicits more admiration than my religious affiliation. Mainly this is because you're putting your sense of service into direct action (through the military) instead of just talking about it the way religion often does.

Do you believe that Paganism is essentially a religion of pacifism? What do you say to those who believe that a military career goes against the Rede?

That's a hard question for me to answer. The Rede doesn't mean that you just allow people to steamroll over you or to take your life. And I don't think that that's what the Gods are intending for us to do. That's not the way it's ever been believed—that we should just act as lambs to the slaughter. It would do more harm if you don't stand up in the face of oppression, if you don't stand up and protect your people. The Rede informs my belief that the military should be used purely for homeland defense and not as an offensive tool. If the military is used in defense, I don't believe that it violates the Rede at all. The Rede is not a road map to pacifism, but rather a tool for living in harmony with others.

In what ways (if any) do you feel that your Pagan beliefs present challenges to the military culture?

By giving me a voice and a moral imperative to speak out against wrong wherever I see it, and that I have a responsibility to act against that injustice, whether it be by taking up arms against an enemy or by speaking out against policies that harm my fellow serviceperson.

How has your spiritual practice been shaped by your combat experience, if at all?

It has helped me develop my concentration in ritual, since it was this ritual work that kept me connected to home when I was far away. In some ways, this ritual work reminded me that I had a home to return to.

Knowing what you know now, what advice would you offer to someone considering enlistment in the military?

It's very hard for me to answer, because I think that the military really does serve the country, but I also realize that more and more of our service is going to support the military-industrial complex and expansion of global business. Sometimes it seems that our service is seen with a sentimentalism that is not in step with the reality of what we do. It seems to me that our missions are more about helping others make more money than we in the military could ever dream of making. As I go on in the military, it's getting harder and harder to see where my service is truly about protecting the country. If you stay in the military for too long, you'll probably become disillusioned. If you truly want to defend the nation, join the Coast Guard.

* * *

10. Family Life During Separation

Can miles truly separate you . . . ? If you want to be with someone you love, aren't you already there?

—Richard Bach

I've described myself for years as the world's worst military wife. I've been yelled at by an officer's wife I didn't even know for not wearing a bra in the commissary. I've happily discussed potty training with a visiting two-star general. I'm well known for my bumper stickers that read "Dissent Is Patriotic" and "Give No Cause to Fight." I refuse to own a magnetic yellow ribbon. Yet, even the world's worst military wife has to deal with life *as* a military wife, with all the pride, frustration, knowledge, and loneliness that it can bring. It is too easy to give in to complacency and become a "textbook" military wife: organizing family-support picnics and sending the children off to school in camouflage T-shirts that read "Daddy's Little Marine." It's a lot harder to retain your sense of balance and community when you fall outside of the predetermined confines of the *Army Wives' Handbook*. And quite frankly, depending upon your base community, sometimes just being Pagan is enough to boot you out of the "good wives" club.

It used to be that I hated it when my husband went on deployment. We are a one-car family, which means that my daily schedule revolves around his, and vice versa. When he's home, we have a nice routine that makes the day fly by. When he's not, things are different. For a long time, I didn't know what to do with myself. I spent whole days waiting for the time that I would usually leave to pick him up for work, and when it came, realized I had nowhere to be. It was awful. I'm not sure what changed, but before he left for Turkey in 2003, I decided that I wasn't going to put myself through those feelings of dependence and loss anymore. I created a list for myself of things to do that basically consisted of everything I'd been waiting on him to do for the past six months: hanging shelves, painting the bathroom, etc. Added at the bottom of my list was "learn to knit."

Wow! What a difference a list makes! It seemed silly at the time, but by giving myself a set of tasks to accomplish, the time flew by. Not only that, but I found out that I *loved* being able to decide when and where and what dinner would be, which movie to rent, or which paint sample to choose. I learned that the best thing any military wife can do is to stop defining herself as a military wife (i.e., one whose personality is dependent upon the presence of her military partner) and reclaim myself as an independent woman . . . who happened to be married to a member of the military. As a Pagan woman and a feminist, I don't know why it took me so long to realize that my identity was not wrapped up in my husband's choice of career, but once I did, I began to enjoy the time away. It created a new dynamic of independence and mutual affection in us both that I cherish. Now, except for combat, I look forward to his deployments!

Holding Sacred Space

One of the most basic ways of holding sacred space for a deployed loved one is simply to hold that person in your thoughts daily. When my husband was away, our son would look at me several times a day and say, "Let's send Daddy some peace." This was our cue to start up a rousing chorus of one of the family's favorite chants, "Peace, Salaam, Shalom." The small act of singing daily—and loudly—with the focused intention of sending our husband and father some peaceful, supportive, and restorative energy worked wonders, not only for my husband, but for the entire family throughout his time away. There are more formal (or, if you prefer, tangible) ways of holding sacred space as well.

The Deployment Altar serves as a focus area for everyone—the deployed parent, for whom the altar serves as the anchor for sacred space being held by loved ones at home; children, for whom the altar is a place to feel close to their parent, as well as a post office and calendar; and for the homebound spouse, to connect energetically with his or her deployed partner. This idea can be applied to any family member, or friend, or covenor, and used as a focus for protective and connective magick.

You will need the following:

- A small table or other flat surface area (this should be dedicated space, as much as possible, separate from your usual working altar)

- A photo of the deployed person, preferably in uniform

- A small lidded box, chest, or novelty mailbox (can be purchased at craft stores)

- Construction paper, cut into one-inch strips

- Anything else you would like to decorate the altar with (symbols of the branch of service, maps of the deployment location, statues or deity images, etc.)

If you choose to do so, decorate and paint your altar. When you are done, bless and consecrate the altar, visualizing it as an anchor or weight tethering an umbrella, parachute, or bubble of protective energy over the deploying person. Family, friends, and religious communities perform a vital task in holding sacred space for personnel overseas. The Deployment Altar becomes the focus for and source of that energy, extending it outward from home to the one it is established to protect.

Place a photo of the deployed person in the center of the altar, and surround it with objects inbued with protective energy placed there by loved ones. These can be anything, as long as they have been charged and blessed by those who are holding space at home. Add images of patron and/or matron deities, addressing them (the Gods themselves, not the statues!) and asking that they protect and guard the deployed serviceperson.

Next, add the lidded box. This is a place to store notes or letters to the deployed loved one. Obviously, actually sending letters to deployed personnel is an important part of keeping up morale. There are some things that are better left unsent (for security reasons, for morale reasons, etc.), and those deeply personal, profoundly important correspondences go into the "mailbox" on the altar, to be read or destroyed upon the loved one's return.

Finally, create a paper chain by gluing or taping the ends of one strip of construction paper together to form a ring, then threading another strip through the center of the first ring and gluing the ends of that one together, until you've formed a chain that has one link for every day of the deployment (don't forget time getting into and out of the combat theatre—these often aren't included in the official count). Drape this around the altar. Mark each day of the deployment by tearing off one link—this is both calendar and tether, magickally pulling the deployed person slowly back to you.

Spend time at this altar every day, if only for a few minutes. This is a safe place to worry, to cry, to scream and yell. If created properly, this is the place you can come to to be closest, energetically, to your loved one overseas. So, take five or ten minutes to remove a paper link, add a note to the mailbox, and "recharge" or reaffirm the energetic connection, as well as the sacred circle cast around the deployed person. You might want to sprinkle the altar with water every few days to disburse the negative energy that is bound to accumulate, and to re-consecrate the altar for a positive energetic bond and a comforting, protective sacred space.

One word of rational caution. The Deployment Altar is meant to provide a protective magickal space around yourself or your loved one. It is *not* a promise of complete prevention of injury or death in battle. I believe that to a certain extent each soul chooses for itself when it enters this world and when it leaves. Magick cannot keep a soul whose time has come to depart, nor protect someone from the will of the Gods. Miracles and magick are most often manifested in ways that we never know. The land mine or IED that was three inches to the left of where you actually placed your foot, for example. I do not want my readers to think that the creation of a Deployment Altar absolutely ensures a safe return. Life (and death) don't work that way. At the same time, it does do an immense amount of good, both spiritually and materially, and its absence can be sorely felt. Magick is like body armor—not a fail-safe solution, but still a vital part of our weaponry. We cannot prevent our destiny. We all do what we can. Often, it makes a far bigger impact than we ever truly realize.

Children's Concerns

When my son was two years old, my husband deployed to Saudi Arabia. This wasn't going to be a long trip, just thirty days, but that is a huge span of time in the life of a toddler. We had done our best to explain that daddy was going on a trip, and our son went with us when my husband got on the plane. He was so excited, seeing everyone in uniforms and all the people milling about. It was clear that he wasn't sure exactly what was happening, but he knew it was something *big!* When the time came, Daddy kissed him goodbye, and he waved so fiercely I thought his little hand would fly off as we watched my husband walk across the tarmac and board the aircraft. Then we went home. Without Daddy. My little boy cried and cried until eventually he fell asleep. About three o'clock that morning, Daddy came home. There had been mechanical problems with the plane, and his departure was delayed until the following morning. Needless to say, the second goodbye did not go as smoothly. This time, our boy knew something bad was going to happen—his daddy was leaving him! The second trip home, and the hours after we arrived were brutal. To make matters worse, my husband showed up at home again

. . . this time, delayed for two days while they acquired another aircraft. All in all, my toddler son said goodbye to his daddy four times. Each time got worse emotionally for all of us. I firmly believe that to this day, my son has some attachment and trust issues that can be traced back to that initial goodbye and return, goodbye and return, goodbye and return.

Thankfully, most deployments do not occur this way. Usually, the base or Family Support organizes some sort of sendoff, with refreshments, speeches, and music. Afterward the departing parents are sent off with kisses and applause. Just because the act of leaving can go smoothly, it doesn't mean that children don't have specific concerns and needs that must be addressed by their parent or guardian in the deployed one's absence. Children are prone to some rather scary leaps in logic and assumption. If left unaddressed, these misunderstandings or misinterpretations can lead to a great deal of stress or trauma for the little ones.

It is very important to prepare your children well in advance of the parent's deployment (acknowledging that this is not always possible) to allow them time to ask questions, process information, and convey their own concerns and ideas about the trip. One great idea is to get a world map and mark where home is, where the parent will be, and perhaps even (if it's known) what other stops Mom or Dad will make along the way. This gives the children a concrete visual to help them begin to understand where Mom or Dad is going and how long she or he will be gone. Keep in mind, however, that little ones don't have a well-developed sense of abstract thinking and are likely to assume that Daddy will be only eight inches away from them while he's "away." My children love to get books about the places that their father goes to, as well. This was especially fun when he went to Turkey and Saudi Arabia, because the children's section of the library has a wealth of information on the lives of children there, the landscape, local costume, and culture.

The flip side of a small child who is still developing abstract thought is the preteen or teenager who knows very well what's going on in the world. My stepdaughter, when told that her father would be deploying to Iraq, trembled uncontrollably for hours after receiving the news. Just as it is important to make sure that youngsters' imaginations are grounded in an understanding of reality, so is it vital that older children be given a chance to express their very legitimate fears about the deployment. As much information as they can be given about the upcoming trip should be conveyed, especially facts that will reassure them of the parent's safety without offering false comfort. For example, a teen should be made fully aware of the safety and security precautions taken by the serviceperson. No children, of any age, should be told that they have absolutely nothing to worry about. Offer as much information as is age appropriate, but never, ever, make a promise you might not be able to keep.

Children may have several emotional responses to the parent's deployment, including depression, social withdrawal, acting out, poor school performance or truancy, frequent tummyaches, headaches, or other nebulous sicknesses, nightmares, urination accidents, regressive behavior, attachment phobias, obsessive fixation on news of world events, and changes in sleep and eating patterns. I strongly recommend that children of deployed parents be encouraged to participate in extracurricular activities and meet regularly either with a children's support group run by your Family Support group or privately with a civilian counselor for the duration of the deployment.

Spell: Connections Mojo for Children

This is a version of the "Home Away From Home" mojo bag that we made earlier for the deploying family member. In this case, we'll be making one for those left behind to carry with them. While the title says that this is for children (and it is particularly effective for them) it can be used by anyone who needs to feel close to someone far away.

You will need the following:

- A small bag or pouch that can be carried in a pocket or around your neck

- 2 small plastic containers (contact lens cases or ¼-dram bottles work very well)

- A few hairs from the absent person, rolled together into a knot or ball

- A picture of the absent person

- Any other special object that you wish to include

Place the hair into one container. In the other container, have the deploying loved one put "kisses" by blowing kisses into the open container and then quickly sealing it. Add in the photograph, and whatever other objects you wish to include (please consider the age of the child who will be carrying this mojo and be aware of potential choking hazards) and then close the pouch. As before, pass the mojo bag around a family circle and have each person breathe upon it. If you have multiple children, you can make this a round-robin game. When everyone has contributed their energy, the deploying parent can formally present the mojo or mojos to the child who will be keeping it. Children can carry it with them and when they feel a need (perhaps each evening at bedtime), they can open the second container and take out a "kiss" from their absent parent. This way, they can be kissed good-night, even though the serviceperson may be far away.

Bedtime Affirmation

My son and I have been reciting this little prayer together for several years now. It is a sweet and simple evening ritual that a parent and child do together, the child repeating each line after the parent, to say good-night and reaffirm the child's place in the world. Military children are often more aware of world events than civilian children—if not because their parents discuss it more, then because civilian children don't usually go through a checkpoint guarded by men in uniform with M16s to go home at night. This short affirmation has been a gentle reassurance to my son that all is right in his corner of the world, and he will rarely fall asleep without it.

> I am peaceful,
> I am happy,
> I am loved.
> My momma loves me,
> My daddy loves me,
> (Insert anyone else your child cares to name) loves me.

Nothing bad will happen to me.
My bed is safe.
My house is safe.
My world is safe.
Only peaceful thoughts.
Only happy dreams.
I am peaceful,
I am happy,
I am loved.

Guided Meditation for Children

Close your eyes, and lie back. Feel the ground beneath you. Feel the air above you. Rest your eyes, and let your imagination pretend that you are flying, as high into the sky as you want to go. Can you see the stars? Do you see our house below? Are you staying close to the ground? Now, once you've gotten used to flying with your imagination, we're going to fly far, far away. You and I together are going to fly over our street, over our town, and far away out to the ocean. Ooh . . . look at how pretty the water is! Do you see any fish or dolphins swimming? Do you see any boats down below us? Do they see us? Wave to them! Let's keep flying over the ocean, until we get to (insert parent's location here, describing the terrain and surroundings as best as you are able to create a good mental image for your child). Do you see Daddy/Mommy? Oh . . . shhh . . . s/he's sleeping! Should we wake him/her up? Okay, whisper to him/her. Look! s/he hears us! Give him/her a big hug . . . tell him/her all about your day. What happened today that you're most excited about? What did you do that you're proud of? Did you get in trouble today? Tell him/her everything you want him/her to know about how you're feeling right now. Okay, it's time for him/her to go back to sleep now . . . s/he has a busy day tomorrow. Give Daddy/Mommy a *big* kiss and a *big* hug and tell him/her we'll come back tomorrow and visit again. Okay, get ready to fly with me . . . one, two, three, *JUMP!* Up into the air we go, back across (describe terrain of deployment locale), back to the ocean. Are the boats still here? Tell them good-night! Are the fish and dolphins still awake? Say,

"See you tomorrow, fish! See you tomorrow, dolphins!" Now we're back to our town. Look, I can see our street from here—can you? Let's follow it back to our house. Do you see our front yard? Let's land there together. Ready? When I count to three, open your eyes and we'll be home again. One, two, *three!*

Note: Take a moment to discuss this exercise with your child. Some children may love it and want to do it often; others may find it makes them feel homesick. Never force your children to go beyond what they are comfortable with and emotionally ready for.

The Dependent Child

Magickal Name: Sparklewater

Primary Duty Station: Offutt Air Force Base, Omaha, Nebraska

Branch of Service: United States Air Force

Status: Dependent Child of Iraq War Veteran, age 13

Tradition/Path: Pagan (Catholic mother, Unitarian Universalist father)

How old were you the first time your father was deployed to Iraq? Do you remember how you felt when you first found out he was going overseas?

I was about ten years old the first time. I remember freaking out at Con-Vocation. My stepmom was annoyed because we had an important family event coming up the next week and now my dad would be gone. My stepmom remembers me crying a lot and shaking. I couldn't stop shaking for a very long time. My aunt and my stepmom were the ones who supported me most. My dad tried to tell me that he was going to be safe, and I kinda believed him, but I knew the facts about what was happening in Iraq.

Did your family do anything special magickally to help you cope with the idea of sending your father to war?

I don't remember much about that time, but my dad gave me a special ring and it made me feel safer to wear. I still wear it. I haven't taken it off since. I was also given my first athame at this time. Before, I'd been told that I wouldn't get an edged blade until I got my first moon. But my parents wanted me to feel brave and to show me that I was mature enough to handle the deployment scariness, so they gave it to me early. The last thing they gave me was a pendant with Dictyna, my patron Goddess, who carries two labryses and protects women and children. So yeah, I guess they did a lot to try and help me feel magickally prepared.

What were you most afraid of while he was gone, and what (if anything) did you do to help cope with your feelings?

The first time he was gone, I was afraid of everything. Everything I heard on the news made me freak out. Whenever Iraq was talked about on TV or in school, I didn't feel good and wanted to leave the room. I wrote in my journal a lot. I got the journal the year before as a gift, and it helped a little to write about how I felt. Sometimes, I would pretend I was writing to my dad. I talked to friends about how I was feeling and what was scariest. I didn't really talk to family much about it though.

How old were you the second time your father deployed to Iraq? Was there any change in how you felt from the first tour?

It was this year, so I was thirteen. There was a lot more deaths on the news this trip, and my dad always checked on the number killed, so that got me even more scared. I was more scared this time, because last year my dad's cousin was killed in Iraq, so it wasn't just something that might happen . . . it was something that did happen to our family.

Did you do anything magickally or religiously to help support your father while he was overseas?

I prayed to pretty much anyone I thought was listening to help protect him and keep him safe. I was (and am) still wearing the ring he gave me before his first trip, so that helped me to feel close to him.

How do you feel about being a military child? Would you consider joining the military yourself when you are old enough? Would you date or marry someone in the military? Why or why not?

Being a military kid isn't terrible, but it's not the greatest either. It's not like I'm the only kid with parents in the military; I have lots of friends in the same situation. Deployments suck. They are scary and sad, and it's hard to go a long time without hearing from your dad. I wouldn't consider joining the military. Definitely *not* one of my future goals. It's not something I'm interested in and especially not when I can't control who tells me what I have to fight for or where. The only way I would join is if there was a president that I very much trusted and believed wouldn't make a stupid decision. I might date someone in the military, but I probably wouldn't marry someone in the military unless I knew that they'd always be safe and wouldn't be deployed.

Do your friends at school talk about the war or the military? If so, how much do you share with them about your experiences and how do they react?

Yeah, they say that "oh, I'm in the same situation," but really they're not . . . they try to reassure you, but it's basically lies and it doesn't really help. Certain friends I share a lot with, but others not so much. They do their best to reassure me and make me feel safer. They try their hardest, but it usually doesn't work. It helps, but it doesn't.

Do military recruiters come to your school? How do you feel about them? What advice do you give to your friends about military service?

The JROTC comes to my school. They talked about what it was like in high school for them, but it did not intrigue me. For the people that want to be in the military, recruiters make them more confident that they can do it, I guess. My friend wanted to join ROTC and the military. I told him it wasn't as much fun as it looks like. In the end, he didn't really care about my opinion.

What do you think that military parents could do to help their children with life as a military "brat"? Are there any magickal or religious activities that you think would be helpful?

Not many people call us "military brats" anymore or make fun of us for being military children. Most people try to help us out now. I don't really know what parents can do to help us out . . . just be there for us.

Is there anything else that you want to share about your experience?

Other military kids need to know that it's okay to talk to people about how they're feeling. They need to learn not to keep things inside.

*   *   *

11. Daring to Confront Danger

I am an apple. I am not alone, but always have an invisible
companion.
Around us his own knife pares the peel and the sweetest flesh;
Swish, swish, swish! I know that this is nature, willed by the divine.
I rejoice in the companionship of the one who wields the blade.

—Author unknown

I cannot speak to the combat experience. Having never served in war myself, I feel that it would be disingenuous of me to attempt to present a reality I have no firsthand knowledge of. That said, I do understand that life in the combat theatre presents its own unique challenges, physically and mentally. It is not easy on the physical body to function at a high stress level for long periods of time. Experiments show that prolonged stress causes biochemical changes in the brain that affect our bodies, making periods of calm and relaxation vital to one's health and well-being.[1]

---

1 Michael Bond, "A Sense of Place," *New Scientist* 189.2541 (March 4, 2006): 50; Ruth Parslow and Anthony F. Jorm, "Pretrauma and Post-trauma Neurocognitive Functioning and PTSD Symptoms in a Community Sample of Young Adults," *American Journal of Psychiatry* 164.3 (March 2007): 509; Tamara V. Gurvits et al., "Subtle Neurologic Compromise

Life in combat can sometimes be dull, with occasional spurts of danger and adrenaline. At other times, the experience can be like that of living inside a box of fireworks—never sure what will go off or when. It is very important that those who are deployed be mindful of their physical health, eating well and properly, and exercising when possible. Mental health care is also extremely important. The experience of war brings with it images, sounds, and feelings that can be hard to process or cope with. By caring for your psyche as regularly as you care for your physical body, you can go a long way toward reducing the harm that the combat experience may cause.

Everyday Self-Blessing

It is difficult to establish a routine of spiritual practice and worship when you are never certain what conditions you will awaken to each morning or what resources you will have access to from week to week. One of the easiest self-blessings you can incorporate into your practice uses nothing other than plain, cool water. Pour a small measure of water into a cup or bowl and repeat the following:

> The Ocean accepts every river,
> All water returns to the sea;
> Wherever my day's journey takes me,
> The path itself shall blessed be.

Dip your fingertips into the water and sprinkle yourself, being sure to get each of the areas blessed in the full self-blessing earlier in this book. When you have blessed yourself, place one hand upon your heart and one hand upon the ground and say:

> My heart belongs to the Mother Earth,
> The Goddess knows her own;
> May she guide me and protect me,
> And when the end comes, lead me home.

---

as a Vulnerability Factor for Combat-Related Posttraumatic Stress Disorder: Results of a Twin Study," *Archives of General Psychiatry* 63.5 (May 2006): 571.

Prayer for the Wounded

May the fires within your body be cooled,
May your brow be calm, may your spirit find rest;
I am with you as the Mother is with you,
Your soul is beloved and your body shall heal.
Sleep brother/sister, sleep. We hold vigil 'til you awake.

Crossroads Hymn

I

Grandmother Hecate,
Hear my mournful cry—
Hear my cry, Queen of the Crossroads,
Hear my heart as it cries out to you.
It is you, Lady, who guards the path
That runs between life and death.
It is you, Lady, who guides those born, those dying.
You take our hands and lead us
From your cauldron to our earthly tomb,
From your coffin to our mother's womb.
No one dies before their time
No one returns before they're due,
And you, Grandmother,
You are Mistress of Us All.

II

It is you we turn to when we cannot find the path,
It is you we cry to when we are torn at the Crossing,
It is you who comes to us to show us our Right Place.
Each of us in our time must meet you at the Crossroads.
At the Crossroads our fate is meted out.
The path of Earth, the path of Spirit,
There in the center, we sit at your feet.
There in the center, we are made whole.
You are the vessel that safeguards our desire,
It is you who restores our hope.

III

Come to us, the Dying.

We entreat your presence here.

We kneel at the feet of the Great Goddess and

We entreat your presence here.

For those who cling to this body, afraid of moving on—

We ask your release.

For those who hold fast to their loved ones,

Afraid of letting them down—

We ask your release.

For those who fear the Crossroads,

Afraid of the pain of loss—

We ask your release.

For those who do not know you,

Afraid of being alone—

We ask your release.

For those who have no faith at all,

Afraid of being forgotten—

We ask your release.

IV

Come to us, the Living,

We entreat your presence here.

We stand at the boundary we are forbidden to cross,

And we entreat your presence here.

For those who love too much to let go,

We ask your strength and grace.

For those who fear too much to let go,

We ask your strength and grace.

For those who hurt too much to let go,

We ask your strength and grace.

For those too lonely to let go,

We ask your strength and grace.

V

There is a land where apples grow
Where all who love shall love again.
There is a land where waters flow
And all who drink are healed.
There is a place where nighttime soothes
And daylight brings no fear.
There is a place where pain can't go
And no one is alone.
We know that we shall find this realm,
Each one in our own time,
And when we leave our mortal home,
You shall greet us at the Crossroads.

VI

I believe that we shall meet again.
I believe we shall be healed.
Body and heart shall suffer no longer,
When we meet on the other side.
We shall meet again on the other side,
Our meeting is preordained.
And when my time comes to join you,
When Hecate calls my name,
You shall be waiting there with her.
When I journey to the Crossroads,
Our paths will cross again.

—Spiral

Funeral/Crossing Ritual

The military funeral is one of the most recognizable military ceremonies, steeped in long-held traditions, some dating as far back as the time of Genghis Kahn. Many of these traditions—such as the playing of Taps and the firing of three rifle volleys and the careful folding and presentation of the flag—have been featured throughout American popular culture and hold an intimate familiarity for our citizens, military and civilian alike. Like the best of Pagan rituals, the elements of the military funeral have been designed with thoughtful consideration toward those participating in and experiencing the ritual, and they elicit a careful blend of pride and mourning, patriotism and personal loss.

The ritual included below is meant to give an example of how to blend military custom with Pagan ritual, to create a holistic and healing experience for everyone present. In times of profound grief, it is difficult to elucidate exactly what our wishes are for our fallen loved ones, and while the Department of Defense provides a casualty officer to help the spouse or parents of the fallen plan the final arrangements, it is unreasonable to expect a person in mourning to explain elements of Pagan belief and ritual to someone who most likely has little knowledge of our faith and its practices. While it is my fervent hope that you will never need this chapter, I have included it so that it might make trying times easier for those who may, sadly, need it. I dedicate this ritual to Patrick Stewart, and the fallen Pagan Warriors of every war.

Crossing the Bridge:
A Pagan Military Funeral

The circle should be cast and the quarters called by the Celebrant prior to the entry of mourners. Family members can and should be present if they desire to be there, and they may call the quarters if they so choose.

East:

> Hail to the East, the Gateway of Dawn. Entrance to the Otherworld. Gentle breath of air, which cools and caresses the souls who cross your threshold, be here with us. Spirit of Air, hail and welcome!

South:

Hail to the South, the Fire-spark of the Soul. Flame which glows brightly within each mortal life, granting warmth and light to those at your hearth. Be here with us. Spirit of Fire, hail and welcome!

West:

Hail to the West, the Waters of Birth and Rebirth. Primordial womb of creation. Your sweet waters offer refreshment and healing to those who cross your shores. Be here with us. Spirit of Water, hail and welcome!

North:

Hail to the North, the Mother Earth herself. Cave of comfort and darkness, our cradle at the end of life. You nourish and sustain our life. You embrace and enfold us at our death. Be here with us. Spirit of Earth, hail and welcome!

Center:

We honor the Center, the Spirit, the Core, all that is greater than ourselves. Above and below, within and without; you existed before our beginnings and embrace us at our ends. Be here with us. Hail and welcome!

At this point the circle should be cast by the Celebrant. If the family decided to conduct these rites in private, the Celebrant should cut a doorway in the circle for attendees and military participants to enter and exit. The military team shall escort the casket into the ritual space in accordance with military custom. When the flag is secured and the military team has concluded its initial service, the Celebrant shall step forward and seal the circle.

Celebrant:

We are between the worlds, and what happens between the worlds affects all the worlds. We are united, spirit and body, for the purpose of remembrance. So mote it be!

> We have gathered this day to honor the spirit of a fallen
> Warrior, (name). S/he who served bravely, with honor and
> distinction, and who gave her/his life in service to country and
> comrade. Who here gathered does not have happy memories or
> kind words to speak of her/him? Who would honor their fallen
> sister/brother? Let them come forward and speak!

At this time, those assembled may come forward (or, if it's a large
crowd, stand and have a microphone brought to them) and tell a short tale
of the departed. When all have said their piece, the Celebrant continues.

> (Name) chose the path of the Warrior, freely and with a heart
> toward justice. We mourn her/his loss as our own. We do not
> weep for (name), who has returned to the Mother and has
> found comfort and rest from the trials of life and the perils of
> war. Rather, we mourn the loss of her/him in our own lives and
> weep for the empty place at our table and in our hearts. This is
> right and good, for it shows (name) how truly well she/he was
> loved. But we must temper our mourning with compassion for
> her/his soul and a true desire that (name) should find healing
> and rest. Let us dry our tears and lift our voices in song, sing-
> ing peace and healing to our beloved beyond the veil.

At this point, a song should be sung. One particular favorite of mine,
"Weaver, Weaver" by Starhawk, would be a lovely selection if you are assisting in making funeral arrangements but are not familiar with Pagan
music. The music for this chant can be found on the Reclaiming tradition
CD *Through the Darkness*, which is available through Serpentine at www
.serpentinemusic.com. If the family or the departed had an alternate preference, obviously that should be used instead.

Now is the time to read the letters from comrades and commanders
in the field, and the presentation of any posthumous honors.

Celebrant:

Mother Goddess, who creates and sustains us, open your arms
to receive the body of our beloved (name). Embrace your child
as s/he travels the path of the Otherworld; returning to you,
returning to the womb. Grant her/him restoration and healing,
and may s/he find peace and comfort with you.

Green One, Father of the Wild, we return your child (name)
to your care and keeping. Watch over her/him as s/he journeys
toward the Otherworld and grant her/him wholeness and restoration. Grant her/him strength to face what comes next and
honor from those s/he leaves behind. May s/he find peace and
comfort with you.

The Celebrant may add any words of personal comfort to the family
and friends assembled to mourn. At the conclusion of these thoughts,
the NCOIC (noncommissioned officer in charge) shall proceed with the
military rituals, including the firing of three rifle volleys, the folding and
presentation of the flag, etc. When the military honors are completed, the
Celebrant comes forward.

Celebrant:

We are comforted by the knowledge that (name) has not left
us completely. We know that the veil separating (name) from
us is thin and mutable, and that while we shall mourn the loss
of her/his physical presence in our lives, we can celebrate the
knowledge that her/his spirit is never far away. (Name) was
born of water, breathed the same air that surrounds us at this
moment, had a spirit of noble fire, and shall return to us again
even as we give her/him back to the earth. As long as earth remains, as long as water flows, as long as fire burns, as long as
the gentle breeze blows—s/he is with us. Let us take comfort
in the certainty of this and carry (name) with us as we depart
from this place. So mote it be.

If there are any other military formalities incorporated into the departure from the funeral site, they may be carried out now. As the mourners leave, it is often cathartic to exit singing. Another favorite of mine, "When We Are Gone," is by Starhawk and Anne Hill. Music can be found on the Reclaiming tradition CD *Second Chants*.

After the attendees have departed, the quarters may be released and the circle taken up. Keep in mind that while this may have been done privately before the ceremony, the vigil will be present afterward.

Center:

Spirit, gem of Deity that unites and unifies us all, embrace (name) and hold her/him close. We thank you for your presence. Hail and farewell!

North:

Earth, mother of our mortality, embrace (name) and hold her/him close. We thank you for your presence. Hail and farewell!

West:

Water, ocean of beginnings, embrace (name) and hold her/him close. We thank you for your presence. Hail and farewell!

South:

Fire, creator of guiding light, embrace (name) and hold her/him close. We thank you for your presence. Hail and farewell!

East:

Air, gateway of life, embrace (name) and hold her/him close. We thank you for your presence. Hail and farewell!

Depending upon your tradition or your family's preference, you may choose to leave the circle in place. Since it was cast with an open doorway, it might be your magickal intention to leave a pathway back for your loved one. If you choose to do this, please take care to "store" the energy away where it will not disturb others coming to participate in future rituals/funerals.

One of the aspects of a military funeral that I appreciate the most is the vigil—the soldier whose duty it is to remain behind and stay with the casket until it is interned. This is a quiet and beautiful service and one that is likely to go unnoticed. The family of the fallen may want to offer private thanks and blessings to this noble watchman, to honor the important symbolic and magickal task he undertakes.

IV. To Keep Silent

*Peace is not an absence of war, it is a virtue, a
state of mind,
A disposition for benevolence, confidence,
justice.*

—Baruch Spinoza

12. Coming Home

Forgiveness is the answer to the child's dream of a miracle by which what is broken is made whole again, what is soiled is again made clean.

—Dag Hammarskjöld

What to Expect from Civilians

Most of the people you will encounter after returning home have two things in common. First, they are well intentioned, and second, they have absolutely no idea what you've been through. There's something to be said for the old Vietnam veteran cliché of "You weren't there, man! You don't know!" But the fact is that the vast majority of those who you will encounter are both ignorant and grateful. Our challenge is to allow them to be both, without expecting more or better from them.

Dealing with Intrusive Personalities

Frankly, no one can fully prepare for the ignorance of the civilian sector when returning from combat deployments. One of the most heartbreaking questions you may encounter is simply, "Oh, is that still going on?" The ignorance about world affairs that so typifies most Americans is all the more heart-wrenching when encountered by one who has been living out the full impact of our geopolitical conflicts. There is very little you can say to these individuals, other than referring them to the daily newspaper. This is one of those times when silence truly is a virtue.

Another common response encountered in the civilian world is the random thank-you. Whether or not this comment is ignorant is a matter of your own perception. I've known some service people who *hate* being thanked, because many return from combat having seen or experienced things that they are not necessarily proud of. They may often be dealing with traumas of their own and do not believe that "thanks" is the appropriate response to their actions. However, there are others who are very grateful to have their service acknowledged by a thankful population—especially when the military is so often overlooked in times of peace.

My husband recently encountered a new form of ignorance: "Oh, you were only gone *that* long? That doesn't count!" This is a reaction that members of the National Guard and Reserves are likely to encounter. I get very frustrated with these comments and have to bite my tongue to keep from asking, "How many bodies have *you* seen blown up in the past few weeks?" Unfortunately, those who make these comments usually will not be persuaded that even one day in combat is at best a life-changing experience and at worst a traumatizing experience. I've often wondered how they would respond to someone who should have been deployed for eighteen months, but who lost his or her legs in the first week of deployment. Was the individual's service too short to count, or is it possible to buy your credibility in blood?

Issues Facing Reunited Families

Power Struggles

For months, sometimes years, the spouses on the home front are responsible for every aspect of home life. They pay the bills, they attend school plays and soccer games, they clean the house and discipline the children. They make every scheduling and budgeting decision alone. For months, sometimes years, their deployed partners operate under stressful conditions wherein snap decisions can save lives. They are a part of a defined command structure, where responsibility is clearly delineated and hierarchically defined. Is it any wonder that these two experiences combined can result in some interesting and frustrating power struggles when the family is finally reunited?

Many units and some branches of the military are now offering "reintegration" or "reentry" counseling to families after the deployed spouse returns home. These sessions are devoted to updating the returned partner on the past year's household management and communicating with each other about the shared responsibilities they are expected to resume. For families that are not offered such assistance, like my own, the homecoming can be a bit of a letdown. It is not uncommon for home-based spouses to look forward to their partners' return date as the time at which they can go "off duty." I told my own husband that when he returned from Iraq, I would not lift a finger for at least a month. It was my expectation that he return home and take over, giving me a break from household tasks equal to the one he had just experienced. Needless to say, these expectations are often let down and feelings of disappointment can tarnish the homecoming experience. I did indeed go off duty for a short period when Rob returned. And not a dish was washed nor a piece of clutter picked up from the moment he set foot in the front door—until I resumed the tasks again.

Communications about one's homecoming expectations should occur well before the deployed person is due home. It is best if these conversations occur prior to the deployment, if at all possible. That way, the division of labor (both during and after the deployment) is understood by both partners and the homecoming transition occurs pleasantly and with minimal conflict and stress. I do think that it is a reasonable expectation that the returning service member will provide a measure of relief to his or her spouse upon the return. However, many returning veterans come back coping with depression or other issues that may require "honey do" lists to take a backseat to other tasks both on base and internally. If possible (and for many military families it's not), bring in a weekly cleaning service or family friend who is willing to take the burden from *both* partners long enough for both partners to rest, restore, and return to normal life together.

Personality Changes

Sadly, I hear it all too often from my military friends: "He came back different . . . distant" or "He's not the man I married." Obviously war is one of the most profoundly life-changing experiences a soul can experience. It is a kiln that hardens minds to suffering (their own and others), fear, and grief in order to focus on survival. This is a necessary factor if one hopes to live long enough to come home—but it can make the homecoming itself difficult if the serviceperson and his or her loved ones are not properly prepared.

I would never say that all personalities experience negative changes due to their combat experience. But I do believe that combat itself is a negative experience and that it does change all who experience it. How depends on the individual's own traits and psychological composition. I know a great many members of the military who came home feeling stronger, more capable of handling the trivial, mundane day-to-day tasks. Many who were not outspoken politically return more insistent upon exercising the constitutional rights they put their life on the line to defend. Sadly, a great many come home with feelings they don't know how to cope with yet. All of these changes—good and bad—will affect the family dynamic and the romantic partnership. If you are able to afford it, or if the military will provide it to you, I strongly suggest family or couples counseling if you find yourself dealing with personality changes that are having a negative impact on your home life.

Domestic Violence

When most people think of domestic violence, they picture the stereotypical "good housewife," wearing dark sunglasses indoors and long sleeves in summer to hide the telltale marks of physical abuse. While physical injury is most definitely one form of domestic violence, there are far more insidious and less-noticeable forms of abuse that happen in conjunction with or instead of physical assault. Marital rape, emotional and verbal abuse, isolation, and financial manipulation are all forms of domestic violence. Often, the abusive partner isn't violent at the beginning of the relationship. He is usually considered the "perfect" husband or boyfriend (since the vast majority of domestic violence survivors are female, for simplici-ty's sake I will use the masculine to describe the abuser and the feminine to describe the abused—if this is not your experience, feel free to modify to meet your circumstances). Often, he is concerned, courteous to a fault, aware of his partner's preferences in food and clothing. He may order for her in restaurants, or suggest outfits to wear out on a date. But over time, he changes. The "suggestions" become demands. The compliments slowly decrease, while the criticisms—of his partner and of her family, friends, or even children—increase. After this grooming period, where the wife or girlfriend is slowly acclimated to the changes in her partner, she believes them to be temporary personality changes caused by stress, anxiety, or any other situation that justifies his behavior in her mind. No one gets punched on the first date. Usually, by the time physical violence manifests itself within the relationship, the abuser has ingrained his behavior into his partner's life in such a way that the physical assault is, if not accepted, then at least excused. Often, the assault is followed by profuse apologies, gifts, and promises that it will never happen again. Sadly, this too is a part of the grooming process, and is an expected event in the cycle of abuse.

But why bring this up in a book about the military? There are many reasons: because domestic violence is the leading cause of injury to women, who make up 15% of the military;[1] because domestic violence rates within military families are three to five times higher than in civil-ian families;[2] because domestic violence incidents are often likely to oc-cur in the wake of a return from combat, especially when symptoms of PTSD and/or depression go unrecognized or untreated;[3] and because do-mestic violence presents an immediate detriment to morale and mission readiness when it goes unaddressed. According to the American Institute on Domestic Violence, 96% of battered workers experience problems at work because of the abuse, 74% are harassed at work by their abuser,

1 United States Census Bureau, "Facts for Features: Women's History Month," http://www.census.gov/Press-Release/www/releases/archives/facts_for_features_special_editions/006232.html (accessed May 21, 2007).

2 The Miles Foundation, http://members.aol.com/_ht_a/milesfdn/myhomepage/ (ac-cessed May 22, 2007).

3 Ibid.

56% are late to work, 28% leave work early, and 54% miss entire days of work because of their abuse.[4] All of this takes a toll on a unit's ability to be mission-ready and on the individual serviceperson's ability to prepare to undertake the tasks of military work. The fact that a woman wears a military uniform, that she is weapons-qualified or even a military veteran, does not mean that she cannot be abused. The National Coalition Against Domestic Violence (NCADV) states that 22% of military women reported experiencing "intimate partner violence" during their military service.[5] Likewise, just because someone wears a military uniform, or has bars, oak leafs, or birds on his shoulders, does not mean that he is incapable of domestic violence. In fact, 62% of the abusers reported in cases of military domestic violence are active-duty military personnel.[6] The fact remains that the military has one of the highest domestic violence rates of any career field.

The NCADV points out several factors that can create an atmosphere conducive to the perpetuation of partner violence within the military environment. First, when an abused spouse decides to report her abusive military partner, she must make her report to his commander rather than the civilian or military police. While her allegations may be backed up by reports taken by law enforcement personnel, the fact remains that the person who determines whether or not to intervene is her partner's boss. This makes many women reluctant to disclose their abuse, because to do so is to risk the financial security of their partners and by extension their families. Second, the standards that the Department of Defense sets for determining the severity of an episode of domestic violence are more stringent than those in the civilian sector. If a female Army private were to be strangled by her civilian husband, the civilian police would consider this incident to be "extremely dangerous." However, if a civilian woman were to be strangled by her Army private husband, the Department of Defense would categorize this assault as "mild" or "moderate"

4 These statistics are obtained from the American Institute on Domestic Violence at http://www.aidv-usa.com/Statistics.htm (accessed January 14, 2008).

5 The National Coalition Against Domestic Violence, *Domestic Violence and Sexual Assault in the Military*, http://www.ncadv.org/files/military.pdf (accessed January 14, 2008).

6 Ibid.

in severity. In fact, only 6% of all reported incidents of domestic assault warranted the label of "severe abuse" by the Department of Defense. These few cases met the DOD's standard of "major physical injury requiring inpatient medical treatment or causing temporary or permanent physical disfigurement." In other words, a serviceperson could break his partner's arm, blacken both her eyes, and assault her sexually, and yet as long as she was seen in the emergency room and not actually admitted to the hospital, this incident would be considered "moderate" abuse at best. In 2002, the Department of Defense noted that less than 7% of domestic violence incidents in the military were met with court-martial proceeding.[7]

So what can you do if you or someone you know is a victim of domestic violence? If you live on a military installation, you need to first be aware of what your rights and protections are, since they are quite different than in the civilian sector. If you are not ready to pursue prosecution, or wish to plan a safe escape from your partner without involving the military command, be careful whom you disclose your abuse to on base. Keep in mind that there is *no confidentiality* within the military structure. Family Support personnel, victim advocates on the base, social workers, and military physicians are required to report any instance of domestic violence within a military family. You know your family situation best. If you feel that it would endanger yourself or your family to involve the military command, then I strongly suggest that you make contact with a local domestic violence shelter in your area. Even if you are not in need of shelter, the agency can often provide you with counseling, safety planning, assistance in locating housing, and legal advocacy. As an added bonus, they will not report your activities or disclosures of abuse to the abuser's commanding officer.

If you do choose to report the abuse to the batterer's commanding officer, keep in mind that civilian wives do have the right to request an MPO, or Military Protective Order, which can include orders that the batterer live in quarters on base instead of in the family home. This would not replace a civilian PPO, or Personal Protection Order, if you live off

---

7 Ibid.

base, however. Keep in mind that the most dangerous time for a battered spouse is the seventy-two hours after her partner is served with the PPO paperwork. While there are no statistics for this, I believe that it is safe to assume that this would apply equally to an MPO—especially when one considers that the report must be made to the batterer's boss. Safety planning is a vital part of this process, and I strongly suggest that you meet with a civilian domestic violence expert when deciding what to do.

Keep in mind that if someone you know is abused, she is not alone. It is important that she gets out of the abusive relationship, and seeks safety and support when she feels ready to do so. Support can be financial and emotional, as well as in terms of security. Often, several attempts are made before a survivor is finally able to separate from her batterer. This process can be even more difficult on a foreign duty station, far from her support network. As a military community, we need to take domestic violence seriously both as a policy matter and as a part of our loved ones' daily lives.

Odds are good that someone you know is abused. Make sure that you tell her that you believe her; do not minimize or make excuses for the abusive behavior. Tell her about local domestic violence programs, as well as any base resources that may be available. Be sure you clarify the confidentiality offered by both options. Tell her (over and over again, if necessary) that she does *not* deserve to be abused, nor do her children deserve to witness the violence against her. Remind her that you are there for her, and will accompany her to court, drive her to counseling, provide her with a safe place to stay—whatever you are willing to do to assist her. Most importantly, do not judge her. Many women face threats of violence against themselves, their children, or their families when they attempt to leave. Some women do not have the financial resources necessary to walk away from their partners yet. A decision to stay may not be the decision you believe you'd make—but that doesn't make it wrong. The most important things you can do for a battered acquaintance are simply support her choices and let her know that you will continue to support her no matter what she decides to do.

If you are in an abusive relationship yourself, tell someone you trust about the abuse. This may not mean reporting the abuse to base personnel; it could mean simply telling a trusted friend. But make sure someone knows what you're going through. Chaplains are the only base personnel who have confidentiality rights; know that if you want some insight into the military command perspective, you do have a right, even as a Pagan, to go to the chaplains for counseling or advice. They will not (or should not) report your situation without your consent. If you are stationed over-seas, perhaps in a country where you don't yet speak the language, the chaplains may be your only option for confidential support. If you are not comfortable speaking to a military chaplain, get in contact with a local do-mestic violence program (if there is one nearby) to discuss safety plan-ning and learn more about your legal options. In the meantime, document the abuse: take pictures of injuries, keep a journal, obtain copies of police or medical reports. Keep these in a safe place (perhaps with a friend) in case you decide to report your partner to military command. Having the resources below, and knowing that there are people you can turn to for support within the military and the local civilian community, can make a difference, quite literally, between life and death.

For More Information, or for Help:

The Miles Foundation: http://members.aol.com/_ht_a/milesfdn/ myhomepage/

National Coalition Against Domestic Violence: http://www.ncadv.org

Military Homefront: http://www.militaryhomefront.dod.mil (click on "Troops and Families" to access the Family Advocacy Program)

Military OneSource: http://www.militaryonesource.com

When it comes to discussing matters of sexual assault and domestic violence, I find it imperative to point out the role that magick and ritual play in addressing these topics. If magick truly is the "art of changing consciousness in accordance with will," we must understand that in or-der to create change in our lives we must work actively in the mundane world to manifest this change. If you are in a situation that is dangerous or violent, please do *not* work magick trying to change your partner or to make the violence stop. Instead, put your energy into manifesting concrete plans to leave the situation. As you create a new life for yourself, work magick for protection and safety. We cannot work magick to violate another person's free will, and frankly, trying to change a batterer into a "different" person is a violation of his will. I am in no way advocating battery, but our spiritual energy is best spent in manifesting a new reality for ourselves—materially, emotionally, and spiritually—rather than in trying to create change within another person, which may or may not be in accordance with the Rede, regardless of your motivations or your partner's own behavior. Magickal work is *one part* of the process of creating change; do not stay in a dangerous situation and ritual waiting for change . . . the gods help those who help themselves.

Children's Special Concerns

Many service personnel are surprised to learn that for children the homecoming can be just as traumatic as the departure. Many parents will send or leave photos of themselves with their children. Depending upon the age of the child, parents can be quite hurt to see that the child relates the photo to "Daddy" rather than the flesh-and-blood person when he's returned. It's important to give your little ones time to adjust to your presence, especially if they were under three at the time of your deployment. It can be quite hurtful to a returning parent, so eager to embrace their child, to have that same toddler recoil and cling to Mom. Deployed parents can become virtual strangers to small children, and they must be willing to ease into the process of rebuilding a relationship rather than rush at the little ones, no matter how eager the adults may be.

Older children have their own concerns. Younger school-age children may experience separation anxiety. They need to be reassured that if the returned parent is leaving the house, he or she is only going to be at the grocery store and will return shortly. It is vital that the returning parent give specific time frames to children of this age to help minimize any anxiety that might come with new departures. For example, instead of simply saying, "Bye! I'll be back in a little while," the parent must be very clear:

"I'll be back in a little while. I have to go to a meeting, but I'll be home before dinnertime, okay?" Giving children a concrete "deadline" they can relate to (saying you'll be home at five thirty means nothing to a child who can't tell time) reassures them that you are not leaving for a year every time you exit the family home.

Preteens and teenagers may react much like their parent and siblings at the time of reunion, but don't be surprised if you are confronted with subtle (or not so subtle) power plays. Teens will demand that your role within the family be reaffirmed. Sometimes, this means expecting you to adjust to a change in household rules that has occurred in your absence (for example, a son who couldn't date prior to your deployment now has a steady girlfriend) or else testing you with manipulations of consistent family policies (for example, the daughter who insists that Mom raised her curfew to midnight in your absence). Be prepared for a mercurial creature who is overjoyed to see you in one moment and, in the next, convinced of your intrusive presence in the domestic order established in your absence. The most important thing to keep in mind is this: children grow a *lot* in a few months or a few years. Parents feel out of step with the household they left. But the one constant is the love—between partners, their children, and each other. It might prove worthwhile to seek counseling for a little while following the deployment, if some of these challenges present serious concern. But never doubt the fact that while everything else may change, the love that was there before you left remains.

13. The Unending Battle

I pray for the strength to accept that lives most often end in tragedy, that quests don't always work, that understanding is a long and lonely hunt, that I can't reason my way to love, eat gold, or live forever, and that none of this matters. I pray to understand that I am here to find my way back to God, whatever that takes, and all the rest save love and duty is an illusion.

—John Taylor Gatto

Issues Facing Returning Veterans

Sadly, one of the flaws within our military system today is the level of intervention and support provided to returning veterans. When my husband returned from his first deployment, he and his comrades were given a checklist to complete while they were still in the field, to determine if they had posttraumatic stress disorder. My husband still laughs and asks, "What part of *post* don't they understand?" This is an all too common experience of veterans, however. I have been told stories of returning troops being offered post-deployment counseling . . . if they stayed in country or on base a few weeks longer. Not many chose to delay reunion with their families, regardless of the level of intervention they might need. Another concern that has been expressed comes from veterans who have been home for a while, or who are perhaps now out of the service. When they do finally seek treatment for their PTSD or depression, many report being told that they do not suffer from combat-related mental illness at all, but rather, had undiagnosed psychological problems prior to their enlistment.

I am sure that there are a great many service personnel who have their concerns met with practical and compassionate intervention as soon as they are reported. For those who might not feel comfortable reaching out to military resources for career or personal reasons, or for those who have experienced situations such as I described above, I would like to discuss some of the most common disorders experienced by returning veterans. I firmly believe that magick is a form of prayer and that prayer is capable of great healing. As a part of this chapter, I have included the Disarmament Ritual, which will work to address these issues at a spiritual level. But I want to stress, *please*, if in reading the rest of this chapter you recognize any of the traits or behaviors I discuss, seek help immediately from a qualified civilian or military professional who you feel you can trust. None of these challenges will simply go away . . . and the sooner we address the emotional health crises that are facing returning veterans, the sooner the restoration can begin.

PTSD

In World War I, they called it "shell shock." After World War II and Korea, it was "battle fatigue." Finally, after Vietnam, it became a formal diagnosis—posttraumatic stress disorder. And while it can manifest in survivors of any traumatic experience, it has remained a dominant mental health concern for military personnel returning home from war. Posttraumatic stress disorder (or PTSD) is defined by the American Psychiatric Association as "characteristic symptoms following exposure to an extreme traumatic stressor involving direct personal experience of an event that involves actual or threatened death or serious injury, or other threat to one's physical integrity; or witnessing an event that involves death, injury, or a threat to the physical integrity of another person; or learning about unexpected or violent death, serious harm, or threat of death or injury experienced by a family member or other close associate (Criterion A1)."[1]

What this means is that many if not most military personnel are exposed to conditions such as combat, shell/mortar attacks, loss of comrades, or simply an atmosphere of pervasive threat conditions, which may directly affect their mental health. The potential result is posttraumatic stress disorder. This fact means that a diagnosis of PTSD in returning military personnel, not to mention diagnoses in military family members, is sadly all too common. As of May 2006, more than one in three soldiers and Marines who served in Iraq or Afghanistan sought mental health care after their tour.[2] Mental health referrals were increased across all branches. Those suffering from PTSD are more likely to suffer from poor physical health in general and are more likely to attempt suicide. You can see, then, why it's important that military personnel and their families be aware of the signs of PTSD and know when and where to seek help.

Comments that I have heard frequently among some members of the military, especially Guardsmen and Reservists, are "I can't have PTSD—I wasn't there long enough to see direct combat" or "Other units' experiences were much worse than mine—I don't deserve to call it PTSD." It is very important that returning veterans acknowledge their psychological responses to combat. To minimize or ignore these feelings can lead to anger management issues up to and including domestic battery and other violent behavior, physical health problems, career disruptions, substance (drugs and/or alcohol) abuse, self-harm, and even suicide. The *Diagnostic and Statistical Manual* of the American Psychiatric Association (APA) does not specify a length of time that one must endure a trauma in order to "qualify" for PTSD. The fact is that experiencing a life-threatening or traumatic experience firsthand or even knowing that a loved one has encountered a life-threatening situation is enough to potentially cause PTSD reactions. This is important because it means that depending upon one's

---

1 *Diagnostic and Statistical Manual of Mental Disorders*, 4th ed. (DSM-IV), as cited at http://www.mental-health-today.com/ptsd/dsm.htm (accessed January 20, 2008).

2 Iraq and Afghanistan Veterans of America, "Mental Health Problems Among Iraq and Afghanistan Veterans," http://www.iava.org/component/option,com_/Itemid,66/option,content/task,view/id,2414/ (accessed January 23, 2008).

resiliency and mental health to recover from even one day in a combat theatre might not be enough because the experience may lead to lasting mental health concerns. Likewise, PTSD can occur in spouses and children of deployed personnel, even if the family members themselves are never in physical danger. PTSD is one of the most pervasive yet under- and mis-diagnosed mental health concerns of the past hundred years.

So, what are the warning signs of PTSD? How do you determine the difference between a true psychiatric concern and a simple readjustment into civilian life? The APA has provided a list of criteria within the DSM-IV that must be observed before a formal diagnosis of posttraumatic stress disorder can be made, and I have included it for you here. However, not everyone is able to decipher the psycho-language, and so a more informal list of possible symptoms is presented for you below. This is not intended to provide a mental health diagnosis, but rather to give you some basic "warning signs" that might indicate a need to seek the help of a therapist, physician, or trusted counselor:

- Nightmares

- Persistent, recurring thoughts/memories relating to the trauma

- Avoiding places, people, or images that might bring up unpleasant memories/feelings

- Feeling hyper-vigilant, even in safe situations

- Being easily startled by sudden or loud noises/unexpected sensory triggers

- Feeling numb, detached, or unable to relate to and connect with those around you—which can include loved ones, commanders, and co-workers

I strongly urge anyone (veteran or family member) who finds that this short list presents an uncomfortably familiar picture to seek appropriate care immediately. The effects of PTSD (and the depression and anxiety that often accompany it) can be devastating if left untreated. There are a few magickal techniques you can incorporate into your spiritual practice *in addition to appropriate mental health care.* Most are fairly simple, such as dream-journaling and meditation. I've also found that a nightly affirmation, with practice, can be quite helpful in reducing or eliminating the night terrors and nightmares that can frequently disturb the rest of combat veterans. Make a habit of reciting something like the following:

> I am peaceful. I am safe.
> I am surrounded in love.
> My home is secure.
> My mind is clear.
> My heart is open.
> There is only love in this place.
> There is only peace in this place.
> The nighttime brings comfort and rest.

This can be recited once before bed, as in a prayer, or over and over in a form of "counting sheep" or chanting. Some might find it helpful to incorporate prayer or meditation beads of some kind. My husband has a set of sandalwood mala beads and has often fallen asleep with them in his hands.

Another idea is a modern interpretation of the Native American dreamcatcher. Take yarn (I like to recommend black, to absorb negative energy) and create a "web" above where your head lies in bed. Add amethyst or turquoise beads, small protective charms or herb bundles, and whatever else "catches" negativity in your tradition or according to your instincts. I've seen small energy webs made around an embroidery-hoop frame, and I've seen webs so large they take up the entire wall behind a bed. But the energetic intent is the same: to trap negative energy, thought-forms, and general "ickies" before they can be drawn toward the already magnetic aura of a traumatized soul. This same idea can be condensed into a simple black string, with a few beads and maybe a charm or two, worn tied around the wrist.

I cannot stress enough how important visualization and breath-work are for anyone experiencing PTSD symptoms. It is so easy to get overwhelmed, or to slip into despair over seemingly "minor" day-to-day occurrences. A mastery of breathing can be the difference between a short period of feeling overwhelmed and an extended length of profoundly helpless fear. Spend time, prior to an overseas deployment, during the experience as much as is practical, and especially after your return, training yourself to find a space of deep, diaphragmatic breath in any situation, as fast as possible. This skill, along with visualization and the sense of calm and restraint it bears, could quite literally save a life.

Simple Visualization Exercise for Any Negative Situation

I first started using this visualization for physical pain, such as migraines or menstrual cramps. When my children got a bit older, I realized that it works very well for emotional and psychic pain as well. By incorporating it into your regular practice (try it the next time you have a headache) and becoming comfortable with the imagery, it can serve as a powerful coping mechanism when you are faced with any kind of trauma, fear, sadness, etc. It's really very simple:

Close your eyes, take a deep, cleansing breath, and focus your attention inward. Examine your physical body and if necessary your mind and heart, to determine the location of your suffering. When you have found the source, do not react to it! It is our natural instinct to immediately rid ourselves of negativity, but you must stop, take a few moments, and examine how you are feeling. Ask yourself: Is how I'm feeling right now a physical sensation? Is it mental? Is it emotional? Probe the tender spot, and determine exactly how it feels. Is it raw or burning? Is it an ache or a throb? Is it purely emotional, like a tightness in your chest? Do not fight it . . . allow yourself time to truly experience the hurt. When you are ready, picture this hurt as a colored light or mist within you. What color is the hurt? Is it black? Red? Gray? Acknowledge the hurt, and keep your focus and your calm attention upon it until you can clearly see it as a colored presence within you.

Now, take a deep breath and visualize your lungs filling up with that negative energy. Exhale, and slowly push all of that colored mist out of your nostrils and away from you. Pause for a moment. Acknowledge the (perhaps tiny) bit of hurt that has exited your body. Now, visualize your body surrounded by light or mist of a second color—a color you associate with healing or peace. Is it blue? White? Green? Take another deep breath and breathe in this soothing, healing light. When you exhale, imagine your lungs pushing it down into your body, and feel it disperse throughout as it displaces the hurting energy you exhaled. Repeat this process over and over, as many times as needed, until you have exhaled all of the negative energy and hurt within you and inhaled enough healing energy to fill the void you've created. If you do this visualization effectively, one of two things will occur: you will either calm down and feel a sense of physical/emotional/mental relief, or you will fall asleep—which often has the same result.

Depression

Depression is an especially common problem for military veterans. It can have biomedical causes (for instance a deficiency of specific neurotransmitters such as serotonin) and also situational causes (arising from specific life circumstances or experiences). When one has experienced life in the combat theatre, where day-to-day functioning occurs in a very high-stress, high-adrenaline environment, it does have an impact on the neurochemical functioning of the brain. This can lead to feelings of depression (short term or chronic) that can be treated with medication. Lt. Col. Grossman writes extensively about the biological effects of life in the combat theatre in his books and papers. I highly recommend (again) exploring his writings if you are planning on a military career of any length. Situational depression is best addressed with a combination of traditional talk therapy and possible pharmaceutical intervention, depending upon the length and severity of the episodes.

In 1998, 19% of military personnel reported experiencing symptoms of depression.[3] Changes in world events (post-9/11) and military usage (we are years into a two-front war) since that study was conducted indicate that military depression rates, and the suicides that can accompany depressive episodes, have risen. Many high-profile instances of military

---

3 Lt. Col. Nancy Chapman, "Depression: The Common Cold of Mental Illness," *U.S. Army: Hooah 4 Health*, http://www.hooah4health.com/mind/suicideprev/depressionCold.htm (accessed May 12, 2007).

suicide have been reported in the news, including the death of Jeff Lucey, who returned home from Iraq and killed himself. In addition, a colonel on active duty in Iraq became the highest-ranking member of the armed forces to take his life either in country or immediately thereafter.

Depression can manifest in many different ways depending upon factors such as gender, duration of episodes, and support networks. It is not an illness that is easily overcome, and even with constant medical and psychiatric treatment, it can last upwards of two years. One of the primary difficulties for military personnel is an unwillingness to seek treatment for fear of having a diagnosis of depression affect their military service or promotion potential. As someone who has lived with a partner who suffers from chronic depression, I cannot stress enough how important it is to seek treatment as soon and as frequently as possible. There are many resources available through the Veterans Administration, which runs vets' centers throughout the country to deal specifically with issues like depression. If you are uncomfortable seeking help through the government, there are literally thousands of private psychologists who are willing to work with people suffering from depression. Keep in mind, however, that these providers will typically cost more and may have less of a foundation in military and veterans' issues.

The disorder itself makes it hard to seek help—depression can manifest in physical fatigue, lethargy, and feelings of futility. All of these factors combined create roadblocks to treatment that can seem insurmountable to the sufferer. If you experience feelings of hopelessness, worthlessness, or apathy that last for longer than two weeks, changes in weight (up or down) or sleep habits (less or more), an inability to concentrate or make decisions, feelings of extreme guilt, unreasonable fatigue, or thoughts of death or suicide, please seek help immediately. If you are contemplating suicide, call a crisis line for immediate advocacy and support. Two national numbers are the National Hopeline Network at 1-800-784-2433 and the National Suicide Prevention Lifeline at 1-800-273-8255.

I believe that Paganism is a healing religion and that a consistent practice of meditation, ritual, and community worship is vital to maintaining mental health. But if you are suffering from depression, or considering ending your life, please do not turn to a spellbook or storefront Priestess for assistance. Get appropriate mental and medical health care *first* and integrate your spiritual and religious practice into your care. Spiritual practice is one aspect of the healing process, but it is no substitute for a mind-body-spirit care model that will support and enable your healing. Peace and light to your spirit.

Anger Management/Hostility

Anger management is one of the many challenges facing returning service personnel. Those who have experienced combat firsthand often have difficulty processing the memories they've acquired and the emotions that these experiences bring up in them. It is all too easy to fall into the habit of taking this anger, outrage, fear, and sorrow out on those closest to us: our spouses and loved ones. Sadly, my husband and I have experienced this phenomenon firsthand. We have come to recognize the signs of this behavior and conscientiously adjust our words and actions accordingly. I believe that this occurs because human beings inherently want to take their sadness to those closest to them. We know that we can scream and yell and vent to our partners and that they will love us anyway afterward. This does not, however, justify or excuse such behavior.

Anger tends to manifest as a result of three primary causes:

1. Internal pain, suffering, or anxiety

2. Confrontation with truth

3. Being injured or criticized by others

The feelings that arise from these stressors are often dealt with in negative ways, such as self-medicating (drug or alcohol abuse), domestic violence, destructive behavior such as excessive gambling or sexually irresponsible behavior, and in some cases injury to oneself or others. These topics will each be addressed separately within their own sections, but I want to speak specifically about violence directed toward loved ones for a moment. I recognize that the legal and military ramifications of domestic violence have been addressed in other sections of the book, but I want to discuss the issue of battery specifically as it affects interpersonal relationships.

In our everyday lives we encounter divinity. The face of the Goddess is in the face of every woman and girl in our world. We see her stages reflected through our grandmothers, mothers, daughters, and lovers. She is there wherever we are. She is the memory held close to the heart on the battlefield. She is the loving embrace soldiers return home to, in many forms. When we return home, but discover that the battles continue to be waged within, we realize that our loved ones don't fully appreciate the extent of the damage. And so resentment leads to further isolation from these very people we cling to as anchors to who we once were and hope to be again. There is no easy answer for any of the things that traumatized soldiers feel as they reenter a world, a place, and a life that feels more foreign to them than the soil from which they returned. The women (and men) you share your life with may not be able to understand, but that doesn't mean they can't empathize. Love from their hearts to yours will open up your being to finding your path again.

This being said, if you fall into a tradition that honors the Divine Feminine, then you cannot diminish or damage another person, no matter how great your internal struggle. Your pain is not entitlement. It is not a justification. Your struggle to find your peace does not come at the expense of partners or children. Causing them to "share" your pain will not alleviate your own. Violence against family members—partners, elders, and children—occurs in every socioeconomic, racial, religious, and cultural dynamic all over the world. Domestic violence is a form of terrorism that bleeds throughout a culture, and its impact on a culture is just as great. The trauma of violent victimization at the hands of someone who loves you is as severe as the trauma of war. This has been studied over and over by academics during the last three decades. Domestic violence forms through patterns of behaviors, actions, words, and threats that leave one partner holding power over another, in the same way that hostages and prisoners of war are conditioned to fear and submit to their captors. These are conscious acts of coercion, obfuscation, and violence. These actions will not take away your experiences from war, nor will creating a war at home stop the onslaught of traumatic responses occurring within yourself. Violence acted out upon others will not eliminate the memory of violence within you. Domestic violence and sexual assault are forms of domestic warfare for the survivors of these crimes.

Honoring the Goddess means honoring the physical forms she takes in your life. You cannot kneel at her altar and then beat her to her knees. Sexual and domestic violence are atrocities in their own right, but to call yourself a worshiper of the Divine Feminine and then to assault another of her children is a magickal failing. You have been through a traumatic and (in some cases) devastating experience. The combat experience leaves no one uninjured. You are the only one who can define the changes caused by your combat experience; no one can know what is going on in your head and no one has the right to minimize your experiences. I am not telling you how to act or how to feel—no one has the right to do this to you. How and what you are feeling is complex and you may require some outside assistance from a counselor or Priestess. However, you have a responsibility to yourself and your family to find a way to come back to yourself on your own terms. No one expects healing to happen overnight. You may not have been in control of your orders, your tour, or your experiences in the military. You are, however, in control of your healing process and your actions now. You can reclaim your power in ethical, gentle ways.

Finding the internal reflection of the Divine Masculine within yourself means connecting to your soul through healing work. This can be done in ways that you are comfortable with and when you are ready. You have spent time deeply bonded with your Warrior self, and connecting to other aspects of the God can be difficult. To reflect on where you have been and where you are going are natural aspects of healing, as is seeking a reflection of the Divine for this personal transition. There are many faces of the God—Warrior, Bard, Lover, Greenman, Divine Child, and Hunter, to name a few.

Recognizing what you have been through and the impact it has had on your life will aid in the transition to a new aspect, one more suited to your stateside service and domestic life, as well as the healing process. But know that while you must work through this soul-work alone, you are never truly isolated from your community, your family, and the Gods. As you work through your pain, each of these support "teams" should reinforce the fact that the violence you experienced on the battle-field needs to stay there, that battles do not have to come home. Honor yourself and you will find God. Honor your life partners (people of any gender and any role in your life) and you will find Goddess. Some techniques that you can utilize to cope with and reduce your angry impulses include the following:

- Practice visualization, coupled with breathing exercises (such as the example found in the PTSD section of this book).

- Avoid using absolutes such as "always" and "never," since these tend to exacerbate our feelings and exaggerate the actual situation at hand. Take a moment to evaluate the situation clearly and with a rational eye. Then address the issues at hand as they truly are—not as your emotions make them seem.

- Remove yourself from the situation. Take a walk, go into the basement, and sit in the dark for a few moments. Do not return until your head stops pounding.

- Address the issue proactively. Instead of jumping into an argument, create a plan of action. This can be helpful no matter what the situation is that's causing you stress.

- Clarify your language. Much anger comes from miscommunication. Use phrases such as "What I'm hearing you say is _____. Is that how you mean for it to sound?" This allows someone the opportunity to either rephrase the statement or else backpedal away from words spoken in haste.

- Physically ground yourself. Go outside and sit on the ground. Dig your fingers (or full hands) into the earth, and do not move until you've felt the soil absorb all the negative feelings you're experiencing.

- Prayer. I'm a big believer in talking out your negative emotions with Deity. Go somewhere private, where you can scream and yell and cry and rant to the Goddess. She will accept your cries without complaint and transform the emotions into something healing.

Addiction

Addiction, in many forms, is a common theme in the veteran's experience. A combination of factors plays into this phenomenon, including a lack of adequate access to mental health care upon returning, ease of access to addictive substances (especially alcohol), and a military mindset that encourages self-sufficiency. It's the latter factor that lends itself toward self-medicating rather than seeking outside support and thus leads me to a brief discussion of substance abuse among veterans and Pagans. When our fathers served in Vietnam, alcohol, marijuana, and hard drugs were freely available in the field. Because of the current combat theatre (primarily Islamic countries), the access to these substances in the field has been relatively diminished. However, it is after the homecoming when many veterans find themselves tempted toward self-medication in order to cope with the stress of reintegration into home life and with painful memories and feelings.

There are a great many substances that can be abused—some legal, some not. I'm going to operate under the assumption that any mood-altering substance you're partaking of is legal, but I want you to understand that while I've phrased the following information in terms of alcohol abuse, it does apply to most other addictions as well. Now, there is nothing wrong with having drinks with friends or enjoying a microbrew in the evening, and that sip of May wine can really add some magick to a Beltaine ritual. But when substances are being used as a way to help you avoid intrusive thoughts or painful feelings, or if your drinking starts to interfere with daily functioning, you need to seek help. So, how can you tell when your drinking has become more pathological than permissable? Here are some of the signs:

- Do your friends or loved ones say that your personality changes when you're drinking? Do you become morose, promiscuous, or aggressive?

- Are you distracted by thoughts of drinking, or do you look forward to times when you'll be able to drink?

- Have people around you expressed concerns about how much you drink?

- Have you missed work, family functions, or other obligations because you've been drinking?

- Are you spending more on alcohol than you can afford?

- Has your drinking caused you legal problems? Have you been arrested for drunk driving or public intoxication?

- Have you placed yourself in dangerous situations in order to access your drink/drug of choice?

If you recognize any of these behaviors in your own life, please understand how vital it is that you seek help. According to Staff Sgt. Kathleen T. Rhem of the American Forces Press Service, 21% of military personnel admit to being heavy drinkers.[4] This is especially dangerous for personnel who may be dealing with undiagnosed or undertreated PTSD, since approximately one-third of suicides involve alcohol use prior to the final act.

There are options for Pagans seeking substance-abuse help. Circle Sanctuary publishes two resources for those in recovery. The first is an inexpensive package called the *Pagans in Recovery Resource Packet*. The second is an academic thesis that discusses the advantages and disadvantages of twelve-step programs and how they can be adapted to meet the needs of Pagans dealing with addiction. It is called *When Goddess Is God: Pagans, Recovery, and Alcoholics Anonymous*. Both resources can be purchased through the Circle Sanctuary bookstore.

The military also offers assistance for personnel dealing with addictions. Counseling referrals are available through www.MilitaryOneSource .com and possibly through your unit's Family Support group. The Veterans Administration provides addiction and substance-abuse intervention as well. The most important aspect of this issue, especially for return-

---

4 Staff Sgt. Kathleen T. Rhem, "Alcohol Abuse Costs DoD Dearly," American Forces Press Service, June 6, 2000, http://usmilitary.about.com/library/milinfo/milarticles/blalcohol .htm.

ing veterans, is to seek an integrated care plan, which will address not only the substance abuse itself, but also the underlying causes—be they depression, anxiety, or stress. Resources are available for those in need, and the Pagan community is becoming increasingly aware of the need for "safe" or "dry" rituals, festival spaces, and covens. The Reclaiming tradition has led the way in assuring substance-free retreats and circles, and it is my hope that other traditions follow their example. In the meantime, the Gods want us to be healthy and whole. Paganism is not a religion that condemns alcohol (or even some other substances, depending upon the path) as outright evil. But it is concerned with balance, wholeness, and a clear connection with Deity. Substance abuse interferes with these goals and needs to be addressed immediately by the user as well as the user's spiritual and military support systems.

Disarmament Ritual

This ritual was difficult for me to write, since I feel an overwhelming obligation to provide a magickal tool not only to welcome returning veterans, but also to allow them to begin the healing process. It is a partner ritual, which I feel is most appropriate for the working, rather than a community endeavor such as the Warrior Class Rite of Passage, or a solitary rite such as the Arming Ritual. The reasoning behind this is simple: it allows a measure of private soul-work while at the same time supporting and upholding the spirit of the soldier. This ritual is best worked with your spouse or significant other, but it can be done by anyone you feel comfortable asking to fill the role of Priest/ess. The veteran should enter into this ritual in his or her battle dress uniform (BDU).

I. The Entrance

The circle should be cast by the Priest/ess alone, in an area conducive to a ritual bath. The space should be darkened as much as possible, using just a few white candles for minimal light. A warm bath should be drawn, with essential oils of lavender and cedar. Mix in a few handfuls of Epsom or sea salts and stir counterclockwise thirteen times to banish negativity while saying:

Womb of Mother, Healing Sea,
All evil present, banished be;
May all darkness from here depart,
Let all that remains be pure of heart.

Then stir thirteen times clockwise to charge the water with peace and healing while saying:

Primordial ocean, place of birth,
Cleanse and heal and affirm the worth;
Of those who seek their healing here,
May their souls emerge both strong and clear.

When the circle is cast and the water is charged, the Priest/ess should open the door and offer the challenge to the waiting veteran.

Priest/ess

Who seeks entry into this sacred place?

Veteran

It is I, (name), who seeks to enter.

Priest/ess

How do you enter?

Veteran

In perfect love and perfect trust.

Priest/ess extends his or her hand and leads the veteran into the room, saying:

Priest/ess

Enter then, and blessed be.

II. Calling the Quarters

The Priest/ess should lead the veteran to each of the Cardinal Points, calling the quarters and presenting the veteran to them. Throughout this process, the veteran should stand in the God position, arms crossed over chest, hands resting on heart.

Priest/ess

Hail to thee, Spirits of the East, come to honor the warrior returned! Be with us here and witness these Rites. Hail and welcome!

Veteran

Greetings, East, place of air and knowledge.

Priest/ess

Hail to thee, Spirits of the South, come to honor the warrior returned! Be with us here and witness these Rites. Hail and welcome!

Veteran

Greetings, South, place of fire and courage.

Priest/ess

Hail to thee, Spirits of the West, come to honor the warrior returned! Be with us here and witness these Rites. Hail and welcome!

Veteran

Greetings, West, place of water and healing.

Priest/ess

Hail to thee, Spirits of the North, come to honor the warrior returned! Be with us here and witness these Rites. Hail and welcome!

Veteran

Greetings, North, place of earth and restoration.

Priest/ess

Hail to the Center, the Spirit, the Core, all that which is
greater than ourselves. Above and below, within and without, the circle is sealed and we are between the worlds.

Veteran

Greetings, Center, the place of balance.

*At this time, the veteran should kneel before the Priest/ess, who shall place
his or her left hand upon the veteran's hand and raise his or her right hand,
palm upward, to the sky.*

Priest/ess

Mistress of healing and magick, Mother of every creature
that walks the face of our Earth, bless your daughter/son
here as s/he seeks return from the field of battle. S/he has
fought honorably, abided by your sacred ways, and desires
now to rest and heal. Blessed Goddess, who both spins and
cuts the thread of life, grant your child peace as s/he lays
down her/his arms and returns to your service at home.
Guide her/his path, ward her/his dreams, and restore her/
him to full understanding of her/his place in the web. So
mote it be.

Great Horned One, who is the Father of every wild thing,
the hunter and the prey, the stalk and the scythe, grant
wholeness to your child before me. S/he has borne the burden of this time of service without rancor or weakness and
seeks now a time of like balance wherein s/he may lay this
load down and become once more lighthearted and at ease.
Noble God, who laughs in the greening of the world, grant
that the winter of this Warrior's heart might give way to the
glorious spring of relief. Guide her/his path, ward her/his
dreams, and restore her/him to a joyous life of safety and
rest. So mote it be.

III. The Ritual Bath

The Priest/ess should help the veteran to rise and shall remove the veteran's clothing. This act should occur in silence, preferably with the veteran's eyes closed. When the veteran has been disrobed, the Priest/ess should take his or her hand and guide him or her into the hot, scented bath. In silence, the Priest/ess should wash the veteran, massaging tired shoulders and limbs in the process. This is a time of caretaking and rest for the veteran, and should be done by the Priest/ess in a spirit of honor and healing. While it may be viewed as such, this is not an erotic undertaking. After the ritual cleansing is complete, the Priest/ess should silently remove the BDUs from the room and allow the veteran some quiet time to soak. When this is done, the Priest/ess shall gently guide the veteran out of the bath and have the veteran open his or her eyes.

IV. The Healing

The Priest/ess should first dry off the veteran with a clean, warm towel. Then, taking up a vial of sweet almond oil, the Priest/ess shall proceed to massage the veteran while saying the following:

Priest/ess

Blessed be your feet, which have roamed so far from home. They have served you well and have carried you home again. Blessed be your feet, beloved of the Gods.

Blessed be your legs, which have held you in strength and steadfastness. They have served you well and have carried you home again. Blessed be your legs, beloved of the Gods.

Blessed be your knees, which have knelt before the Gods alone. They have served you well and have carried you home again. Blessed be your knees, beloved of the Gods.

Blessed be your groin/womb, which has held the seat of your power. It has served you well and has carried you home again. Blessed be your groin/womb, beloved of the Gods.

Blessed be your chest, which has guarded your Warrior's heart. It has served you well and has carried you home again. Blessed be your chest, beloved of the Gods.

Blessed be your arms, which have borne your weapon in courage and restraint. They have served you well and have carried you home again. Blessed be your arms, beloved of the Gods.

Blessed be your hands, which have worked for swift victory. They have served you well and have carried you home again. Blessed be your hands, beloved of the Gods.

Blessed be your shoulders, which have carried your equipment and your worries without complaint. They have served you well and have carried you home again. Blessed be your shoulders, beloved of the Gods.

The Priest/ess should place a hand upon the veteran's head and say:

From the top of your head, to the soles of your feet, you have served well your people and returned home again. Blessed be (veteran's name), beloved of the Gods.

V. The Completion

The Priest/ess should give the veteran a new set of civilian clothes to put on. When he or she has dressed, the quarters should be released and the ritual completed.

Priest/ess
We turn and bow to the Spirits of the North, who have supported (veteran's name) in this Rite. We thank you for your presence. Hail and farewell!

Veteran
Place of earth and restoration, I carry you within me always.

Priest/ess
We turn and bow to the Spirits of the West, who have supported (veteran's name) in this Rite. We thank you for your presence. Hail and farewell!

Veteran

Place of water and healing, I carry you within me always.

Priest/ess

We turn and bow to the Spirits of the South, who have supported (veteran's name) in this Rite. We thank you for your presence. Hail and farewell!

Veteran

Place of fire and courage, I carry you within me always.

Priest/ess

We turn and bow to the Spirits of the East, who have supported (veteran's name) in this Rite. We thank you for your presence. Hail and farewell!

Veteran

Place of air and knowledge, I carry you within me always.

Priest/ess and Veteran together

Spirit of the Center, place of balance. We carry you within us as we depart from this place. May our work in this place and between the worlds influence all the worlds as together we strive for peace and healing. So mote it be.

PAGAN PERSPECTIVES
* * *

Military Widow

Name: Roberta Stewart, Widow

Status: Widow of Sgt. Patrick D. Stewart, Army National Guard, Kandahar Air Base, Afghanistan (killed in action)

Tradition/Path: Wiccan

Please share a bit about your husband's life and service, as well as the circumstances surrounding his passing.

Sgt. Patrick Stewart had a lifelong dream of flying. He enlisted in the military on his eighteenth birthday with the intention of learning how to fly. Patrick decided in boot camp that he wanted to work on helicopters. After basic training, he served in Korea and then Kuwait during Desert Storm. Patrick was part of the cleanup crew at the Kuwait Airport, and cut down the bodies of women and children that Saddam Hussein had burned and hung from the lightposts at the airport just before he fled the country. Patrick bagged the bodies for transport. There are some things that no one should have to see. And yet, in Afghanistan Patrick experienced the same horrifying scenario. He told me he was growing tired of dropping off crew members and picking them back up in body bags, and said, "I don't think I can go through another ramp ceremony." Patrick's next ramp ceremony would be his own, in Kandahar, Afghanistan.

After September 11, 2001, Patrick re-enlisted. He joined the Nevada National Guard and became a technician working on the Chinook CH-47 helicopters. He also assisted as a firefighter during the fire seasons in Nevada and California. In 2004, he was called to serve in Afghanistan and in March 2005, he was deployed to Afghanistan as chief flight engineer. He was one of the only flight crew members with prior combat experience. On September 25, 2005, Sgt. Patrick D. Stewart was shot down and killed. It happened just a matter of hours after speaking with me by telephone and telling me that he loved me and was looking forward to coming home. A part of me also died that day, along with all of my hopes and dreams for a future with my husband. The nightmare began with the knock on the door and the news that Patrick had performed the ultimate sacrifice and would not be coming home alive.

During the time of your husband's deployment, did you have a support network within the military and Pagan communities? Was there any overlap? Why or why not?

Patrick and I were sole practitioners and did not participate in ritual except with ourselves. I was very involved with the military communities and was part of the Family Support. I also worked the SRPs and helped the JAG prepare documents. During deployment the wives did several things and the Family Support group gathered donations. And we were able to do things with each other, like take our kids to Wild Waters Fun Park. Overall the Family Support was good. I went to all the meetings prior to deployment and after they were deployed to learn all I could. We were close to his military comrades as he also worked with some of them full time at the facility as a federal employee, where he was a CH-47 technician and did firefighting during the fire season.

You were instrumental in pushing the Veterans Administration to approve the use of pentacles as a religious symbol on military tombstones. Prior to your husband's death in Afghanistan, how public were you about your Pagan practice?

I would say we were not public. Patrick's unit knew, all our family and friends knew, but we still didn't tell people unless they asked. We worried for our children due to the discrimination surrounding our faith.

How did the military relate to your needs as a Pagan war widow? Did the casualty officer work with you to incorporate Pagan elements into the military funeral rites? What did you do, ritually or magickally, to cope with your loss?

I was dealing with our local military, not national, so I experienced a great deal of love and compassion and they granted me everything I wanted. Patrick's funeral was military with full honors and I incorporated our Wiccan faith; a circle was cast and wrapped with red, white, and blue ribbon with one entry. The entry was lined with Indian rocks that Patrick had collected, and after they brought his casket in the circle the Honor Guard closed the circle with those rocks. It was the most beautiful ceremony. We had our spiritual advisor and friend along with other friends and the military speak. My local military and the state of Nevada truly honored our faith in all aspects of Patrick's death. They truly honored Patrick completely.

I have now gone public and have broad Pagan support around the country. What I do to cope is to try and honor my husband and our love. I will continue to speak out against the discrimination that I experienced, and I now travel to different states to participate in rituals. I do my rituals at home too, but to tell you the truth, I am just now dealing with it. I had focused so much on the Pentacle Quest, I didn't cope.

Please give a short history of your dispute with the Veterans Administration. How did your local military and Pagan communities react to your call for an approved pentacle?

My dispute with the VA started in 2006, when I applied for Patrick's plaque at the VA cemetery and I was told I could not have the pentacle placed there because it was not an approved emblem of belief. I started my research and was shocked at what I had found. I then started to speak on this issue and also called my political appointees. The state of Nevada overrode the VA and granted Patrick his plaque with pentacle, and it was installed on December 2, 2006. I continued the fight so that all our Pagan soldiers would be recognized and hopefully this discrimination will not happen to another military family. I then spoke with Under Secretary [for Memorial Affairs] Tuerk and realized this issue was nothing but discrimination. I then decided to sue the VA. Along with Circle Sanctuary and other veterans' widows, we continued to speak about this issue to the press, and the entire state of Nevada worked on this issue along with other political people. We finally had settlement in April of 2007.

You've become something of a heroine to military Pagans in America. Have you been contacted by service personnel who are still in the "broom closet"?

Yes, I have. I have also been in touch with current military and their wives. Most of them came out of the broom closet when we settled the case, and I was notified by other Pagans in the military that there was a rush of people changing their dog tags. It was a very moving day. Other military also honored Patrick by wearing his unit patch during their deployment during the fight with the VA. In fact it is this contact that gave me the strength to continue the fight after Patrick received his plaque with pentacle from the governor of Nevada in November. I continued litigation for all our soldiers with great pride.

How has your Pagan practice influenced your life as a military wife (now widow) and vice versa?

I don't believe my faith is different from anyone else's. The Pagan practice influences my life daily—it is a part of who I am, and I am proud of who I am today. I do believe, however, that my Pagan practice helped me accept my husband's role in this lifetime. I believe by understanding that life is eternal and that we would meet again helped me to deal with his deployment and other missions. As a widow, it has helped me deal with the loss of Patrick. I am still dealing with it, and I have good days and I have bad days, but my Pagan faith has helped me in so many ways.

What advice would you give to someone currently considering joining the military today?

I would advise them to check into all of their rights as a solider and ask themselves if they are willing to sacrifice some of those freedoms for our country. Personally at this time I would not advise anybody on that issue.

* * *

Blessings and Acknowledgments

It doesn't seem enough to simply "acknowledge" the people who have helped make this volume possible. Everyone mentioned here has blessed my life in so many ways that I can't begin to describe. This is my simple way of returning my love and blessings to them here.

Rob Barner: My partner and best friend. Without you, I would never have recognized the need for this book. Without you, I would've missed out on many great adventures and conversations. Without you, my life would not be the same. I love you, I love you, I love you. Can we be civilians yet?

My family, especially Mom, Wayne, and Nana: For being proud of me, even though I turned out completely different than you expected. For supporting me, even when you disagree with me. For understanding that even though my path is different from yours, it is still your light that guides me. I love you . . . even if I do confuse you most of the time.

Renee Graham: For being a constant source of inspiration, strength, and love. For allowing me to drag you along for (and into) all sorts of crazy experiences, experiments, and assorted adventures . . . and for doing the same to me. For the dozen phone calls we trade per day. You are the sister of my soul.

Rod Powers: The best About.com guide around and a wealth of information about every aspect of the military. You made this accomplishment so much easier to research, and I am forever grateful.

Cesiwir Serith: Master of poetry and prayer. I've carried your little green book with me everywhere and have been blessed by your work. Thank you for the support you've shown to me throughout this project.

Efufulele: My teacher and Priest for the past five years. Your friendship means the world to me. I am a better person for having you in my life. Thank you.

Trillium Reclaiming: For bringing a little magick into my life. You won me over with your perfect harmony and bottomless well of chants. You are the chewy center of my spiritual practice. Peace, salaam, shalom, friends.

Military Families Speak Out and IVAW: Most especially Charlie Richardson and Nancy Lessin, for helping me find a voice and a positive channel for my anger and outrage. In peace and solidarity, always.

The magickal members of the United States Armed Forces: All those military personnel who shared their thoughts, opening up their military and magickal lives to me—I only wish I could have included you all! Those Pagans in uniform who put their bodies, minds, and lives on the line every day in defense of a nation that still doesn't fully understand. I pray that you may be brought home safely and soon, and properly cared for upon the homecoming. May your sacrifices be honored.

The individuals who made this possible: Friends and loved ones who offered advice, encouragement, and inspiration, notably:

> Laura Ross, exciser of errant commas and exterminator of extraneous "howevers"
>
> Lisa Givens-Dubay, for providing much needed first aid
>
> David Hogg, resident flirt, passer of notes, voice of reason, and personal cheerleader

Angie Hogg, for her endless patience and willingness to share a giggle or a gasp on Sunday mornings

Randy Magner, who inspires me to let my imagination soar

Nanette Holkestad, who reminds me that being grounded is also important

David Smith, my big brother

Stacy Hafley, my traveling companion and co-conspirator

Kimmi Keith, the woman I aspire to be when I grow up

Paula and Brett Liddle, just for being who they are in every way

Everyone else whose touch has influenced this work

Each and every one of you is beloved.

Brightest blessings on you and yours!

Appendices

Appendix A: Warrior Deities

Agrona (British): The name literally means "carnage." The Welsh river Aeron is named for her.

The **Alaisiagae** (Roman/British): Worshipped in Roman Britain and Germany, the Alaisiagae (or "dispatching terrors") were sisters, Beda (deifying burial) and Boudihillia (victory's fullness).

Anat (Semitic): The sister of Ba'al, Anat is a warrior goddess, often depicted wading knee-deep in blood. She is described as wild and joyful in battle. Anat has also been linked to Set in Egypt, Astarte in Mesopotamia, and Athena in Cyprus.

Ankt *or* **Anouke** (Egyptian): Minor warrior goddess of Egypt, often portrayed wearing a crown that was feathered and curved and bearing arrows or a spear.

Ares (Greek): Literally meaning "battle strife," and also called Mars by the Romans, Ares is usually the first warrior god we learn about—often in elementary school. Son of Zeus and Hera, Ares was often viewed with mistrust by the other Olympians. His sister Athena rules over strategic battle, and Ares over war for war's own sake. His symbols include a chariot driven by four stallions, armor, the spear emblazoned with a poisonous snake, and the vulture.

Astarte (Semitic): Astarte appears in various guises throughout the Middle East, including Judea, Mesopotamia, Phoenicia, and into Egypt. Her symbols, as a warrior deity, include the lion and the sphinx, although she is also seen as a goddess of sexuality and love, associated with the planet Venus.

Athena (Greek): Athena is the tactician of the Olympians. She rules over wisdom and war, and tends to combine the two, engaging in battle only when it is most logical to do so. Her symbols are the chariot, shield bearing the image of Medusa, and owl. Athena (called Minerva by the Romans) is one of the most famous goddesses known to us today.

Badb (Irish): Badb, or the Crow, was known for causing confusion amongst the opposing soldiers in order to assure her people victory. Along with her sisters, Macha and Morrigan, Badb is one of a trinity of Irish warrior deities.

Belatucadros (British): Belatucadros was worshiped exclusively in northern Britain, especially near Cornwall and Westmoreland. Also worshiped by rank-and-file Roman soldiers, he was often equated with Mars (Ares). Altars that have been discovered are small and unadorned, even plain. He seems to be a deity that was particularly honored by what would today be considered enlisted and junior enlisted soldiers.

Brigid (Irish): Ruler of everything "high," including the high-ground, Brigid is equated frequently with Athena/Minerva. She is a triple goddess, with one of her aspects ruling over smithcraft, and thus the forging of weapons.

Bugid Y Aiba (Haitian): A loa of war in the Vodoun tradition.

Catubodua (Gaulish): Meaning battle-crow, not much is known of this goddess. Speculation is that she might be related to Badb (Irish), Nike (Greek), or possibly Sigyn (Norse).

Chi You (Chinese/Hmong): An ancient emperor, possibly from the fourteenth century, who was legendary for his skill as a warrior. Responsible for uniting twelve feudal states, and undefeated in seventy wars, his symbols are weapons such as arrows, spears, and helmets, as well as the color red and red flags.

Cocidius (British): Another deity worshiped mainly in northern Britain, Cocidius was also equated with Mars as well as with Sylvanus, the god of the wild. Dedications to him have been found in Cumbria, including a small figure portrayed as standing spread-armed and spread-legged, holding a sword in his right hand, a shield in his left, and wearing a scabbard, belt, and tunic.

Esus (Gaulish): Portrayed cutting tree branches with an axe, Esus's name means literally "master." He has been equated with Mercury and (far less convincingly) Jesus, and some ninth-century sources suggest that he may have been offered human sacrifice. His symbol is the tree.

Honos (Roman): God of military justice and honor, his symbols are the cornucopia and lance.

Huitzilopochtli (Aztec): National God of the Aztec people, this "Hummingbird of the South" ruled over war and warriors as well as death, storms, and the sun. The Aztecs believed that fallen warriors return as hummingbirds.

Indra (Hindu): Chief deity of the Rigveda, Indra is the God of war and weather. He is often referred to as Sakra, the mighty one. Indra is usually portrayed as having four arms, and often riding a four-tusked white elephant. Deceased warriors spend eternity in the Hall of Indra, called Svarga.

Kukailimoku (Hawaiian): Kukailimoku, which means "Seizer of the Land," is considered to have existed for all time, without the need to be created, and is responsible for causing light to shine.

Laran (Etruscan): Portrayed as naked, except for a helmet and spear, Laran was the god of war and consort of Venus. His mythology and worship were later merged with that of Ares.

Mars (Roman): Originally a god of agriculture and vegetation, Mars later evolved into the god of war. His dual identity meant that he ruled over both springtime and the battlefield, where he appeared with his sister, Bellona.

Menhit (Nubian/Egyptian): Meaning "she who massacres," Menhit (like Sekhmet) was associated with lions. Egyptians believed that she rode ahead of their chariots and rained down firey arrows on their enemies.

Minerva (Etruscan): Counterpart to Athena, Minerva was part of a triumvirate of goddesses: Minerva, Uni, and Tinia. Symbolized by the owl and the shield, Minerva's dominion was war and wisdom.

Menthu (Egyptian): This god was originally viewed as one aspect of the sun god Ra, in his aspect of the scorching heat. This destructive attribute eventually evolved into a warrior deity. Menthu's sacred animal was the Bakha, a white bull with a black face, and Menthu was depicted alternately as bull-headed and hawk-headed.

Mextli (Aztec): Born as a fully armed adult warrior, Mextli was the Aztec god of storms.

Morrigan (Irish): This "phantom queen" is a terrifying figure in Irish mythology, often compared to the Lamia, the Valkyries, or the Furies. Personified by the carrion-eating crow, her sisters are Badb and Macha.

Neit (Irish): God of war, and husband to Badb.

Neith (Egyptian): Neith, like Athena, was a goddess of both war and weaving. Because of these attributes, the Egyptians also naturally associated her with the linen strips used to wrap mummies. She is said to guard the bodies of the dead, and it is in this capacity that she serves as warrior.

Nemain (Irish): Nemain, who was often seen as a weeping woman, washing clothes in the river, was said to foretell the coming deaths in battle—upon close inspection, the garments she washed belonged to those of the doomed soldiers. It is little wonder that her name means "panic."

Odin (Norse/Germanic): The chief of the Norse gods, counterpart of Woden in the Anglo-Saxon pantheon, his roles are many. He is the god of battle and wisdom, hunting and magick, wisdom and poetry, as well as divination. Odin is most famous for sacrificing his left eye on the tree of life, in order to obtain the secrets of the Runes.

Ogun (Haitian/Yoruban): Ruler of all things iron, including weapons, Ogun carries a machete and is one of the three warrior orisha. He is one of the most fearsome and most protective of the Yoruban deities and is not one to be trifled with or approached by those unfamiliar with the Yoruban path.

Oro (Tahitian): God of both war and peace in many Polynesian tribal cultures.

Perun (Slavic): Chief god of the Slavic pantheon, he shares roots with Odin. Like many war deities, he rules thunder and lightning. His symbols are the mountain and oak tree.

Resheph (Semitic): Gazelle-headed god of the plague, Resheph was later assimilated into Ungarit and Egyptian pantheons. His wife was Qetesh, goddess of sexual acts.

Rudianos (Gaulish): Depicted as a rider on horseback, bearing five severed heads, Rudianos was connected to Mars.

Samulayo (Fijian): God of war, and the souls of those who died in battle.

Segomo (Gaulish): With a name literally meaning "victory," Segomo was worshipped in Gaul, as well as in some parts of Ireland and Britain.

Sekhmet (Egyptian): One of the more famous Egyptian deities, this lioness-headed goddess rules over both beer and war. As the avenger of wrongs, she was seen as more vengeful than Bast. As the Scarlet Goddess, she ruled over blood and menstruation.

Set (Egyptian): Seen as almost a "Devil"-like deity, Set was the murderer of Osiris and thus rules as god of killing, as well as of the desert. Famous as the jackal-headed god, he is associated with crocodiles (Egypt's most deadly creature) as well.

Smetrios (Roman/Gaulish): Depicted as a bearded man about to kill a snake with a club, Smetrios is equated with Hercules.

Teoyaomqui (Aztec): A god who is the protector of dead warriors, and ruler of the sun and the sixth hour.

Thor (Dutch/Norse): God of thunder, famous for rushing into battle with his hammer, Thor is the red-haired son of Odin. Thor is the protector of Asgard and Midgard, and, second to Odin, probably the most famous of the Norse deities.

Tyr (German/Norse): One-armed god of justice and treaties, Tyr is a god of the end of war, as well as of single combat and heroic acts. In this capacity, Tyr allowed the great wolf Fenrir to hold his arm in his mouth while the other gods chained him. When Fenrir realized that he had been tricked, he bit off Tyr's arm, resulting in his assumption of the title "Leavings of the Wolf."

Woden (Anglo-Saxon): Leader of the Wild Hunt in Anglo-Saxon English mythology. (See also Odin).

Appendix B:
Worldwide Resources
for Military Personnel

Covenant of the Goddess

www.cog.org

> COG has been around for twenty-five years and has taken a leading role in creating a viable, reputable Pagan presence in American culture. Its local councils are located in the United States, including several near major U.S. military bases.

Lady Liberty League

www.circlesanctuary.org

> For nine years, the Lady Liberty League, a part of Circle Sanctuary, has fought for the right of fallen Pagan service personnel to have the pentacle inscribed on their tombstones. Rev. Selena Fox, High Priestess of Circle Sanctuary, has led the battle for full legal recognition of Pagan veterans in what has become a protracted, ongoing dispute with the Veterans Administration. LLL and Circle Sanctuary offer a great deal of support to Pagan service personnel, including advocating for the appointment of a Pagan military chaplain, and they are wonderful resources to be aware of.

Military Pagan Network

www.milpagan.org or Military Pagan Network, Inc., P.O. Box 1225, Columbia, MD 21044

The MPN's mission is to assist those military personnel who are facing harassment, discrimination, or other hostile situations because of their religious beliefs. Founded in 1992, the MPN has staff members who specialize in each branch of the military, and they can advise you on the rights and regulations specific to your service. Membership in the MPN, both for moral and legal support, is dirt cheap ($10 per year) and highly recommended!

Sacred Well Congregation

www.sacredwell.org

SWC was founded in part by military personnel, with a primary focus of offering support to other military personnel. It acts as the sponsoring body for DFGs worldwide and, like Circle Sanctuary, is currently in the process of trying to sponsor a Wiccan military chaplain. SWC offers a military liaison, who is an absolute wealth of knowledge and help, as well as contacts on bases around the world and in several combat zones. Sacred Well does require that its DFGLs study Greencraft, the Sacred Well tradition that draws heavily from Tolkien and Elf-lore.

Unitarian Universalist Association

www.uua.org

www.cuups.org

The UUA is not a Pagan organization; however, the UUs are known for being an incredibly inclusive denomination, and most congregations draw at least some of their inspiration from Goddess- and Earth-based paths. For those who find themselves feeling like the only Pagan on Earth, the Unitarian Universalists can provide a wonderful home away from home. There is also a separate website for CUUPS, the Covenant of Unitarian Universalist Pagans.

The Witches' Voice

www.witchvox.com

To be honest, there aren't many Pagans who aren't aware of Wren Walker and The Witches' Voice. This website is the town square of global Paganism, with listings for individuals (including military personnel) and groups around the globe, as well as tons of articles, editorials, news, and more. I can't say enough about it—the world is a better place because of this site.

Appendix C: Political Groups and Governmental Agencies

The White House

Attn: (insert official here)

1600 Pennsylvania Ave. NW

Washington, DC 20500

Comments: 202-456-1111

Switchboard: 202-456-1414

Fax: 202-456-2461

www.whitehouse.gov

> Regardless of one's political views, I firmly believe that every American should have the White House's main line on speed-dial.

Your Elected Officials

www.usa.gov

> The absolute best resource for contacting elected officials is www.usa.gov. Through this website, you can contact your senators and congresspeople, as well as just about anyone within the U.S. government. Do you want to see the commission of a Pagan/Wiccan chaplain? Don't just write to the president, write to the head of the Veterans Administration!

That's the beauty of www.usa.gov: it gives you access to everyone, so your voice can truly be heard.

Military Families Speak Out
www.mfso.org

MFSO is not a government agency. It is a nonprofit group established to speak out against the Iraq War. MFSO's founders, Nancy Lessin and Charley Richardson, define their mission as twofold: Bring the Troops Home Now and Take Care of Them When They Get Here. MFSO is not an anti-war group and it takes no position on Afghanistan. It is specifically focused on the current conflict in Iraq and the dramatic toll it's taking on the U.S. Military. The membership of MFSO is 100% friends and family members of U.S. service personnel.

Gold Star Families Speak Out
www.GSFSO.org

GSFP is a sister organization of MFSO. Founded by Gold Star families who wanted to be able to voice their opposition to the war in Iraq without being affiliated with some of the more left-wing politics of Cindy Sheehan.

Iraq Veterans Against the War
www.ivaw.org

IVAW is another anti-Iraq War group, made up entirely of the veterans themselves. Obviously not a general anti-war group, these young combat veterans have committed themselves to speaking out against what they perceive to be an illogical war.

Note: None of the above groups—MFSO, GSFP, or IVAW—take a position on the conflict in Afghanistan or any other war. They are strictly focused on ending the war in Iraq as soon and as safely as possible. None consider themselves to be anti-war groups.

Veterans for Peace

www.veteransforpeace.org

VFP is composed of veterans from conflicts ranging from World War II up through Afghanistan and Iraq. Mostly, though, its membership consists of the Vietnam-Era veterans who founded it. VFP does consider itself to be a peace group, and therefore it can be considered an anti-war group. However, VFP members are wonderful resources to have and very supportive people to know.

Military Family Voices of Victory

www.mfvov.org

In the interest of being as balanced as I can, I'm providing information on this group as well. It was founded in response to Military Families Speak Out and Gold Star Families for Peace, and while this organization says it is nonpolitical, a brief stop at its website indicates a definite partisan preference, especially when it comes to what sources it draws information from. However, not every Pagan is politically liberal, and if you're a fan of Fox News, then this might be exactly what you're looking for, in which case, here's the website info.

GI Rights Hotline

www.girightshotline.org

This is the place to turn for information on discharge. Any and every question you have about leaving the military can most likely be answered here. You'll also find information on recruiting and other helpful tidbits to review before you sign your enlistment contract.

Please note: Several of the groups in this section take stands either "for" or "against" either an individual war or war in general. The fact that I'm providing this information should show only that a growing number of military personnel and their families are looking for groups such as these. If one or more of them is not your cup of brew, that's okay too.

Appendix D: Family Support and Veterans Programs

Veterans of Foreign Wars

www.vfw.org

> The VFW's mission is to "honor the dead by helping the living" by focusing on community and veterans' assistance, as well as promoting a strong military and national defense. With over 2,400,000 members and 9,000 posts nationwide, you're pretty much guaranteed to have one nearby. However, keep in mind that the VFW tends to run a bit (or a lot) on the conservative side, so this isn't necessarily a Pagan-friendly environment. It is, however, a great place to have a beer or soda with a fellow vet, swap war stories, and contribute to your local community.

American Legion

www.legion.org

> The American Legion definitely falls into the "conservative" end of the spectrum. The organization is not what I would call Pagan friendly, but again, it is a nice resource for military personnel to be aware of. The American Legion has over 3 million members at over 5,000 posts

nationwide, so again, if you're interested in community service and military camaraderie, this is the place . . . just don't go in wearing your Military Pagan Network T-shirt.

Vietnam Veterans of America
www.vva.org

The motto of the VVA is "never again shall one generation of veterans abandon another." While membership is open only to those who served during the Vietnam Era, the VVA does a great deal of work to benefit all veterans, especially those dealing with the challenge of homelessness, as well as MIAs/POWs.

Vet Centers: www1.va.gov/directory/guide/vetcenter_flsh .asp?isFlash=1

AMVETS: www.amvets.org

Evan Ashcraft Memorial Fund: www.evanashcraft.org

Iraq and Afghanistan Veterans of America: www.iava.org

Kristin Brooks Hope Center: www.hopeline.com

National Association of Black Veterans: www.nabvets.com

National Center for PTSD: www.ncptsd.va.gov

National Coalition of Homeless Veterans: www.nchv.org

National Veterans Foundation: www.nvf.org

Purple Hearts Project: www.purpleheartsbook.com

Soldiers Project: www.thesoldiersproject.org

U.S. VETS: www.usvetsinc.org

Veterans for America: www.veteransforamerica.org

Vets 4 Vets: www.vets4vets.us

Wounded Warrior Project: www.woundedwarriorproject.org

Glossary of Relevant Military Terms

AAFES: Army and Air Force Exchange Service (pronounced "a-fees"); operates the shopping facilities on Army and Air Force bases. See "Exchange."

AFRTS: Armed Forces Radio and Television Services.

AGR: Active Guard Reserve.

ANG: Air National Guard.

AWOL: Absent Without Official Leave.

BDU: Battle Dress Uniform.

BHA or BAH: Basic Housing Allowance; what you get for the cost of housing in addition to your pay.

CDC: Child Development Center.

Chaplain: Military officer charged with providing spiritual support to personnel.

CINC: Commander in Chief (pronounced "sink").

CO: Commanding Officer.

COB: Chief of the Boat.

CONUS: Continental United States.

DADT: Don't Ask, Don't Tell.

DEERS: Defense Enrollment Eligibility Reporting System.

DEROS: Date of Estimated Return from Overseas.

DFAS: Defense Finance & Accounting System.

DFG: Designated Faith Group.

DFGL: Designated Faith Group Leader.

DOD: Department of Defense.

ETS/EAOS: Estimated Time of Separation; point at which your time of military service ends, unless one chooses to re-enlist.

Exchange: Primary shopping mart on the facility; the acronym varies depending upon your branch of service. The Air Force calls it the Base Exchange (BX) while the Army says Post Exchange (PX), the Marines go by MCX, and the Navy shortens it to NEX. But it's all the same thing. See also AAFES.

FRG: Family Readiness Group.

FSG: Family Support Group.

GI: Government Issued.

JAG: Judge Advocate General; military officers and attorneys, specialists in military law.

LES: Leave and Earnings Statement (military paystub).

MOS: Military Occupational Specialty.

MP: Military Police (see also SP).

MRE: Meals Ready to Eat.

MWR: Morale Welfare & Recreation.

NCO: Noncommissioned Officer.

NCOIC: Noncommissioned Officer In Charge.

NG: National Guard.

OCS: Officer Candidate School (or **OTS,** Officer Training School, in the Air Force).

OIC: Officer in Charge.

OSI: Office of Special Investigations.

PCS: Permanent Change of Station; to move from one base to another on permanent assignment.

POA: Power of Attorney.

POC: Point of Contact.

POV: Personally Owned Vehicle.

PTSD: Posttraumatic Stress Disorder.

QTRS: Your living quarters (house or apartment) on base.

SP: Special Police (see also MP).

SRP: Soldier Readiness Processing.

TDY or TAD: Temporary Duty/Temporary Assigned Duty; relocation of service member to another base for a short time. Varies from PCS in that most likely family members will not accompany the serviceperson to the TDY or TAD location.

UA: Unauthorized Absence.

UCMJ: Uniform Code of Military Justice.

USS: United States Ship.

XO: Executive Officer; second in command to the Commanding Officer (CO).

Bibliography
and Works Cited

About.com. "Post-Traumatic Stress Disorder: Reliving Trauma." http://
seniorhealth.about.com/library/mentalhealth/bl_PTSD.htm?terms=
PTSD.

American Institute on Domestic Violence. "Domestic Violence in the
Workplace Statistics," 2001. http://www.aidv-usa.com/Statistics
.htm.

American Psychiatric Association. "Posttraumatic Stress Disorder,"
309.81 in *Diagnostic and Statistical Manual of Mental Disorders*, 4th ed.
Washington, DC: APA, 2000. Available online at http://www.mental
-health-today.com/ptsd/dsm.htm.

Bannerman, Stacy. *When the War Came Home: The Inside Story of Reservists
and the Families They Leave Behind*. New York: Continuum International
Publishing Group, 2007.

Baybrooke, Marcus. *The Bridge of Stars*. London, England: Duncan Baird
Publishers, 2001.

Bond, Michael. "A Sense of Place," *New Scientist*, March 4, 2006.

Bush, Kenneth W. "Military Worship Wars: Blended Worship as a Pastoral Response," *The Army Chaplaincy*, Winter–Spring 2003. http://www
.usachcs.army.mil/TACarchive/ACwinspr03/bush.htm.

Center on Conscience & War. "Advice to Those Considering Enlistment." http://www.centeronconscience.org/literature/pdf/enlist
ment_advice.pdf.

Chapman, Nancy. "Depression: The Common Cold of Mental Illness,"
U.S. Army Hooah 4 Health, 2007. http://www.hooah4health.com/
mind/suicideprev/depressionCold.htm.

Conahan, Frank. "GAO Report on Gays in the Military," June 12, 1992.
http://www.fordham.edu/halsall/pwh/gao_report.html.

Coyle, T. Thorn. *Evolutionary Witchcraft*. New York: Tarcher Penguin
Publishing, 2005.

Dowd, Alan W. "Faith Through Service," *The American Legion*, September
2006.

Grossman, Dave. *On Killing: The Psychological Cost of Learning to Kill in War
and Society*. Boston: Little, Brown & Co., 1995.

Grossman, David, and Bruce K. Siddle. "Psychological Effects of Combat." In *Encyclopedia of Violence, Peace, and Conflict*, edited by Lester R.
Kurtz. San Diego: Academic Press, 2000.

Gurvits, Tamara V. et al. "Subtle Neurologic Compromise as a Vulnerability Factor for Combat-Related Posttraumatic Stress Disorder: Results of a Twin Study," *Archives of General Psychiatry* 63.5 (May 2006):
571.

Iraq and Afghanistan Veterans of America. "Mental Health Problems
Among Iraq and Afghanistan Veterans." http://www.iava.org/compo
nent/option,com_/Itemid,66/option,content/task,view/id,2414/.

Joannides, Paul. *Guide to Getting It On*. Waldport, OR: Goofy Foot Press,
1996.

Kirby, David. "Serving Out Loud." *The Advocate*, October 26, 1999.
http://findarticles.com/p/articles/mi_m1589/is_1999_Oct_26/
ai_56529317.

Mas, Alexandre, and Enrico Moretti. "Peers at Work," University of California at Berkeley, 2006. http://faculty.haas.berkeley.edu/amas/peersatwork.pdf.

Miles Foundation. "Facts and Findings." http://members.aol.com/_ht_a/milesfdn/myhomepage/.

Military OneSource. "Drug and Alcohol Abuse: Warning Signs." 2004. http://www.militaryonesource.com.

Monaghan, Patricia. *The Goddess Companion: Daily Meditations on the Goddess*. St. Paul, MN: Llewellyn, 1999.

National Coalition Against Domestic Violence. "Domestic Violence and Sexual Assault in the Military." 2005. http://www.ncadv.org/files/military.pdf.

Parslow, Ruth, and Anthony F. Jorm. "Pretrauma and Posttrauma Neurocognitive Functioning and PTSD Symptoms in a Community Sample of Young Adults." *American Journal of Psychiatry* 164.3 (March 2007): 509.

Pavlicin, Karen. *Surviving Deployment: A Guide for Military Families*. Woodbury, MN: Elva Resa Publishing, 2003.

Powers, Rod. "The Perfect University." http://usmilitary.about.com/od/joiningthemilitary/a/academies_4.htm.

Powers, Rod. "Top 10 Lies (Some) Recruiters Tell." http://usmilitary.about.com/od/joiningthemilitary/a/recruiterlies.htm.

Regan, Judy, Freida Outlaw, Gwen Hamer, and Arvis Wright. "Suicide in the Military," *Journal of the Tennessee Medical Association*, July 2005. http://tennessee.gov/mental/omd/suicideMilitary.pdf.

Rhem, Kathleen T. "Alcohol Abuse Costs DoD Dearly." American Forces Press Service, June 6, 2000. http://usmilitary.about.com/library/milinfo/milarticles/blalcohol.htm.

Roberts, Elizabeth, and Elias Amidon. *Prayers for a Thousand Years*. San Francisco: HarperSanFransisco, 1999.

Serith, Ceisiwr. *A Book of Pagan Prayer*. Boston, MA: Weiser Books, 2002.

Smith, Michael. "APA: Troops with Post-Traumatic Stress More Likely to Be Physically Ill," *MedPage Today*, May 23, 2006. http://www.medpage today.com/Psychiatry/GeneralPsychiatry/tb/3377.

Smith, Stew. "10 Steps to Joining the Military." http://www.military .com/Recruiting/Content/0,13898,rec_step09_bootcamp_tips,,00 .html.

Steen, Joanne M., and M. Regina Asaro. *Military Widow: A Survival Guide*. Annapolis, MD: Naval Institute Press, 2006.

Tessier, Marie. "Sexual Assault Pervasive in Military, Experts Say," *Women's eNews*, March 30, 2003. http://womensenews.org/article .cfm?aid=1273.

U.S. Army. *Religious Requirements and Practices of Certain Selected Groups: A Handbook for Chaplains*, U.S. Government Publication No. 008-020-00745-5. (Section on Wicca available at http://www3.bc.sympatico .ca/hillwalker/milwicca.htm.)

U.S. Census Bureau. "Facts for Features: Women's History Month: March 2006." http://www.census.gov/Press-Release/www/releases/ archives/facts_for_features_special_editions/006232.html.

U.S. Department of Defense. *Guidelines for Handling Dissident and Protest Activities Among Members of the Armed Forces*. DOD Directive 1326.6. http://www.dtic.mil/whs/directives/corres/pdf/132506p.pdf.

U.S. Department of Defense. "Population Representation in the Military Services," http://www.defenselink.mil/prhome/poprep2001/chap ter2/c2_raceth.htm.

U.S. Department of Defense. "Sexual Assault Prevention and Response Program Procedures," June 23, 2006. DOD Instruction 6495.02. http://www.dtic.mil/whs/directives/corres/pdf/649502p.pdf.

U.S. Department of Defense. *Sexual Assault Prevention and Response*. SAPR Homepage. http://www.sapr.mil.

U.S. Department of Defense. Uniform Code of Military Justice. http://www.army.mil/references/UCMJ/ucmj2.html.

U.S. Department of Veterans Affairs, National Center for Posttraumatic Stress Disorder. "FactSheet: What Is PTSD?" http://www.ncptsd.va.gov/ncmain/ncdocs/fact_shts/fs_what_is_ptsd.html.

Vandevoorde, Shellie. *Separated by Duty, United in Love: A Guide to Long-Distance Relationships for Military Couples.* New York: Citadel Press, 2006.

Volkin, Michael. "Top 10 Things to Expect When Preparing for Basic Training," *ArmyStudyGuide*, October 26, 2005. http://www.armystudyguide.com/content/Prep_For_Basic_Training/basic_training_prep_articles/top-10-things-to-expect-w.shtml.

Wikipedia. "List of War Dieties." http://en.wikipedia.org/wiki/List_of_war_deities.

Wilson, Barbara A. "Myths, Fallacies, Falderol and Idiotic Rumors about Military Women." http://userpages.aug.com/captbarb/myths.html.

Free Catalog

Get the latest
information on our
body, mind, and spirit products!
To receive a **free** copy of Llewellyn's consumer
catalog, *New Worlds of Mind & Spirit,* simply
call 1-877-NEW-WRLD or visit our website at
www.llewellyn.com and click on *New Worlds.*

☽ LLEWELLYN ORDERING INFORMATION

Order Online:

Visit our website at www.llewellyn.com, select your books, and order
them on our secure server.

Order by Phone:

- Call toll-free within the U.S. at 1-877-NEW-WRLD
  (1-877-639-9753). Call toll-free within Canada at
  1-866-NEW-WRLD (1-866-639-9753)
- We accept VISA, MasterCard, and American Express

Order by Mail:

Send the full price of your order (MN residents add 6.5% sales tax) in
U.S. funds, plus postage & handling to:

> **Llewellyn Worldwide**
> **2143 Wooddale Drive, Dept. 978-0-7387-1194-2**
> **Woodbury, MN 55125-2989**

Postage & Handling:

> **Standard** (U.S., Mexico, & Canada). If your order is:
> > $24.99 and under, add $3.00
> > $25.00 and over, FREE STANDARD SHIPPING
>
> AK, HI, PR: $15.00 for one book plus $1.00 for
> each additional book.
>
> **International Orders** (airmail only):
> > $16.00 for one book plus $3.00 for each additional book

Orders are processed within 2 business days.
Please allow for normal shipping time. Postage and handling rates subject to change.

The Witch's Shield

Protection Magick and Psychic Self-Defense

CHRISTOPHER PENCZAK

Is it possible to gain spiritual enlightenment even in difficult or threatening situations? In this thorough and thoughtful handbook, readers are urged to take responsibility for their own actions, ask what the situation might be teaching them, and hold compassion for those viewed as doing the harm.

Popular Wiccan author and teacher Christopher Penczak takes a threefold approach to protection magick in this guide for Witches, pagans, shamans, and psychics. First, find out how to protect yourself using personal energy, will, and intent. Next, discover how to connect with your guardian spirits, angels, and patron deities. Finally, learn how to use traditional spell craft and ritual for protection.

978-0-7387-0542-2

216 pp., 6 x 9, illus., includes CD   **$19.95**
with protection meditations read by the author

Magickal Self Defense

A Quantum Approach to Warding

KERR CUHULAIN

As a Wiccan who spent twenty-eight years on the police force, Kerr Cuhulain knows a thing or two about self-defense. The author of *Wiccan Warrior* and *Full Contact Magick* returns with a powerful program for magickal protection—based on the principles of the Witches' Pyramid, chi energy, and quantum science.

From everyday stress to the emotions of people around you, negative energy is everywhere. This innovative guide not only advises on how to cope with negative energies, but it also offers a fascinating explanation of how magick works in our quantum universe. Beginning and advanced magical practitioners will learn how to safely thwart psychic attacks, develop threat awareness, balance chi, create an astral temple for refuge, and use magickal tools for defense. Cuhulain also evaluates traditional methods of self-defense—energy traps, mirroring, fire, fumigation, sigils—and debunks many protection myths.

978-0-7387-1219-2
240 pp., 6 x 9 $15.95

Pagan Visions for a Sustainable Future

Ly de Angeles, Emma Restall Orr, Thom van Dooren

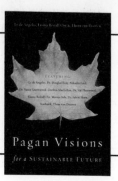

Do Pagan practices lead to an ecological approach to life? What is the role of magic in contemporary Paganism? How can ancient Pagan codes of behavior be applied today?

Representing diverse arenas of Paganism, eleven established activists, authors, and academics passionately debate the critical issues facing modern Pagans. These provocative discussions—exploring feminism, magickal ecology, ancient Egyptian ethics, political activism, globalization, the power of truth, sacred communities, and environmental spirituality—challenge readers to reconsider what it means to be Pagan in the twenty-first century.

978-0-7387-0824-9

312 pp., 6 x 9 $17.95

Solitary Witch

The Ultimate Book of Shadows
for the New Generation

SILVER RAVENWOLF

This book has everything a teen Witch could want and need between two covers: a magickal cookbook, encyclopedia, dictionary, and grimoire. It relates specifically to today's young adults and their concerns, yet is grounded in the magickal work of centuries past.

Information is arranged alphabetically and divided into five distinct categories: (1) Shadows of Religion and Mystery, (2) Shadows of Objects, (3) Shadows of Expertise and Proficiency, (4) Shadows of Magick and Enchantment, and (5) Shadows of Daily Life. It is organized so readers can skip over the parts they already know, or read each section in alphabetical order.

978-0-7387-0319-0
608 pp., 8 x 10

$21.95

Pagans & Christians

The Personal Spiritual Experience

Gus diZerega, Ph.D.

Pagans and Christians have been polarized within the spiritual landscape for two millennia. Recent media reports even talk of efforts by the Christian Right to boycott the U.S. Army for allowing Wiccan soldiers to practice their religion. There is no better time for Western civilization's most prominent religion and humanity's oldest religion to enter into intelligent and respectful dialogue.

Providing something for Pagans and Christians alike, Dr. diZerega presents an important and original contribution for contemporary interfaith understanding. For Pagans, his book deepens the discussion of Paganism's theological and philosophical implications, penetrating its inner truths and examining the reasons for its modern growth. For Christians, it demystifies Paganism, offering respectful answers to the most common criticisms levelled at Pagan beliefs and practices.

978-1-56718-228-6
264 pp., 6 x 9
$16.95

Instant Magick
Ancient Wisdom, Modern Spellcraft

CHRISTOPHER PENCZAK

What if you could practice magick anytime, without the use of ceremonial spells, altars, or magickal tools? Items such as candles, special ingredients, and exotic symbols are necessary to perform many types of magick, but these items aren't always feasible, attainable, or even available. The purest form of magick—tapping into your own energetic awareness to create change—is accessible simply through the power of your will.

Popular author Christopher Penczak explains how to weave natural energies into every facet of life by inspiring readers to explore their own individual willpower. This book features personalized techniques used to weed out any unwanted, unhealthy, or unnecessary desires to find a true, balanced magickal being. Penczak's innovative, modern spellcasting techniques utilize meditation, visualization, words, and intent in any situation, at any time. The results can seem instantaneous, and the potential limitless.

978-0-7387-0859-1
216 pp., 6 x 9 $12.95

Spanish edition:
Magia blanca al instante
978-0-7387-0956-7 $13.95

To order, call 1-877-NEW-WRLD
Prices subject to change without notice

Pagan Spirituality

A Guide to Personal Transformation

JOYCE & RIVER HIGGINBOTHAM

In a world filled with beginner books, deeper explanations of the Pagan faith are rarely found. Picking up where their critically acclaimed first book *Paganism* left off, bestselling authors Joyce & River Higginbotham offer intermediate-level instruction with *Pagan Spirituality*.

Respected members of their communities, the Higginbothams describe how to continue spiritual evolution though magick, communing, energy work, divination, and conscious creation in a pleasant, encouraging tone. Learn how to use journaling, thought development, visualization, and goal-setting to develop magickal techniques and to further cultivate spiritual growth. This book serves to expand the reader's spiritual knowledge base by providing a balanced approach of well-established therapies, extensive personal experience, and question-and-answer sessions that directly involve the reader in their spiritual journey.

978-0-7387-0574-3
288 pp., 7¹/₂ x 9¹/₈ $16.95

To order, call 1-877-NEW-WRLD
Prices subject to change without notice

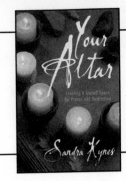

Your Altar

Creating a Sacred Space for Prayer and Meditation

SANDRA KYNES

Sandra Kynes demonstrates how to create personal altars and empower these sacred spaces according to your needs. Discover how to harness energies to manifest change, make decisions, receive wisdom, find balance, explore your soul, and grow spiritually. Kynes's unique approach provides nine overall matrices—each one corresponding to the number of objects placed on the altar—and the numerological significance of each. You'll also find suggested meditations and a wealth of helpful information—spanning chakras, colors, days of the week, elements, gemstones, gods/goddesses, runes, and more—for choosing appropriate symbols and objects that reflect your needs.

978-0-7387-1105-8
240 pp., 6 x 9 $15.95

The Circle Within

Creating a Wiccan Spiritual Tradition

DIANNE SYLVAN

Anyone can put on a robe and dance the night away at a Sabbat, but it takes courage and discipline to be a Wiccan twenty-four hours a day, seven days a week, for the rest of your life. Every act can be a ritual, and every moment is another chance to honor the Divine. This book shows you how to do just that.

The Circle Within guides the practicing witch toward integrating Wiccan values into his or her real life. The first part of the book addresses the philosophy, practice, and foundations of a spiritual life. The second part is a mini-devotional filled with prayers and rituals that you can use as a springboard to creating your own.

978-0-7387-0348-0
216 pp., 5³/₁₆ x 8   **$12.95**

To order, call 1-877-NEW-WRLD
Prices subject to change without notice

To Write to the Author

If you wish to contact the author or would like more information about this book, please write to the author in care of Llewellyn Worldwide and we will forward your request. Both the author and publisher appreciate hearing from you and learning of your enjoyment of this book and how it has helped you. Llewellyn Worldwide cannot guarantee that every letter written to the author can be answered, but all will be forwarded. Please write to:

Stefani E. Barner
c/o Llewellyn Worldwide
2143 Wooddale Drive, Dept. 978-0-7387-1194-2
Woodbury, MN 55125-2989, U.S.A.
Please enclose a self-addressed stamped envelope for reply,
or $1.00 to cover costs. If outside U.S.A., enclose
international postal reply coupon.

Many of Llewellyn's authors have websites with additional information and resources. For more information, please visit our website at:
www.llewellyn.com